Information Architecture with XML

A management strategy

Peter Brown

JOHN WILEY & SONS, LTD

Other Wiley Editorial Offices

John Wiley & Sons Inc., 111 River Street, Hoboken, NJ 07030, USA

Jossey-Bass, 989 Market Street, San Francisco, CA 94103-1741, USA

Wiley-VCH Verlag GmbH, Boschstr. 12, D-69469 Weinheim, Germany

John Wiley & Sons Australia Ltd, 33 Park Road, Milton, Queensland 4064, Australia

John Wiley & Sons (Asia) Pte Ltd, 2 Clementi Loop #02-01, Jin Xing Distripark, Singapore 129809

John Wiley & Sons Canada Ltd, 22 Worcester Road, Etobicoke, Ontario, Canada M9W 1L1

Library of Congress Cataloging-in-Publication Data (to follow)

British Library Cataloguing in Publication Data

A catalogue record for this book is available from the British Library

ISBN 0 471 48679 5

Typeset in Helvetica Neue and Times Roman by WordMongers Ltd, Treen, Cornwall TR19 6LG, England

Printed and bound in Great Britain by Biddles Ltd., Guildford and Kings Lynn

This book is printed on acid-free paper responsibly manufactured from sustainable forestry, in which at least two trees are planted for each one used for paper production.

Contents

Preface

We are not responsible for the brain we are given…
But we are responsible for what we do with it.

Anon

This book started life at sea level, on the beach of a small Greek island, was written on leave, at home or away, and finished in the Swiss Alps. It was an uphill struggle in many ways unrelated to the geography, but I like to think that I've kept my feet on the ground throughout the journey.

I have been lucky in that my professional life to date has been immensely varied. Although considered a disadvantage in some disciplines, being a 'Jack of all Trades' has served me well. It has given me a wide range of skills – in politics, communications, international relations, publishing, administration, linguistics, training and of course, information technologies – and enabled me to keep an eye always on the wider canvas, beyond the speciality of the day. For once, all these valuable experiences have come together and been useful together on the same project.

Why this book?

I was inspired to write for three reasons.

Firstly, I have always maintained that XML is not a 'toy for the boys'. It is a set of strategically vital data standards, and *not* a programming language. It will allow an enterprise to manage, and extract maximum advantage from, one of its most valuable assets: information. XML's importance cannot be underestimated, and its introduction and use must be carefully and firmly managed, and not remain the exclusive preserve of the 'back room boys'.

Many enterprises are rightly worried about the risks of becoming locked into proprietary systems and of being at the mercy of a single vendor. Badly managed, XML can be worse: locking an enterprise into a home-grown proprietary standard that only a handful of programmers can fathom.

This is meant with no disrespect to programmers or analysts who want to dive in and get things done, many of whom I have admired in my years of work. It is merely my conviction that XML should only be allowed into their hands once the senior management of an enterprise has understood its implications, power and scope in all areas of their business and administration. The target audience for this book is therefore mainly management.

The book is not intended to keep the reader up to date with the latest XML specification to be wheeled out – an issue I return to in my conclusions – but rather is the fruit of a little distance and reflection. Some authorities have already suggested that as much as two thirds of the $ millions invested each year in XML modelling activities is wasted. The problem is not the technology: it is the lack of good management.

Secondly, most XML books focus on data – in the sense of structured data destined to be managed within a database. Managing text, however, has been notoriously elusive, seen by human and machine alike as little more that a sequence of characters with a beginning, an end and a lot of unpredictable characters in between. Text can be generated from standard form letters or reports, where the structure is well understood and defined, as would be used – for example – in a mail merge program. Many XML books that take this approach make major assumptions about data organization that is simply not the reality for many 'text-centred' organizations. My experience has been that text is far, far, more complex than this, and can rarely be understood using this simple 'database plus form letter' approach. For this reason, the focus of this book is strongly text and document-centred.

Thirdly, with a focus on data processing, many XML books jump immediately into databases and programming modes. The assumption seems to be that information is already well structured in the first place and that the principal function of XML is to write programs. If it comes to merely managing well-structured data, a high-quality database is probably satisfactory as it is without converting to XML. But XML is much more than this, and many potentially valuable XML-centred projects have never left the starting block due to the perception that XML is more of a hindrance than a benefit.

This book attempts to draw the mildly-curious manager – understanding that IT strategy is important but hesitant to take the plunge – into the world of the XML standards, but using the familiar environment of their day-to-day work rather than the techno-speak of IT specialists.

The information management work of the European Union (EU) institutions and some national administrations with whom I have worked provided me with some ideas for the strategy outlined in the book. Unlike many 'data rich' environments, these administrations are 'text rich': preparing texts, notably drafting legislation, *is* their business.

Although this case might be considered as unusual, it is actually very useful for a book such as this. It has offered me important insights for large scale, complex organizations. The EU's considerable language service infrastructure is unique in the world, currently inter-working among eleven languages and moving to twenty-one by 2004. The complexity of this multilingual environment is an ideal testing ground for the advantages that XML offers. The few coding examples I give, however, are fictitious and entirely my responsibility.

Why XML?

XML is not a *technology*, but rather a *standard* that serves as a powerful medium for describing, communicating and implementing a true information management strategy. It is a computing standard that does not – or should not – belong to the IT specialists, although their support is vital, as we will see. Its basic concepts – that allow you clearly to define and express business entities and terminology – are close to management concerns. Its expressiveness is of immense value to the growing field of information architecture.

As a potentially powerful and expressive management medium, therefore, XML, and the family of standards around it, is too important a business asset to be treated as merely a technical issue.

The expressiveness of XML-based systems will come from their ability to associate real meaning to simple text and thus facilitate knowledge management. If we accept that knowledge is an organized progression and aggregation of data and information, we must come to terms with what this implies, particularly as more and more data and information are available only in electronic form.

Computer programming languages put *processing* – actions – at the centre of their concerns. XML, on the other hand, is and should remain centred on what can be processed: content – *objects*. Processing is only a means to an end. An enterprise's information – the content, whether text, data or information in all its guises – is often an end in itself. It is an increasingly valuable business asset, and XML can help manage it wisely and profitably. XML is *not* a programming language: it is a powerful standard that allows you to package and label your objects in such a way that they can be processed in whatever way is most to your advantage.

Why Information Architecture?

Well-designed information systems should be like well-designed buildings. Good buildings have a strong and stable infrastructure, foundations and supporting walls. All aspects of plumbing, wiring, choice of materials, dimensions and proportions, safety and ergonomics are the fruit of centuries of architectural standards and experience. A well-planned city will ensure that all buildings exist together harmoniously and that vital networks and utilities are adequate.

An information system that is built without foundations, without attention to the choice of materials or without standards may look good on its own, but is going to be difficult to integrate in the IT 'urban landscape'.

A preoccupation with architecture and standards will ensure that whatever you choose or need to build will stand the test of time and be fully inter-operable.

Why a management strategy?

Senior managers beyond the confines of IT departments and business units are unlikely to express much, if any, interest in the complexities of computer technology. Nor should they, and with reason: it's not their job, even if they should be concerned about resources allocated to IT and how those resources are deployed. Interest in XML, on the other hand, should become as familiar as human resources management or cost-benefit analysis in the tool-kit of any manager who wants to ensure that IT use properly reflects the needs of their enterprise.

This is because XML is different. It offers a *lingua franca* not only between analysts and developers in the IT world, but also planners and decision-makers from the management world.

Deployment of XML, and the increasingly confusing series of standards that go with it, forces an enterprise to reflect upon how it manages one of its most valuable of assets: information. At the same time, deployment is not solely a matter for the 'IT people'. Indeed, the biggest danger to long-term stability in the deployment of XML in an enterprise is that it is introduced 'by stealth', and purely in the field of application development and programming. What is needed – as I will argue throughout the book –

is for its use to be studied, understood and implemented further 'upstream', at the heart of business management.

XML's introduction should not be technology-driven, or discussion of its use limited to the IT community. My approach argues that all users can be drawn in and offer valuable contributions to XML's intelligent deployment, without getting bogged down in the technical jargon.

Who should read this book

- *Project sponsors*. If you are relying on subcontracting development work, to a specialist team or beyond the enterprise, it is important to know which issues you must keep in hand, which you can safely delegate and how, and which upstream issues need addressing, before even launching into any project.

- *Middle-managers and business analysts*. If you are to avoid the disastrous problems of proprietary formats, lack of inter-operability and wasted resources that have plagued too many IT developments in the past, it is not sufficient to believe that 'doing it in XML' is necessarily going to make the situation any better. It is vital to see the 'big picture' of what the XML family of standards can offer, and ensure cross-service cooperation, strategic planning and well-argued business cases. Initial investment in developing XML-centred systems might seem alarmingly high for no obvious initial return. A clear understanding therefore of its immense power will help in value analysis, showing favorable cost/benefit ratios and short returns on investment.

- *IT Managers*. Developers adore being let loose on a new programming language and IT environment. XML is different. If not properly thought through, you are likely to be left explaining why all your different XML projects don't and possibly can't work together, despite all the hype. You need to understand when and how to bring senior management on board and force them to address issues regarding XML that are not technology problems, but are firmly in their realm and require their decisions.

- *Senior management*. You are likely to be excited by the idea of reduced IT costs, improved inter-operability, faster returns on investment (RoI) and application development cycles – but can the claims made for XML all be true? What are the right questions to ask, and of whom?

The structure of the book

The book presents a hands-on approach for management, an approach essential to XML's successful deployment. It introduces the key concepts of XML in terms that managers can appreciate and subsequently deploy. It proposes an approach that enables managers to outline their desires and strategy in terms that IT specialists can appreciate, while keeping a firm management hand on the tiller.

After the introductory chapter, Chapters 2 to 4 detail the roles played by information management and XML and the need for a management-driven strategy.

Chapters 5 to 9 cover the planning, development and management of an XML-centred information architecture.

Chapters 9 to 13 then look at specific areas of XML deployment.

Food for thought

Something to chew on

Throughout the book, readers are invited to chew over a number of important and interesting issues.

This 'food for thought' is precisely the sort of insight that ought to get your management juices flowing. Savor it, share it and take your time to digest it.

It is *not* the intention of this book to delve into the technical intricacies of the XML and related standards. What little code there is, is provided to give some insight into the power of XML, and as such is not intended for use 'as is'. An overview of the key XML standards of interest and concern to management is however included in the reference section.

Food, glorious food

Analogies and metaphors can be very powerful, particularly when explaining unfamiliar ideas. An ever-curious cook myself, I use analogies to food in particular, and have found a resonance for this metaphor with managers: the separation of pre-packaged information 'dishes' (documents) into their constituent ingredients is central to managing the way in which information is created, identified, processed and ultimately consumed.

When recounting a recipe, it is rare to focus on the utensils: certainly the right tools are important to get the job done. But it is the content – the ingredients – and the recipe – the processes – that are ultimately the most important considerations. You will need the tools necessary to get the job done, no more. Some will improve efficiency – occasionally drastically – but they are not going to achieve anything unless you put them to work. That is why there is little attention given in the book to tools: I have tried to give some indications of the criteria you might apply when selecting your utensils, but your choice really depends on what meals you intend to prepare.

With these thoughts in mind, it remains for me only, therefore, to wish you…

Bon appetit!

Peter Brown

Acknowledgments

I have been helped along a difficult journey by a number of people who have contributed, often unwittingly, to the book's final publication: Michael Fitzgerald and Karen Mosman, for starting me on the road and to many others for keeping me going: Christiane Bracher, Bryan and Carole McHugh, Ralph McIntyre, Nick Marsh, Emmanuel, Alexandre and Andreas Pappamikail, Jack Fairey, Dick Stevens, Selina Barnett, Mark McLeod, Andrew Carter, Maddy Scott, Anne Wrightson, Bernard Vatant, Caroline Philips, Clive Mills, Sandra Kyriacou, Dianne Dodsworth, Suzanne and Keith Sivyer, Paul Mills, Claire Bicknell, Yuri Layhe, Helen Sims, Judi Bond, John Innes, Michelle Crozier, Stacey Robbins, Steven Stingemore, Anita Best, Leonie Riches, Anne Corkhill, Melita Jones, Sigrun Hoppmann, Colin Belchamber, Anabela and Pedro Frade, Gordon Jenner, Mark Buss, Simon Binns, Zoki Tsoi, Gary Dunleavy, Craig Walters, Anna Somerford, Rio Romanucci, Stuart Pate, Stuart Harris, John Frehley, Kate King, Rebecca Allison, Victoria Daly, Thomas Kloiber and others from the 'Eastbourne Crew'.

My sincere thanks also to Gaynor Redvers for picking up the baton at Wiley halfway through the project and soldiering on, to Steve Rickaby for timely advice and consistent support through the sometimes hair-raising last lap before publication, and to Nassos at the Sportscafé in Heraklion, Crete, without whom I might have been three chapters light.

A very big 'thank you' to you all. But especially to Christiane.

1 Introduction

Our diet will change dramatically in the future, although the essential components that we need to eat in order to stay healthy remain the same

Brian J. Ford, *The Future of Food*

A culinary tale

In the 'good old days' before food labelling, sell-by dates and competitive brand promotion, you placed yourself at the mercy of your local village store manager. After the painful wait for the previous customer to bid his farewells and finally let attention turn your way, you placed your trust in the nice old guy who knew his store and his supplies. You often ended up with more than you bargained for, with a tip thrown in on the best and freshest deals of the day, a few extra ingredients to spice up that special recipe and a summary of the latest village gossip.

The intelligence of the 'system' – the management of a wide range of foods and ingredients – was human: a customer's questions dealt with personally and a cumulative knowledge of their needs and interests allowing a truly personal service to be offered.

'Caveat emptor' The model doesn't scale well, however. Customers today want wider choice and availability, better prices and faster service, so the supermarket revolution was born. The downside for customers was the need to 'internalize' that grocer's wisdom and assess their purchases for themselves: the shelf stackers could point you to the flours but would be hard pushed to tell which one was best for waffles. Even if they did have an opinion on the matter, they probably wouldn't have been allowed to express it, for fear of being seen to promote one brand over another.

Then is there is the question of quality and trust. In many countries, it has taken major food quality and health scares to prompt public authorities to interpose themselves between producer and consumer and insist on food labelling, quality control regulations and inspection. In parallel, the growth of the fast food outlet offered 'no-questions-asked, no-answers-given' solutions to the busy and/or unimaginative: fast and cheap, benefiting from economies of scale and industrial-style production, as long as you accept the pre-determined and pre-packaged realization of someone else's flight of fancy.

'Parse the salt'

Have you ever tried to order – let alone receive – a salt-free quarter-pounder and fries? Or asked for a reassurance that the beef is hormone or BSE free? If you are lucky, you will receive a sympathetic shrug and an explanation that "I only cash and wrap" – in other words, a simple reminder that you can take it or leave it. The consumer has no control over what is delivered and little idea of what goes into it.

If customers want a varied and balanced diet, control over the ingredients and guarantees of quality, they should not rely on fast food outlets, but rather opt for the organic store, find a reputable restaurant with a patient Maitre d', shop around or grow their own.

Food for thought

In the good old days, committing ideas to paper was labour intensive, copying messy, impracticable or expensive, and re-using typed material without retyping unheard of. The corporate collective memory of an enterprise was a rich mix of human experience and well-filed documents.

A century ago, a secretary was a highly skilled, valued and usually male employee. The rôle of the humble and now largely defunct filing clerk was key to the corporate memory, ensuring the safe deposit and retrieval of documents.

In smaller enterprises, it was the clerk that would meet information retrieval and storage demands, often with an undocumented and highly personal system. In bigger organizations, master file classification systems were developed and documented: labelling became more sophisticated, cross-referencing introduced between files and individual documents, check-in/check-out systems and routing slips introduced. It was still often the filing clerk that would add those personal touches to the corporate system to keep it in tune with personal quirks of managers. It was still *people* that moved the documents and files around. Humans commented on their contents, their whereabouts, *who* had to do *what* to *which* text. The 'intelligence' of the system – like the grocery store – was human.

The increased use of electronic means of information storage – whether 'traditional' documents, e-mail, accounts or statistics – has lead to an immeasurably larger pool from which ever-greater information-hungry customers want to draw. But electronic files don't carry the same baggage, and it is still humans that are called upon to interpret and comment...

Except that the filing clerks, the well-documented and structured file classification systems aren't there any more – hard-pressed secretaries and administrators rely on their wits and highly personalized systems to provide the intelligence sought.

Except that the secretary isn't there on the evening the manager needs to piece together information from several documents, databases and other sources, and the report is due yesterday, as usual.

What, why and 'why me?'

This book is less about the '*how?*' of XML but first and foremost the '*why?*'

We will also see what XML can be used to tackle and who should be involved and responsible.

It is not therefore primarily a book for the programmer or application developer, who wants to explore the intricacies that the XML family of standards has to offer. There are already plenty of good books on the market that do this. This is rather a book for managers, whether they be responsible for managing resources, information and data content, editorial and design policy, business rules and processes or IT infrastructure. There are two important messages for them, which can sometimes seem contradictory:

- 'Keep the toys from the boys' – ensure that development and implementation of XML-based systems are kept firmly in the hands of management and not left to the back-room boys without any framework or guidance.

- 'Resistance is futile' – as several business analysts have pointed out, doing nothing about XML is not an option: the potential benefits of XML in so many areas of an enterprise's activities mean that it is going to pop up somewhere sooner or later. As such, it is better to be prepared and have a strategy to manage a coherent implementation before things get out of hand.

It is however valuable for a programmer or developer who wants a better grasp of the wider or senior management perspective of information management, who wants to see the entire wood before examining the trees. This is sometimes difficult when you are knee-deep in parsed external entities and library callback functions but – as we will see throughout – is absolutely essential for a robust and well-designed implementation strategy.

To start with, we examine three main questions:

- *What* problems can XML address?
- *Why* is XML important?
- *Who* should be involved and responsible for XML?

Before looking at XML, however, we should start by examining and understanding some the principal concerns under the general heading of 'information management'.

Information management

Few of us are today not involved in information management to one degree or another. Whether our main concern is managing personal accounts and an address book or a multi-Terabyte data warehouse, we are all confronted by four major challenges in our increasingly 'digital everything' world:

- Information overload
- 'Digital rot'
- Content and transaction management
- Multiplicity of formats and media for the same content

Information overload

In contrast to the early days of computing, until the last decade, the cost of long-term mass storage of digital information has fallen dramatically.

In the years when digital storage space was at a premium, and programmers ten-to-a-penny, major efforts were made to optimise code and compress content. Organizations were careful about what data and text they would save and archive, as these represented considerable overhead in the IT budget.

The emphasis was on optimising code and compressing content. Such economies were considered acceptable: why, for example, express a year as four digits, when two will surely do?

That particular problem will not arise again, for either 90 years if you didn't do anything about the Millennium Bug, or another 7000 if you did but considered four digits enough. Unfortunately, there are plenty of equally costly 'semantic short-cuts' around. A high and often costly premium is still placed on brevity.

In contrast, we are now entering the age of digital everything, rendered feasible by a combination of:

- Massive increases in storage and processing capacity – a full length feature film will fit on a DVD disk, together with dubbed soundtracks and subtitles in a handful of languages. Similarly, an average home PC will now ship with a processor a thousand times more powerful than a decade ago.

- Plummeting costs for mass storage.

As well as generating and storing more information, we are moving more of it about, copying more of it to more people and as a result storing increasing numbers of copies of the same content, while retaining more drafts and versions of incomplete texts.

There has been a vast increase in the total volume of information produced and stored digitally in the world, and yet we are not – according to the report – consuming any more than years earlier.

> ### *Food for thought*
>
> ### Bulimia?
>
> A total data consumption in the USA of 3,344,783 Megabytes in 1999 alone sounds impressive.
>
> According to a study in 2000 by the School for Information Management and Systems (SIMS) of the University of California at Berkeley, however, it is not significantly more than in 1991.
>
> Is it possible that we actually have a relatively fixed capacity to digest information, and that we have to start dieting?

If the growth in volume of source data continues, therefore, we are faced with an equally growing need to filter and select. To do this, we therefore need to be able to identify our information more easily before selecting what we want to consume.

'Digital rot'   In the days when enterprises still employed filing clerks and corporate filing systems, everyone knew that someone was looking after the files. The ubiquity of the desktop computer file system has brought that era to an abrupt and often messy end: each user has a very personal understanding of what 'correctly filed' means, and this has heralded a breakdown of corporate-wide classification and filing systems. Complacency is compounded by the belief that one can 'always do a search' to find an elusive file, or that your software will somehow manage the problem for you.

But 'digital rot' has taken hold. A number of studies have concluded that, far from guaranteeing the longevity of knowledge, many digital collections actually undermine it because of three dangerous assumptions.

Firstly, there is the assumption that everything is kept, that disks don't crash, get wiped by users or reformatted by system administrators wanting to free space on a network. The mere existence of the electronic filing *medium* (a technology issue) complacently assumes the existence of a filing *system* (a management one).

Secondly, there is the assumption that the digital format can capture everything. Contextual information can be provided to augment the understanding of a particular real-world artefact, but it will sometimes fall short of need or expectation.

Thirdly, there is the assumption that 'the library can always sort it all out later'. Leaving information management to the end of the road means that much potentially helpful information is not 'captured' until it is too late.

Food for thought

A comment about context

Digital media cannot capture everything.

An HTML text rendition on a Web page of a real-life account of battle is no substitute for seeing a bloodstained original letter.

Similarly, there could be no digital parallel of the 'vinegar search engine' described by Paul Duguid in *The Social Life of Information*, or a suitable description of the import of the eleven words written by Richard Nixon when tendering his resignation as President of the United States.

These examples show that the full significance of a non-electronic original can have as much to do with *context* as with *content*. The electronic versions of such originals are but information world 'surrogates' of the real-world artefacts.

Text is not everything.

In a situation of digital rot, when the electronic file goes missing, everyone looks back for the paper copies, still considered as *the* reference format. Paper is still often the defining medium in corporate information management culture: unless 'it' is on paper (or at least, *also* on paper), a document or information is often still not taken seriously. Accounts departments notoriously often maintain that they need paper receipts or proofs of purchase. One can attach to a sales invoice a copy of the artwork that your enterprise has paid for, but how does one do the same for an on-screen animation?

One reason for this, and the more general obsession with the paper format, is that a document on paper is considered as being committed irreversibly. Whereas an electronic data file can be modified, a Web page may change, paper is a 'terminal format' – once printed it is considered immutable, even if it might yellow and fade a little.

Multiplicity of formats and media

Electronic filing systems have rapidly evolved beyond being mere digital copies of their paper equivalents. The multiplicity of formats, whether:

- different formats of the same content, such as a Web page, a WAP phone or a word-processor file), or

- radically different content, such as a word processor file, a movie, an architectural plan or a workflow chart,

share the common denominator of being able to be stored on the same digital medium, magnetic or optical.

The 'all digital' approach would seem therefore to answer a librarian or documentalist's prayer to dispose of or replace the multitude of storage systems necessary for media as diverse as thirteenth-century illuminated manuscript and newsreel footage.

Food for thought

'Keep a copy'

In one Central European state, the archives service – facing serious shortage of storage space – was instructed to weed out those papers and documents that could be safely disposed of or digitized.

Presented with a recommendation to throw out hundreds of thousands of paper files and thus free up valuable shelf space, the service head gave his go-ahead with one awkward proviso: 'Photocopy everything first.'

Apocryphal? Maybe. Believable? Certainly.

Furthermore, each medium and each content type has seen the evolution of specific cata-loguing systems in response to their particular needs, from the humble record card for a book collection to more complete reference information, abstracts and keywords to identify and describe the catalogued item. Insufficient effort seems to have been dedi-cated however to developing cataloguing and description systems independently of medium of format, with consequent duplication of effort and, worse, incompatible information across different formats.

A further problem related to formats is concerned with the management of *similar* information in *dissimilar* – and often incompatible – data formats.

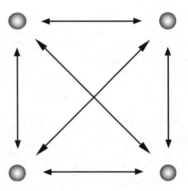

Figure 1. With only four 'nodes', there are already twelve connectors...

With four different systems, we can see that there are already twelve 'interfaces' – six bi-directional connectors between each pair of systems. If information is to flow between all four, and all four maintain their respective content in four different formats, a different 'translation' of that information is required for each of the twelve interfaces.

The number of interfaces increases exponentially with the number of systems added to the 'matrix':

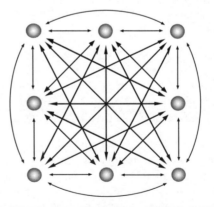

Figure 2. ...and with more, the situation becomes rapidly unmanageable

It is clear that the overall infrastructure will rapidly become unmanageable and costly to maintain and scale. Indeed, one consultancy group has estimated that 35-40% of recurrent IT costs in many businesses are consumed in transforming data from one application format to another.

Transaction and version management

We are no longer satisfied merely with digitally rendering and storing content, we increasingly want a digital trace of its history:

- How has a file evolved from a first draft through to its final, 'polished' version?

- To whom has it been sent and by whom has it been seen and approved?

- Has it been received, has such receipt been acknowledged and dealt with appropriately?

Files are attached to electronic mail messages and copied around an enterprise, modified and sent around again. The electronic mail system that transports this data is no longer a transparent conveyor, but rather a collective memory storing valuable evidence of transactions undertaken. Storage and management of the electronic mail messages themselves therefore start to become a business requirement. We don't want just to manage the content, but also the transactions, versions and processes – they too must be maintained, catalogued, archived.

More powerful word processors can keep track of all the modifications, deletions and comments made on a text and of who has done what. Well-designed database management systems with 'commit and roll-back' allow a user to move backwards or forwards in a process' history to see the situation at a particular moment. Maintaining this 'freshening history' for all transactions takes space. Archived electronic mail, particularly if you wish to preserve the access security that the system offers, is voluminous.

But as 'digital space' becomes less and less of a problem, we want it all and no longer feel the need to delete or tidy up. But that doesn't necessarily mean there is any order or structure to stored data, or that such transactional information is accessible beyond the confines of a particular application's proprietary standard.

We will be looking at these four main concerns in more detail in the next chapter – *Information Management* – but in this overview it is important to establish why XML fits into the picture as a universal currency for information systems.

Why is XML important?

XML must be understood in the context of the 'Web paradigm' – the set of technologies and information management practices that have led to the explosion of the World Wide Web. This paradigm has broken down previously existing barriers between computing platforms and applications that manipulate data, by providing a high level of interpretability across heterogeneous systems through the use of three key standards:

- TCP/IP, the already well-tried and tested protocol for transmitting data across the Internet

- HTTP, the protocol that manages the transfer of web pages from a server to a client browser in response to requests from a client

- HTML, a coding scheme – existing in several versions with different functionalities – for packaging and labelling information within such files and rendering them on screen in a client's browser

The robustness of these protocols led many organizations to replicate the same concept, as a way of overcoming similar problems of incompatibility across different platforms.

This paradigm has led not only to an explosion of public Web sites from 1994 onwards, but to the ubiquitous presence of these technologies within the enterprise.

The expressive power of HTML – the language of web page construction – is geared, and largely limited, to page presentation. To accommodate more sophisticated page generation and presentation, HTML began to be used more as a convenient 'wrapper' around proprietary or application-specific code and content, and was already up to Version 4 in 1997. HTML had to evolve rapidly to respond to new needs, or face serious fragmentation as different vendors pursued divergent strategies to convince users of the suitability of their 'HTML extensions'.

XML was developed as an answer to the straitjacket that many developers felt HTML represented, while attempting to preserve the interoperability and open approach that characterized HTML. It is understandable therefore that in this context XML is often seen, wrongly, as only an extension of HTML – described as 'HTML on steroids', for example – with a focus on Web environments and Web publishing.

However, XML is much, much more. When listening to an XML proselyte, you will often hear a list of benefits that is certainly impressive and important to any enterprise, including:

- 'Content repurposing' – the capacity to generate information content across multiple channels and in multiple formats and media from a single source

- Massive reduction in the additional costs associated with production and publication turnaround time

- 'Future proofing' – the guarantee that, whatever delivery mechanism or format is thrown at you in the future, you will be able to deliver from the same single source

- Dramatic improvements in 'intelligent', and thus less wasteful, searching for content

- The simple reusability of content in different contexts

- The easing of content exchange between heterogeneous information systems

- Better management of content production at source, implying reductions in down-stream problems

- Greater possibility of automation in workflow systems and ease of adaptability

All these claims, and many others, are certainly true. In addition, the immediate beneficiaries of a full-blown XML-centred information management system would be those that are involved in:

- The production of large, well-structured works such as technical and reference manuals

- The management of documents that contain complex structures, or involve many interlocking elements and dependencies

- High volume, often repetitive information exchange

Food for thought

Proprietary lock-in

You have at last found a product on the market that meets your every need, or nearly – a bit of customisation, and 'presto', you have the authoring and management tools you need. Then the application is taken off the market. If there is the slightest problem in the future, or a need for further user licenses, you are at a dead end. You have two choices:

- Pay – almost certainly dearly – for someone to convert all your content to another format, manageable by another system, always with the inherent risk that something may be overlooked during the conversion

- Buy or upgrade to the latest release of the same application – assuming that there is one and that the application you bought into hasn't disappeared – which 'of course' ensures upwards compatibility

Some call this 'brand loyalty' – others, proprietary lock-in. If you opt for the first choice, this is the moment to study very carefully whether the target format ought not to be XML. If you have to convert in any case, do it once and for all.

Sceptics have argued that large undertakings have sufficient resources to develop whatever they want, according to their absolutely and finely defined criteria. What could be the incentive for them, therefore, to 'compromise' their information systems by using a standard or a technology defined by someone else? The question, therefore, 'what can XML offer' is a false one, precisely because the principal concern of XML is not *what* but rather *how*.

The 'how' can be summed up easily:

XML offers a means of managing information in a standardised manner that guarantees interoperability and stability over time and avoids proprietary lock-in.

How a specific XML document is actually rendered within a Web browser depends on other factors, particularly with the use of style sheets to transform the semantic blocks that XML uses into the presentational blocks that HTML favours. XML is not restricted to use via the Web, although it is important to remember that:

- XML content is transported in the same way as HTML, using the main, tried-and-tested – in many Electronic Data Interchange (EDI) initiatives – networks.

- XML is character-based and not binary, and as such is accessible both to humans and to the simplest text processor, rather than only the application that generated it. Put another way, you have complete ownership of your content – something that is *not* true when content is dependent on a proprietary standard.

- XML content is transported in the same way as HTML, using the main, tried-and-tested, protocols that drive the Internet and the Web, TCP/IP and HTTP. As those standards are in the public domain, you will not have to worry about the cost of keeping your information moving around, as was the case in many Electronic Data Interchange (EDI) initiatives that relied on proprietary and private networks.

- XML is sufficiently similar to HTML to offer an accessible entry point and shallow learning curve to new users, unlike other 'heavyweight' vendor-specific systems.

- All the XML family of standards, with a couple of rare exceptions, use the same grammar and syntax. This means that a developer working with one XML application and vocabulary can be 'recycled' easily into another area without encountering a steep learning curve.

- XML can be rolled out with low overheads and short design-to-delivery cycles.

One aspect of the World Wide Web 'phenomenon' is central to a management understanding of the role that XML can play as a unifying force in enterprise-wide information management. Along with the now ubiquitous desktop computer or terminal, the Web has introduced hordes of non-IT professionals to the world of computing through a set of accessible and easily-mastered standards, in particular HTML. Graphic designers and programmers rub shoulders with authors, accountants, database administrators and librarians, all finding in HTML a way to publish their work.

Table 1. A few raw comparisons between HTML and XML

HTML	XML
Emphasis on presentation (format)	Emphasis on representation (structure)
Fixed set of tags	Any number of user-defined tags
Tag meaning usually clear	Tag meaning not necessarily clear
Tags rendered by most browsers	Tags have to be processed through a stylesheet before a browser can render them
Browsers extremely fault-tolerant	Processors need to strictly validate every tag
Essentially a 'terminal format' aimed at an end user	A format that can be used to deliver, exchange, process or manipulate data in any way whatsoever

What HTML started, XML takes further, involving an every-widening community of users, developers and managers.

As XML has grown on the 'coat tails' of the Web, it is valuable to examine how the 'maturing Web' has highlighted some major management questions that are equally applicable to the development and use of XML.

Before doing so, however, we should bear in mind a comment by Tim Berners-Lee in a May 2001 article in *Scientific American*: that the Web has developed as a medium for 'documents for people' rather than for 'data and information for machine consumption'. An essential difference, as we shall see, between HTML and XML and important in the strategy for bringing IT disciplines – notably database management systems – into the scope of a coherent XML-centred strategy.

It is too easy simply to extend the current model with its focus on Web publishing – it must encompass much more. However, it is a useful exercise to examine how the this phenomenon of 'Web publishing' has evolved through a series of rapid generations.

Responsibilities in a maturing Web

Many medium- to large-scale Web sites have gone through a maturation process that exhibits rapidly evolving generations, starting with the 'one-geek show', through a highly-specialized but often disconnected 'Web team', finally to stabilize around a model used for decades by the newspaper industry.

Food for thought

The Webmaster

If there is one job title that is poorly-defined and the subject of bitter turf wars, it is that of 'Webmaster'. A dozen or more people can legitimately claim the title, as it masks a multitude of responsibilities.

Start by asking the dumb question: what do *you* mean by 'Webmaster'? The range of answers will surprise you...

We will see the value of these comparisons when examining the respective roles that should be played by each actor in our XML-centred strategy.

The 'one-geek' show

Web development started off in the same way in many enterprises, large and small – as a programmer's 'lunchtime side-show' that rapidly caught the attention of middle management, sucking in resources as everyone demanded more features on the corporate Web site.

The problems were many:

- There was often too much emphasis on 'bells and whistles' – arguably necessary to draw management attention, as impact brings resources. This often meant that poor or nonexistent development methodology was often completely overlooked.

- Web servers were firmly and exclusively in the hands of IT departments, who often denied access – sometimes in good faith, with worries about security, quality of service, or other legitimate technology concerns – or obfuscated legitimate questions raised by traditional publishing and information management services in the enterprise.

- Many IT professionals insisted that HTML publishing was a 'computing question', which led many enterprises to initially miss the boat, with programmers designing desperately poor Web sites, often resembling tedious database query reports. Concepts such as corporate style or authoring guidelines were often foreign to IT departments, as in many cases was the idea of enterprise-wide metadata management.

- Writing HTML is easy: reverse-engineering code from a good-looking site, copying icons and graphics. Anybody could do it – so everyone did, with multiple, often competing internal Web sites taking over more and more resources and – irony of ironies – being sometimes incompatible and unable to share information with each other.

The specialized 'Web team'

Very soon it became clear that a 'one-geek show' was not enough. A Web site was no longer considered as just a question of writing code. Your average programmer is not a graphic designer, an author, journalist, editor or proofreader as well, and certainly not a librarian or information manager. Specialized profiles were needed for specialized tasks.

There are two major problems, however, with a 'Web team' approach:

- Each of the team players may have their own 'language' and tools, often limiting the possibilities of working together smoothly.

- The team itself may be cut off or downstream from the mains flow of corporate information and content generation – producing a Web-page version of such content was still an afterthought to the production of the paper-based original.

As content is intimately tied up with its presentation, it was often difficult to avoid duplication of effort, resulting in paper-based content being re-coded for Web pages by separate and parallel procedures. Such parallel administration, required to maintain Web sites alongside other publications media, has caused significant additional costs for many enterprises.

The newspaper paradigm

As a further stage of evolution, I have argued in favour of the 'newspaper paradigm', for developing and managing Web sites and in all areas of information and content management. In the newspaper paradigm:

- Everyone has a distinct role – the staff in the print room do not decide what goes on the front page or what is selected for print, any more than a journalist would buy in stocks of newsprint or a 'sub' unilaterally increase the number of pages to print.

- There was – admittedly until IT blurred the lines – strong respect for each trade, but equally a respect for house rules and corporate identity or house style.

- Production does not mean publication – a journalist's content could be spiked or held over to a later edition. It is not the journalist who decides on publication.

- A strong sense of house style is enforced using 'boilerplate' approaches both for producing content and for displaying it. These provide strong verbal and visual cues for the reader.

- All aspects of the newspaper's production can be contracted out, except for ownership.

- All stages of production are managed through judicious use of standards, to ease the exchange not only of textual content, but also of images, reference information and data. Although there may often be no central repository of content, there is always a central catalogue referencing that content.

These clear lines of responsibility must be applied to the managed introduction of XML, avoiding its use in one area without a higher-level appreciation of how it might be used throughout.

Areas of responsibility

In the rapidly evolving Web publishing domains, the problem of job definition becomes more and more acute, even if some more 'traditional' functions are clearly reappearing along the lines of the newspaper paradigm.

In such an environment, with so many actors with different responsibilities and a wide diversity of content, from simple text to complex multimedia, it is of immense value to have a *lingua franca,* not only for managing the exchange and use of content, but also for expressing management rules.

Web publishing, as with information management in general, involves many actors with different and distinct responsibilities, including:

- Functional and organisational questions

- Infrastructure and tools

- Coordination, management and arbitration

Understanding – and more importantly getting agreement over – the distinctive roles and responsibilities is the key, not only to successful Web publishing, but also to the wider canvas of potential use of XML across the enterprise.

The 'one-geek show' model highlights how easy it has been to roll up several roles and functions into the work of one person. In developing a management-driven strategy, we will see the importance of separating out and identifying these different responsibilities.

In addition, equally important management issues must be taken on board. Business units that need to work together require a 'common currency' in their discussions and negotiations. There will have to be firm but diplomatic arbitration over responsibilities.

Table 2. Responsibilities in a mature Web-publishing environment

Functional and organisational responsibilities	Infrastructure and tools	Coordination, Management and arbitration
All the process-oriented responsibilities associated with information management will have distinct inputs from: • Content providers, whether these are authors, photographers, recording technicians, translators, illustrators or anyone whose focus is producing content • Managers keeping track of business rules, processes and quality-control work • Editors, publishers, syndicates and all others involved in aggregating content sources into a packaged whole • All those involved in information delivery, whether 'pushing' content, developing navigation pages or more sophisticated knowledge-management systems	Project-oriented responsibilities for those concerned with infrastructure and tools, whether it concerns: • System and information architecture • Tools for content creation, edition and management • Data and document storage systems • Business processes and workflow • User and system interfaces	Decision-oriented responsibilities: • Resource allocation and sharing • Attributing responsibilities • Rule-fixing and arbitration
This work is a permanent feature, with possibilities for modelling and automating the repetitive aspects.	This work tends to require periodic investments of time and effort for a particular need.	This work involves input from senior management when called upon

Who is responsible for your content?

Understanding – and more importantly getting everyone else to understand – their respective roles is *the* key to the management-driven strategy that this book expounds.

Among the most important responsibilities, as we will see, is the management of content. A proper understanding of the power of XML will come from realizing that it is primarily concerned with content – your data, information, in short, the entirety of your 'digital objects' – and not with its processing, the focus of 'traditional' computing languages.

XML by stealth

I refer to 'XML by Stealth' occasionally through the book – it was even a working title in the early stages of the book's evolution. Its use is deliberately ambiguous.

The vast majority of actors involved in developing and using what will become an XML-centred information management strategy do not need to be encumbered with the technical jargon of XML. I later argue that they would in fact play their part all the more effectively if they stuck to what they are good at and avoided becoming lost in technical detail. They will be introducing XML without necessary knowing it – thus 'by stealth'.

On the other hand, developers and programmers should not be carried away with the intricacies and undoubted 'beauty' of the XML family of standards, but concentrate upon what they are best at. This means, in particular, being open and mature enough to recognize that many of the questions that XML deployment will necessarily throw up, and that require answers in order to proceed, are beyond their remit and require input and decisions by management, sometimes at the most senior level. As we will see, this is all the more important when IT expertise is decentralized within an enterprise.

'XML by stealth' can therefore be understood both as:

- An IT-centred approach to be avoided, because it introduces XML 'by stealth' without sufficient reference to management – or positively as

- A management-centred strategy that enables a complete XML-centred information management system to 'emerge' coherently without having been explicitly earmarked as such.

That said, there is no silver bullet – it won't come about by miracle or without a clear plan of action. It is necessary to develop and pursue the strategy in the same way as any other high-level project, by establishing a business case or engaging and motivating a project sponsor, mobilizing resources, establishing milestones and evaluation criteria, all the while keeping on board the wide range of sponsors, managers and users alike.

One important catalyst to the whole process may be the input of an XML 'evangelist'. Such a person must command sufficient authority to overcome the biggest potential threat to a coherent strategy: as XML is 'all things to all people', it contains within it the seed of many potential turf wars as the strategy unfolds. Keeping this in check and developing a cooperative approach is the focus of Chapter 4, *Developing a Management Strategy*.

Conclusions

In this introductory chapter we have taken a first look at the three main themes of the book, each of which is a subject for the following chapters.

Firstly, the main challenges that a 'digital everything' information society poses in terms of management of content, processes and media. All these issues will be examined in detail in the next chapter, *Information Management*.

Secondly, we saw some initial pointers to why XML might be sufficiently powerful and extensible to offer a 'global' response to these concerns. In Chapter 3, *Why XML?*, we will look at XML's capabilities, start building the management case for its use and identifying some key issues in deployment.

Thirdly – and precisely because XML extends into so many areas of work – we have seen the range of 'actors' likely to use and benefit from an XML-centred system. The of bringing those actors together will be examined in detail in Chapter 4, *Developing a Management Strategy*.

2 Information Management

The bane of my existence is doing things that I know the computer could do for me.

Dan Connoly

Introduction

In Chapter 1 we looked at four main challenges in the area of 'information management', challenges that have come to typify the 'digital-everything' world.

Information management is a vital starting point for our understanding. Information itself is becoming more complex, managing it even more so. Information reuse is often still limited to 'cut and paste', but users are expecting more, better and faster, delivered to and by a bewilderingly array of devices.

In this chapter we will start to investigate how these challenges are best addressed. In order to do so, we will develop a first high-level management perspective and introduce some working principles used by XML. These principles are developed in later sections of the book as we unfold an implementation strategy.

Handling information overload

The four challenges of information management that we encountered in the last chapter were:

- Information overload
- Digital rot
- Transaction management

- Multiplicity of media and formats

How then are we to handle these four issues? We will address each of the challenges in turn.

Quality and choice

The key to handling information overload must lie in giving the user more control over which information is selected and how. We can use our food-shopping metaphor again:

- The 'village store' is often very intimate, the shopkeeper having a degree of knowledge of a customer's interests. This personalization of service, however, is very labour-intensive and as such does not scale well to high volume delivery. The consumer is tied to a single 'outlet' and is extremely dependent on the abilities and qualities of the shopkeeper. It can work like a dream or be a descent into hell!

- The 'fast food' outlet offers pre-packed solutions on a 'take-it-or-leave-it' basis. The user can shop around between competing outlets, but it is unlikely that fast food will satisfy more than immediate needs.

- In a restaurant, a wider range of solutions is on offer with – depending on your waiter and the mood of the cook – some margin of manoeuvre. On the downside, the quality is likely to be more variable than the fast-food joint.

- In the 'supermarket', users are in control of the ingredients that are chosen, but left very much to their own devices regarding quality control, although compulsory food labelling and trades description legislation helps.

- If you grow your own food, you have complete control over what ingredients to cultivate and select, but you have to 'internalize' every skill, learn everything yourself and have no economies of scale.

It is clear from these metaphors that users have the greatest scope and independence for meeting their specific information needs when:

- There is a large range of clearly-identified or labelled content, preferably with a standardized or regulated 'vocabulary'

- The user is 'equipped' and sufficiently aware to make informed and intelligent choices

- The user is prepared to invest the extra effort required in putting together recipes and dishes.

- The danger for users – by picking their own ingredients – is not knowing the value or existence of useful and related ingredients that might help complete a particular recipe. In a supermarket scenario they are out there on their own, whereas in the other scenarios, they are quite literally 'catered' for by the chosen outlet.

This growing area of 'resource discovery' and information 'linking' will be examined in Chapter 13, *Navigation Strategies*.

Identifying your ingredients

If you want to order pizza just as it comes, fine. But if – like one of my sons – you don't eat cheese, you would want mozzarella to be explained to you and have a means of isolating it.

The capacity to pick out the content you want is heavily dependent on two factors:

- Knowing the constituent ingredients and being able to identify them: in a salad where all the ingredients are still identifiable and discrete, this is possible. It is less obvious in a blended soup.

- Isolating the ingredients from the whole: not so easy if you have to pick out the molten mozzarella from a pizza.

A healthy information 'diet' requires that a user is able to trim away the fat and concentrate on the essentials. This is difficult, however, if content is presented as composite and untextured 'lumps'. It is considerably easier if:

- The information is properly packaged and labelled in a coherent and consistent manner

- Its ingredients are identifiable and separable

- The user can be guided to related ingredients that might be of interest

By ensuring that all information – whether in structured data sets or free-flowing text – is identified and identifiable according to an agreed set of terms, an XML-based information system allows a user greater control of information load.

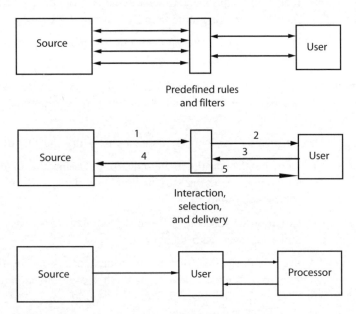

Figure 3. Three scenarios for handling a healthy information diet

This might involve:

- Defining a series of rules and filters to determine what information is to be seen or handled. By structuring 'information chunks' and offering extensive explicit or implicit labels to those chunks, XML allows, for example, extensive personalization of a Web page or Web service. It offers a means of creating and displaying a common vocabulary for understanding diverse information sets.

- Presenting a series of options, menus or other means for determining a specific selection. The user interface will interpret these choices and dynamically create a query or filter that determines which information chunks are presented to the user, and how.

- Delivering a complete 'information pack' to the user together with the entirety of the contents, XML packaging and labelling. Once in the hands of the end user, different filters, queries and analyses can be applied at will.

In all three scenarios, the key is refinement from a vast data source.

Handling digital rot

The image conveyed of 'digital rot' is one of decay – a failure of an information system to remain fresh and offer content fit for consumption.

Past the sell-by date

What should you do if your information is locked into a proprietary format and the supplier of that format goes bust? Or no longer supports the data format – but will of course help you migrate to their newer format at a 'small charge'? Or your organization is tied to another format after migrating to another system? Who owns your information content, after all?

One classic approach has always been to 'dumb down' data, saving to a format that represents a lowest common denominator, thereby ensuring accessibility by anyone at the expense of the formatting or presentation offered by a proprietary application. That lowest common denominator was all too often ASCII. This is acceptable if your business is producing English-language texts made up of simple paragraphs and little else. Otherwise, you were condemned, until recently, to a bespoke approach to handling the character sets of other languages or managing more sophisticated formatting needs.

The advent of the World Wide Web and the ubiquitous 'hyperlink' added a new dimension to information management, offering the possibility of transforming 'dry' cross-references or citations in a text to the dynamic form with which we are now so familiar. The Web also offered a text-based means of mixing on-screen text with other media and formats, from the earliest digitized images, which at the start often required a 'viewer' external to the Web browser, to the sophisticated multimedia Web pages that we see today.

Keeping afresh

We are faced with an apparent conundrum: to maintain text as data in a lowest common denominator format to preserve interoperability and ensure that it can evolve to meet the needs of new formats and new media.

By being both the lowest common denominator and offering the richest and finest detail of any given content, XML is a guarantee against obsolescence. It avoids the pitfalls of vendor lock-in to proprietary forms while offering a bridge to those formats should they be needed. XML content is stored in character format rather than binary. Whilst it is not really intended to be 'human readable' in everyday usage, this format for XML content is a permanent safeguard of readability and accessibility.

XML is evolutionary, adapting itself to its environment over time. Evolution is all too often falsely associated with the notion of survival of the fittest – a question of performance and efficiency. XML is certainly not the most efficient information storage standard (being verbose) but then evolution is centrally concerned not with the *fittest* but with survival of the *most adaptable*.

If a new storage medium or classification system requires additional information or attributes to be associated with some or all items of content, XML can easily adapt to these new demands through the application of transformation rules.

Identifying the contents

A further problem concerns 'packaging' and 'labelling': any serious system of information management could not rely wholly on filenames to describe the content adequately, particularly in systems with severe limitations to the length and structure of a filename.

If mere filenames have never been adequate, some other form of 'labelling' or description of the contents needs to be deployed. Many applications provide such facilities ('document summary', 'properties', and so forth) as an 'on-board' function. This is fine in an environment in which you know that data files will only be accessed by users that have the same application.

Alternatively, document management systems offer proprietary solutions to managing the information about files and content, but you are then dependent – in some environments, one could argue, deliberately so – on that system to make and maintain the links and 'pointers' to your files.

Imagine being the proprietor of a store with vast stocks of tinned goods, following a disastrous flood: all the stock is intact, the tins survived unscathed, but all the labels have dissolved or washed away. Is it soup or coffee? You will only ever know by opening every tin. The link between content and its description has rotted. Yet we seem to spend an inordinate amount of our valuable time with that high-tech 'can opener', the 'full text search'. Surely there is a better way?

This issue – managing the information about your content, text or not – is a critical starting point to the strategy outlined in this book. This information, or metadata, will provide many of the 'hooks' upon which systems will depend and that will be used to fish out content in an effective and targeted manner.

What is metadata and what is it for?

Often described as 'data about data', metadata is an important reference resource that can describe an information object or artefact. Its value, as with the labels on produce on a supermarket shelf, is to allow some understanding of what to expect the object to be or to contain without having to access it.

It is valuable therefore in automating any system that needs to act or react in a particular way, by providing programmatic access to the information content. This can be anything from a structured search query such as:

```
'indicate the location of all document whose title includes the word
XML and published since 2000'
```

to a program statement such as:

```
'if the access rights on the current element are more limited than
restricted then skip to next step'
```

Types of metadata

There are three broad uses for metadata:

- To 'wrap' unknown or uncontrolled content. When documents are received from or referenced from outside your scope of control, you sometimes need to add your own labelling information to keep track of it. Such metadata might include source or supplier, nature, description, keywords and so on.

- To meet business needs. Metadata might indicate a process or a line of responsibility within a business unit for a particular document, keywords, title or other user-readable reference information.

- To meet technical needs. Metadata might indicate storage location details, versioning information and so on.

Whatever the metadata types that your business identifies, use them consistently. The metadata set proposed by the Dublin Core (DC) Metadata Initiative offers a valuable starting point that confers the bonus of interoperability. Their basic, core, set of metadata provides a useful starting point for many enterprises and often requires little modification or extension for specific uses.

If the Dublin Core or its extensions are not suitable for your needs, investigate whether work has been done by similar organizations. The work of government agencies, public administrations and libraries are probably the best sources of inspiration and material from which to develop your particular needs.

How such metadata is conceived and designed will be examined in detail in Chapter 6, *Building on the Foundations*.

Handling multiplicity of formats and media

We saw in Chapter 1 that the maturing Web led to a shift from the 'specialist Web team' to the newspaper paradigm. One of the major reasons for this shift was the problem, in increasingly complex and large Web sites in particular, of synchronizing content. A printed text – a brochure, for example – would be used to create an equivalent Web page or pages, or occasionally vice-versa. In time critical organizations this inertia, or time lag, caused a domino effect.

Events that start here...

...take time to be felt here

Figure 4. Events occurring in a system take time for their effect to be felt further on

Even with the most efficient workflow cutting turnaround time to a minimum, there is still a conceptual problem with which philosophers are familiar: you can never step into the same stream twice. In other words, in an environment of ever-changing content, the only way to ensure that your Web pages correspond to another medium at a given moment is to use the same content! That is, to be able to generate whichever medium or format that might be required from a common source: a printed page, a Braille-enabled Web page, a WAP screen and so on. Such an approach has a number of advantages:

- It provides security and control over the versioning of a particular content. By modifying a single source text, the changes are automatically passed downstream as each format or medium requires.

- It underlines a proper division of responsibilities. If the content of a document changes, it is the content author who is solely responsible for changing it. Otherwise, a Web team member has to change the Web page, someone else the PDF version, a third the WAP channel and so on. These people have their respective responsibilities, but updating other people's content as it changes shouldn't be one of them. At whatever stage content finds itself within a production chain, the content owner should always remain responsible for it.

- It is easier to secure your content if it can only be changed in one place – its source – rather than in many.

- If the content of a document is strictly separated from its presentation and form, it is possible to develop more agile publishing environments. If your source text is tied to a specific format, it is less easy to 'repurpose' that format for other uses, as all the formatting has to be changed.

- If there is a 'master' source document, it is possible to extract smaller chunks. This has several advantages: to split a document into manageably-sized Web pages, for example, to limit a particular format to a subset of the document, for example for a WAP service, or to mask certain parts of the master completely, perhaps for security reasons.

By strictly separating content, its structure and its presentation, XML can ensure that the same content can be transformed, dynamically if necessary, into whatever format or medium might be required and according to clearly-defined rules. In this way we can eliminate the all-too-familiar sequential 'domino' effect and inertia-ridden processes of transforming content from one format to another, together with the insecurity of not knowing precisely *which* format and which version holds the authentic content.

If certain formats or media require greater or lesser granularity than others, XML offers the means to include or exclude content at will. From a single XML content file, it is possible to produce many data streams, including:

- A word processable document

- A printable file laid out and presented according to given paper size and visual identity rules

- A Web page table of contents with separate pages for each content section

- A WAP menu allowing the content to be sent as an e-mail or SMS message

We recall from the last chapter that the number of interfaces increases exponentially with the number of systems added to the 'matrix':

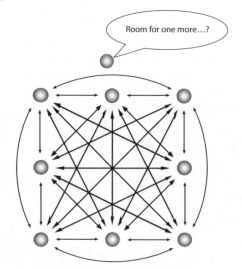

Figure 5. Our increasingly complex matrix…

It is the clear that the overall infrastructure of transformations, managed one at a time from one format and need to another, become rapidly unmanageable. The rational approach would be to move towards a 'hub and spoke' approach:

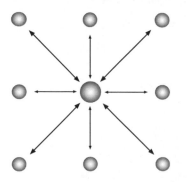

Figure 6. …can be simplified by first adding a central 'hub' and connecting the 'spokes'

By initially *adding* a further system to the centre, we can route all transactions through this hub and later eliminate all the direct, bilateral interfaces between 'satellite' systems.

Furthermore, adding one more delivery format now involves adding only one more transformation from the hub format.

Handling transaction and version management

Even at the simplest level of a company internal memo, we are faced with a number of questions concerning version control, transaction management and processing. In the 'good old days' a text was typed and presented for signature. Because of the time and effort involved and the lack of correction facilities, many typed texts were formally 'signed off' with hand-written annotations and corrections. Many legal texts, such as notarised documents, still use this approach.

The advent of the word processor and, in particular, the laser printer rendered the whole process a secretarial nightmare: for as long as the paper version of a document represented the authentic version, revision after revision was made because the technology permitted it.

Why is this important? If the paper version of a text is considered authentic, then the electronic version has to be updated *ex post facto* to ensure integrity. If different layers and different steps of correction have to be identified (author 1 adds 'ABC', author 2 deletes 'XYZ', author 3 deletes 'Z', author 4 modifies 'AB'...) then some method is required to maintain track of these changes and evolutions.

In many organizations, draft versions of a document hold little or no value. It's what is printed out and signed that counts. In others, modifications have to be tracked and logged, as is the case for organizations with ISO 9000 accreditation. Some word-processing packages now offer relatively sophisticated tools for managing chronological versions of a document, as well as auditing the changes made in a collaborative authoring environment.

If the entire collaboration is between a group of users using the same software, there will be few problems with this approach, but what if a wider group of users are interested in the evolution of a text from its first draft through to finished product? Or wish to analyze similar actions and revisions across a set of documents by a certain author or authors? Or are on the other side of the planet from the author and use different software?

This problem is familiar to anyone involved in analyzing complex documents that involve many authors and stages of preparation, such as legislative processes, in identifying who modified what and at what stage. It is the bread-and-butter of political consultants across the world. In highly-regulated industries also, it may be a requirement to be able to identify who modified what and when and – if necessary – 'roll back' the document to a previous version.

The key must lie in the capability, firstly to associate relevant control information with any piece of text, indicating the 'what' ('added', 'deleted', 'modified'), the 'who' and the 'when', and secondly to maintain that information either within the document itself, or externally but referenced from within.

With ever-greater automation of document and content production, other types of control information must increasingly be embedded within a document, serving to trigger actions downstream according to clearly-defined workflow rules. Until recently, a document was a 'passive artefact' that had processing done to it. If a document can contain within its bounds all such information, it is able to break free of proprietary document management systems that permit such workflow or understanding of version history only within the confines of the application.

How this control information can be built into your documents and how it can subsequently help your workflow and business rules will be examined in Chapter 11, *Process Management and 'Web Services'*.

Unlike most other data and text processing formats, XML does not make any hard and fast distinctions between content and control information or 'attributes'. This means that a string of characters understood by one conforming application as a valid content element might also legitimately be understood as critical workflow control information by another.

This ability to be all things to all people is a result of XML content being self-describing. It means that it is not restricted to being the object of manipulation or processing by an application, but can also be the subject – the *actor* – of a process whose behavior is triggered by the document's content. The values themselves can determine the outcome of a process that in turn might alter, add to or delete the original content.

As information about the transactions themselves can be handled as content, this in turn allows content management over time in a way that 'linear' workflow tools cannot, even with the most sophisticated rollback options.

IT responses to information management

So what do the problems outlined in the previous sections have to do with XML? Although information technologies have offered help for each of these problems in turn

– and some with enormous success in specific, specialized areas – it is rare to find a technology however that is able to offer a response to all four challenges. Certainly not without being proprietary, and thus limited to those who share the same infrastructure, or rendered obsolescent by more recent and better attempts, and thus limited over time.

Alongside these concerns, the World Wide Web has revolutionized and generalized a previously little-exploited concept, the hyperlink, allowing the possibility of relating otherwise unconnected content, irrespective of structure, flow, source or – thanks to the Internet – location.

The domain of link management will probably grow for another important reason. We saw in the last chapter that we seem to have a more or less fixed capacity to digest information, irrespective of the capacity to deliver ever more. In this scenario, the ability to associate diverse content in meaningful patterns will be a key to extracting maximum benefit from a fixed capacity.

Information technologies have never provided a 'Grand Unified Theory' to tackle all these issues, providing a common, stable and vendor-independent *lingua franca*. Information management and information sciences have their own standards, but they are often not information *technology* standards, and the worlds of information management and information technology do not seem to have met each other's needs. Until recently…

Enter XML

As an information-coding standard, XML offers, by design, a powerful means of tackling these and other information management concerns.

XML provides a standardized means of capturing, storing and describing:

- Information content and structure
- Rules and information about how that content should be understood, managed, stored and referenced
- How the content is transmitted, transformed and/or presented according to context, rules, user profile, medium or format
- How content is related to each other.

To do this is the challenge that XML has set out to achieve on the back of the infrastructure of the Internet:

- XML encodes content and its structure in a standardized manner but according to patterns that any user or enterprise can define

- XML allows you to embed, in the same standardized manner, any information about particular content or metadata, as well as rules and processing instructions that can be exploited downstream by users and applications

- XML allows content to be picked, mixed, transformed and presented as necessary, according to rules that themselves can be stored as XML

- XML builds on the 'hyperlink' concept that has become ubiquitous with HTML and the World Wide Web to offer a standardized solution to complex linking and resource discovery problems

Before delving further into XML, we continue this chapter with a deeper exploration of these information management domains and start, hopefully, to see why XML can offer a comprehensive and standardized solution.

Food for thought

What is a standard?

Standards are stable and are formally expressed in such a way that predictable outcomes can be assumed and planned for.

The World Wide Web Consortium (W3C) that developed XML goes to great length to explain that it is not a standards organization, unlike – say – the ISO. The W3C 'only' produces *recommendations*.

This may be legally correct but is overly modest. The ISO and national standards bodies may produce *de jure* standards that can stand up and even be cited in law courts. The W3C's work nonetheless, given its nonprofit status and very wide membership base, provides what are to all intents and purposes *de facto* standards.

As such, I refer throughout the book to the 'XML standard' or 'XML family of standards'.

Information content

Text is not just an undifferentiated stream of characters framed only by a beginning and an end, but is structured. The nature and complexity of a particular text's structure will depend on the nature of the text, from the relative simplicity of an office memorandum through to massively complex documents. Those structures can be explicitly indicated with labels or supporting text (the 'To', 'From' and 'Subject' lines of a memorandum, for example) or by conventions or visual cues that associate particular structures or elements with a specific presentation or layout, such as bold, centred text for a new chapter in a book, *italics* for emphasis and so on.

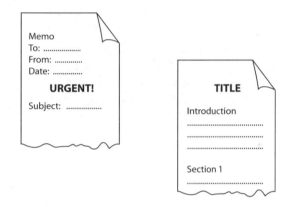

Figure 7. Visual layout offers us 'cues' to a text's structure

Electronic mail is an example of how such a structured approach to text is applied by information technology: most basic e-mail systems copy the model of an office memorandum but cut out the message clerk, and in many cases the secretary. It is the most used application in many enterprises. On one hand, it *constrains* a user to introduce content in a structured manner, but on the other it offers rewards in return:

- Addresses must be indicated in predefined fields, and in the case of e-mail sent within an enterprise are often checked against an internal directory for validity. This is not always the case with paper mail.

- The message content is introduced in a clearly defined area.

- Electronic files can be attached in their 'native' form without modification.

Food for thought

E-Mail as document manager?

Electronic mail is sometimes used as a 'lightweight' search and retrieval tool for documents: users often remember from whom or to whom a document has been sent – most commonly as a message attachment – as well as the subject matter, and can define an approximate timeframe.

Why is it so easy? The simple answer seems to lie in the nature of the 'packaging': in situations where an electronic mail message is being used as the transport mechanism for a document, the package is labelled with 'To', 'From', 'Subject' and is usually accompanied by an explanatory note.

Unintentionally, therefore, your e-mail system is acting as a metadata manager for such documents. Searching metadata is considerably more efficient than full text searches: the metadata fields are standard, and the documents themselves – the attachments – are together in a known location, your inbox, which you can sort, filter and manage.

In addition, the user is more or less able to manage aspects of the message's behavior: to determine when the message is sent, to assign it a degree of importance or urgency and to encrypt or otherwise protect the contents.

Finally, the recipient also has a degree of control over the behavior of incoming messages:

- To filter out or even automatically delete messages on the basis of undesirable known and identifiable senders

- To notify the recipient with an alert for messages indicated as urgent

- To launch other processes or applications when triggered by the presence of a key word or phrase in the subject line or body of text

This example of electronic mail is used to demonstrate an important concept:

Information is data structured for a purpose.

Before electronic processing, structure – and the presentational styles that are associated with the different elements of such structures – certainly improved clarity of a text. But why is this relevant? Because clarity of presentation facilitates visual processing of the information that the structure presents. A message clerk needed to know to whom a message should be delivered. If marked 'urgent', he would assure personally that the message was delivered directly to the recipient, rather than somewhere in the internal mail system.

This physical, paper-based system did not require a rigidly applied format for the different information elements, but the visual cues were the key. A message clerk would be able to distinguish between a subject and a recipient, a misspelled name or a message that did not need to be delivered because the contents were already redundant. Structure certainly helped, but was not indispensable as long as a human was interpreting and processing the information. The 'intelligence' of the routing and messaging system was human.

XML now offers structure to our information again, but without necessarily having to know its purpose or potential uses in later processing. This is a vital point to bear in mind: there are often immense pressures to 'add a little bit more' at the source, but which actually end up limiting the content's potential reuse later in a wider range of situations that may be unforeseen at the time.

Take away the human messenger and such imprecision is no longer tolerated. The most powerful computer systems in the world are still more stupid than a cockroach, so any automated system has to be absolutely rule-based. A mis-addressed e-mail will not be delivered, but a redundant message announcing a meeting that took place the previous day will. Where physical presentation and visual cues were important for human processing, strict respect for predefined and predictable structures is the key to automated or computer-assisted processing.

Electronic mail is a good example of tightly-structured information processing, but it also highlights one big shortcoming: the structure is normally predefined by someone else, and you must take it or leave it. As it follows the office memorandum structure, most people will take it, as it reflects the core needs of light 'messaging'.

A much richer example of content 'structured-with-a-purpose' came with the advent of the World Wide Web. Electronic mail had already developed conventions by which different computers, whatever their operating systems or physical location, could exchange message content, but many were unhappy with its text-character based 'flat file' approach.

HyperText Markup Language (HTML) offered three new advances over text-only messaging:

- Text could be *structured* using a set of common structural and presentational elements from word processing and publishing – headings, paragraphs, justification and type style. These elements could be identified by human and electronic processor alike by means of '*markup tags*' that act as labels to delimit the text to which they refer:

```
<H1>This is a first level heading</H1>
<P>This is a paragraph of text</P>
<H2>This is a second level heading</H2>
...
```

Figure 8. A 'classic' HTML layout

- The file containing the text could be processed like a computer program: being character-based rather than binary, it was easier to establish conventions – the markup tags – that could be recognized and thus processed across different computing platforms and operating systems. An HTML file acts as a program that the client browser processes, interpreting the markup tags as instructions to display the text content in a particular manner:

Figure 9. A browser interprets each tag as an instruction on how to display content

- As well as tags to control display behavior, one particular tag type manages the hypertext. This ability to embed a reference to a target location in the same, or another document on a computer on the other side of the planet, is most commonly expressed as the Web page 'hyperlink' and is executed by a user action. The key to the success of hypertext is that the mechanics of the link reference – the content, destination and transfer protocol involved – is hidden from the end user, as Figure 10 illustrates.

Figure 10. The structure of a hyperlink

The browser interprets a mouse click over the hyperlink as an instruction to fetch another resource, as indicated in the code for the 'target'.

The key to the early success of HTML was the simplicity of its vocabulary – 50 or so basic tags were defined, but useful structures were possible using less than a dozen – coupled with a processor, the browser, that was very tolerant of poor syntax. The combination of a character-based format and the visibility of the 'source code' to the recipient encouraged copying, experimentation and reverse engineering in a way never seen before in conventional programming languages. Millions of users with no experience or interest in programming were nonetheless writing computer programs with each Web page they created.

In those early days of Web production, the emphasis was on content-from-scratch Web pages created specifically for the medium. References to substantive existing content were often off-loaded to a particular and often proprietary format external to Web standards. Soon emphasis was placed on the need to *convert* existing content, further upstream in a proprietary format such as a text processor or database management system, into Web content.

As the Web phenomenon took hold, the emphasis was on 'quick and dirty' development. The client browser remained very tolerant of what were, technically, scripting and run-time programming errors, but as the key factor was 'time to Web', these were ignored. A whole cottage industry developed using lightweight applications, macros and batch processors that would convert content into HTML.

Aside from some basic packaging, HTML did not impose any significant rules regarding the structure of a Web page's content – a basic tag set that permitted a page designer to designate content as a heading, a paragraph or a bulleted list was often enough. Most converters contented themselves with identifying similar structures in a text-processed document and adding the required tags to create the HTML version.

This novelty rapidly wore off, as:

- Hyperlinks had to be manually encoded more often than not

- Text had to be checked for processing errors

- Proprietary codes and behaviors in text or data processing applications sometimes gave unpredictable results

- There was little control over the correspondence between a Web page's layout and the text version

A Web page's tags should define and delimit a structure for the content, but that structure was rarely explicitly laid out, originating rather from the structure handed down from the text processor that provided the content. The emphasis in both was all too often on presentation – 'this is a heading', 'this is in bold', 'this is a new paragraph' – rather than structure.

This was all very well as long as the objective of the Web page remained for an end-user to process information visually, in much the same way as for a word processed text. However, as 'Web technologies' offered a *lingua franca* by which information, text and data could be transmitted across otherwise incompatible computing platforms, HTML came to be seen as a valuable tool for the machine processing of information.

In crude terms, a Web browser could recognize and process a particular HTML tag to display a particular content in a predictable manner. However, the browser remained ignorant of the significance or meaning of a particular tag. A word in **bold** could denote emphasis, a key word or a heading – it was up to the user to interpret the visual cues. A table of information laid out in columns and rows might contain text that a user 'understands' as column headers or row descriptors, but the browser was ignorant of the roles played by different cells.

Early attempts at 'machine interpretation' of HTML content made use of many assumptions and guesswork, for example 'the second column of the fifth row in the first table encountered on the page indicates the unit cost of the product described in the second row of the same column'. This is acceptable provided that no-one changes the page design, you have complete control over the entire Web production cycle, and of course that nothing ever goes wrong.

In theory this will work: in practice, how many times have you seen a corrupted database file in which half the data relating to a product description ends up in the price column? It *looks* wrong, it *is* wrong, the processor only knows that it should contain digits but doesn't, and therefore hangs. Equally, a single code omission or error in interpreting a Web page could leave a machine interpreter hanging. Software needs more clues to identify unambiguously the meaning of specific content.

One approach that gained favour involved adding some keyword or descriptor to a tag in such a way that it would be ignored and invisible to the Web browser, but that could nonetheless be identified by an application. This involved adding *attributes* to a tag's name:

```
<TR>
<TD class='def'>Price</TD>
<TD class='price'>95.99</TD>
</TR>
```

The 'class' attribute is used normally in its role of governing the presentation of different elements of a Web page that uses style sheets. In this example, it is used to give a description of the 'tagged' content. Web browsers will either not 'see' these attributes, or fail to make sense of them, ignore them and move on. The information therefore remains hidden until seen by a processor configured to identify such nuggets. It could for example be required to identify the price of a product on the basis of a search for the appropriate string of characters and process the information it finds.

This works well with one proviso: that the use of such attributes and the names and descriptions given to them are all known and controlled within a particular environment. Furthermore, it is still limited to squeezing the maximum out of a relatively limited set of markup tags, and is still 'hard-coded' in each page. What will happen if you take over the management of someone else's Web pages that also use this approach, except that – in our example – price indicates UK sterling in one tag set and US dollars in another? Or one part of your enterprise underlines the names of its staff while another part reserves use of underlining for its glossary of technical terms.

Interoperability becomes a big problem.

XML is an attempt to answer these problems. In the chapter on content management, Chapter 10, we will see how XML offers a comprehensive approach to managing the way in which content is created, managed and described to suit the need of a particular enterprise or community of users.

Link management and link rot

The wonderful simplicity of Web hyperlinks has a serious downside for information and content managers: 'link rot'.

On the surface, the hyperlink acts as a magic transporter to another location. The link description that is displayed is the cue to clients of what they can expect to find beyond the link. Because the target of the hyperlink can be located anywhere and called anything, that's often precisely what happens – anywhere and anything!

> ## *Food for thought*
>
> ### 'Container Management'
>
> We hear more and more about 'Content Management Systems' for Web sites that take over major aspects of good housekeeping such as file and link management, development, pre-production and production phases.
>
> It would be more correct to refer to them as 'Container Management Systems' as, with few exceptions, they are concerned with operations at the level of files and distinct Web pages, rather than the management of actual content.

I have lost count of the number of times I have seen collections of Web pages built up with no file-naming or storage conventions or, at best, one known only to the original developer. A large majority of reasonable Web 'container management' systems will take charge of these problems. However, they often deploy either a proprietary naming and organization convention over which the developer has very little real control, or require considerable reconfiguration, presupposing a coherent and well thought-out policy to be established beforehand.

'Link rot' is the phenomenon that has gone hand in hand with such lack of container management: as a developer loses track of the references and pointers created by an increasingly complex mesh of hyperlinks, the dangers of one of one or more of such links going 'bad' increases.

One answer to this, which is addressed later in the book, is to ensure a coherent naming convention for all your content 'chunks' that can be applied to both to paper and electronic content. Such a convention must be robust enough to survive changes of output format without disruption. There is nothing more frustrating for the end user than to see diligently bookmarked pages resulting in a series of 'Web page not found' errors simply because the .htm extensions had been replaced throughout by, for example, .php.

Conclusions

In this chapter we have looked at some major information management challenges, how design and human endeavour has met them, and highlighted the shortcomings of the different solutions. We have very tangentially connected with XML for the first time and have been introduced to some expectations of its use by looking in some detail at information management questions that XML sets out to address.

In the next chapter, we will look more explicitly at XML's design goals, meet the family of XML standards and gain an insight into their functions and uses. We will then be able to start to build a detailed picture of how these standards can be used to develop comprehensive information and knowledge management solutions.

3 Why XML?

For text and other media to be combined, exchanged and published, it must be organised within some kind of infrastructure. The XML standard provides such a platform

Neil Bradley, *The XML Companion*

Introduction

In the first two chapters we examined some major concerns of information management and had a glimpse of how they might be addressed with XML. The time has come, therefore, to meet the family, of XML itself and some of its offspring.

We will start by examining XML's origins briefly and, more importantly, the design principles and goals that its creation was intended to address. We will then examine XML itself and the range of related standards, and the principal means by which XML can be processed, particularly in the light of information management problems that we have set out to address.

We should be clear on one point, however: this chapter is not intended to be a comprehensive guide to the technical intricacies of XML, and no developer should launch into any substantial project armed only with this information. The guide to further reading at the end of the book should help as a pointer to more in-depth material.

Having examined the range of standards, and to which problems they might be applied, we then aim to set out a high-level business case for the use of XML, and identify the implications that its deployment throws up for management, thus tackling the core concerns of the book.

Design principles

The team that developed the original XML standard set out ten goals by which they intended to evaluate the outcome of their work. Of these ten, five are of particular interest to us:

- The standard should be usable directly over the Internet, using its existing infrastructure, protocols and standards.

- XML must have a wide range of possible uses – it scope should not be not limited to Web pages, databases or text processing, but preferably cover all three and many more besides.

- It should be easy to write XML documents.

- It should be easy to create applications that process XML documents. This is of particular significance in businesses where design-to-production time is important.

- XML documents should be readable by humans, not just by machines. This has meant that the entirety of XML documents – content and 'markup', as we shall see later – is written in plain text rather than a binary format. This also explains why we refer to XML files as 'documents'.

These goals have helped to shape a set of principles that are central to the effective use of XML. Although XML has certainly not invented these principles, it makes them more easy to apply. We will look at these principles before examining the XML standard itself, in order to keep in mind the strategy we develop through the book.

XML functions on the basis of a number of key principles:

- Separation of form and content

- Authoring of documents within a constrained or 'bridled' structure, often referred to as a 'schema'

- Storage of structure, labelling and content in clear text rather than binary format, and created according to an agreed standard

- 'Semantic' labelling of content 'chunks'

- 'Keys' to understanding the labelling accessible to all

- The entirety of the rules regarding the structure of a text or document type, as well as additional functions including further processing, linking and management, should themselves be written in XML

Let us look at these principles in turn.

Separation of structure, content and presentation

I remember my very first text processor. It was a small program that ran on a VAX750 minicomputer, and it very literally 'processed' my text. Three stages had to be rigorously followed:

- Firstly, I would write my content in a simple text editor, oblivious to format, layout or pagination

- Secondly, I would annotate or 'mark up' my text with processing instructions such as 'from here: in bold' and 'from here: end bold' or 'define a page header', and save the file

- Finally, this 'source file' would be processed – or 'parsed' – through the dedicated word-processing batch program on the computer, generating a formatted output file designed to be passed to a printer

The principal drawbacks of this rather primitive system are obviously a very limited control over presentation and the difficulty of predicting results. However, this supposedly primitive approach embodies one of the central principles and strengths of XML: that content, structure and presentation are three distinct facets of information management and must be treated as such.

The output from this early 1980s system reflected a limitation of the printing and processing possibilities of the time, rather than being conceptually flawed. The same cannot be said of many popular, so called 'WYSIWYG' ('what you see is what you get') word-processing systems, where presentation and content are entirely mixed, with few opportunities to identify underlying information structure.

Text is not simply a stream of words, even if it might seem so to many authors and readers alike. There are structures, from the simplest titles and paragraphs, which are presented to the reader or user in a particular way. This structure will normally precede the actual content, even if only implicitly.

Constrained authoring

Much information content is in fact quite tightly structured, although often those structures may be only implicit in the manner that authors prepare their content. As we saw in the example of e-mail in the previous chapter, some structures are more explicit – often necessary for the automatic processing of the content or to improve presentation and management.

In order to ensure processability, and underline the separations of content, form and presentation, it is useful to *force* authors to respect agreed structures at the point of creation. In this manner, authors are required to place all content within appropriate markup tags. This requires both that these structures are defined and that they are available to authors in a way that they can conveniently use.

Although it is possible to write an XML document directly – as can be done also with HTML – authoring tools have inevitably emerged to help the user concentrate more on content and less on defining the actual tags. Unfortunately, however, many XML-compliant applications still make such structured authoring look too much like the form-filling front-end of a database and not enough like authoring tools. Further, what authoring functions that do exist are more concerned with presentational constructs than with the business of providing relevant structures to a text.

That the structures are agreed *is* important. Users could be constrained to use a structure defined by someone else, as we saw with the example of e-mail, but XML offers more. It is concerned with allowing users, user communities and enterprises to develop and agree shared structures to be used for given types of information and text.

Text not binary

The choice of clear text for the storage of XML documents, rather than any binary format, is important, if controversial for some. A binary solution would have been more efficient from a machine-processing point of view and would allow much smaller files. Having XML documents in plain text, however, means that users can intervene manually to examine or edit them if they wish. Keeping both the content and the containing markup as plain text allows users and programs alike to identify easily not only the structures foreseen by an author but also the intention of those structures.

In reality, many XML systems – whether processing or storing XML – use proprietary binary formats internally to improving operational efficiency. XML in its native plain text form is most useful when exchanging information between systems.

As we saw in the opening chapter, there is no longer a premium on 'terseness', so the added verbosity of XML is not a problem from the point of view of storage. Literally 'spelling things out' is the key to XML's role in interoperability between information systems.

Semantic labelling of content structures

The story of the 1999 Mars Climate Orbiter Mission has passed into folklore amongst XML specialists, and with good reason. That this important NASA mission ended in the orbiter crashing on the surface of the planet as a result of computational error is not in dispute, but the origins and causes of the expensive mistake are telling.

According to reports of the investigations after the crash, a part of the navigation software that controlled the small booster rockets failed to distinguish between the imperial measure of pounds of thrust and the metric measure of Newtons. Each instruction sent to correct the error simply made the situation worse.

While it cannot be claimed that XML on its own can eliminate such errors, its use does involve one vital principle: information about how content should be understood must be made available, via the markup, in the content itself. An application that has certain values passed to it – in the Mars example, for rocket thrust – is also told *explicitly* how to interpret those values. Their intended meaning is not left to assumption, in this case costing NASA more that $250 million. There is clearly a cost to spelling everything out, but this is relatively small compared to the benefit or cost of *not* being clear enough.

It is a fallacy, however, to imply that any machine will actually 'understand' the markup – 'Newtons' or 'pounds of thrust' are both just strings of characters. What XML provides rather is a standardized mechanism by which such semantic constructs – 'understand this term in *this* way' – are exposed and made available.

What is vital, therefore, is prior agreement on the meaning to be attached to particular markup. XML allows you to draw up a 'contract' of common understanding of the meanings to be attributed to the markup, done using an XML schema. This makes XML documents easier to create, validate and manage when the tags used for the markup are human-readable, as they offer insight on their meaning to any human user, particularly those not party to the original contract.

Rules and functions expressed in XML

The entirety of the rules regarding the structure of a text or document type, as well as additional functions including further processing, linking and management, are themselves all written in XML. This *lingua franca* can be applied not only to the sharing of semantics between information content, but also to the sharing of meaning in respect to content processing and management.

All aspects of an integrated information management system could therefore be expressed in XML, including:

- Managing your information and documents themselves – the essence of XML: storing data in a neutral format

- Applying your business rules: your business processing 'middleware'

- Constraining format and structure of data and documents, plus workflow and access

- Controlling user interfaces and information display, including user control over display without affecting underlying content

- Extracting knowledge from information

Usable directly on the Web

One important factor in XML's usability is that it is passed between clients and servers using the same protocols that manage HTML Web pages, so that the tried and tested infrastructure of the Web and the Internet can be used 'as is'.

The genetics of XML

XML is a standard that is designed to encode information in a structured and accessible manner. It is a stable and reliable standard, vendor-independent and managed by the World Wide Web Consortium (W3C) and supported by a wide range of application and system vendors. A number of related standards, each using the core XML standard itself, have also been developed to respond to the specific demands of information management.

Some of these additional standards have been criticized for their apparent complexity and for creating a potentially tangled web of dependencies that might make their deployment less effective or less straightforward. This overlooks the fact that it is in the 'genetic' makeup of XML to be evolutionary, and even more standards are likely to emerge. As with DNA, the complexity of an XML standard or an XML document that uses it is proportional to the complexity of the 'organism' or the task for which it has been designed. For simple tasks and simple document structures, XML can be deployed in a simple manner – this is the principle of extensibility that we find in the standard's name.

To understand the anatomy of XML, we will look at an analogy using natural human language. A single alphabet or character set can underpin a range of languages. This is important of course to keyboard manufacturers, typeface copyright holders and anyone involved in displaying information to an end user. A character set on its own, however, does not constitute a language, any more than being able to recognize individual letters constitutes an ability to understand a language that uses the character set.

In order to understand, there are a number of different layers of recognition:

- That a text is written in a particular alphabet: that καρπός is written in the Greek alphabet, but that фрукт is in the Cyrillic alphabet.

- Which particular language within a given alphabet: 'frucht' and 'fruta' are respectively German and Portuguese, but the word 'fruit' is in which language? English? French? And is фрукт Russian or Ukrainian? This starts to become a little trickier.

Figure 11. "It's all foreign to me…!"

- The meaning of the particular string of characters that make up a word. In the previous example, we could make a stab at meaning, and make the reasonable assumption that 'frucht', 'fruta', and 'fruit' all mean the same thing in each of the four languages (as does фрукт once you recognize that it is pronounced 'frucht'). On the other hand, what are 'plod', 'toradh', 'hedelmä' and 'gyümölcs'? And in which languages?

- In the case of words with multiple meanings, the specific intended meaning can often be deduced from context. If the French word *avocat* appears in a recipe book it is most likely to have a different meaning than if the same word appears in a legal tome. The context provides valuable insight into the probable meaning in a particular situation.

Food for thought

'Faux Amis'

Visiting the elderly grandmother of a French friend, I was invited to taste her home-made jams. We got into a discussion about bottling and preservation. Little did I know that my innocent inquiry about sensible preservatives – rendered literally into my then poorly-mastered French – actually meant 'sensitive contraceptives'. These *faux amis* ('false friends') demonstrate that it is not always sufficient to recognize a word and assume that it belongs to your own vocabulary. Context can help, but beware!

The alphabet and syntax

XML on its own already offers the computing equivalent of a common alphabet and syntax. Each building block of an XML document is constructed in exactly the same manner. Reading an XML document sequentially, a label or 'tag' identifies the start of a particular building block:

```
<fruit>
```

as a means of indicating to human and computing processors alike that what follows is content wrapped by this label:

```
<fruit>orange
```

and that it continues until a matching closing tag indicates the end of the content making up the block:

```
<fruit>orange</fruit>
```

At its most primitive, only three characters:

```
< > /
```

are needed to create basic XML documents if used in this clearly defined manner. This means that conforming XML processors must tackle this first layer of character recognition by giving a special significance to these character combinations.

On its own it may not seem much, and there is a lot more work to do before we can claim understanding. However, the intended meaning of:

```
<fruit>orange</fruit>
```

can be reasonably guessed at by an English speaker. As it happens, for this example, a French speaker would understand exactly the same. Using a language identifier would remove any shadow of doubt.

In programming languages, as in the real world, such labels are often 'members' of a particular group, or vocabulary:

```
<fruit>
<utensil>
<recipe>
```

or:

```
<part number>
<tool>
<process>
```

This is of added value in situations where there might be ambiguity as to the context or meaning of particular content. We came across the French word *avocat* earlier: it can mean either the avocado fruit or 'lawyer'. Most of the time the context will guide the user as to which translation and meaning is the correct one.

An XML tag, on the other hand, can banish any possible ambiguity, particularly for the stupid computer:

```
<fruit>avocat</fruit>
<profession>avocat</profession>
```

To do this, XML allows you to declare particular element names as being part of a particular vocabulary.

Understanding the labelling: the vocabulary

Labels can often be ambiguous when different people use the same term to signify different ideas:

```
<title>Mr</title>
<title>Information Architecture with XML</title>
```

We therefore need a mechanism that allows humans and computers alike to be warned that the name or label on a particular building block is to be understood in a specific way as part of a vocabulary – particularly if different vocabularies use the same labels:

```
<title (by which I mean Mr, Dr, etc)>
<title (by which you mean title of a book)>
<title (by which she means a piece of legislation)>
```

XML tackles this second layer of meaning – identifying to which particular set a specific building block belongs – through the use of 'namespaces'. A namespace is an arbitrary label which, according to its specification, takes the particular form of a 'Uniform Resource Identifier' (URI) such as:

```
xmlns:book="urn:xmlbystealth-net:book"
```

The namespace declaration does not actually have to 'point' to anything: it is merely an arbitrary but unique label, reserved for a particular set of tags or vocabulary. It serves to warn that a specific meaning has been attributed to a set of tags and that specific treatment of those tags is expected according to that meaning. In a piece of markup the namespace prefix is then used to declare unambiguously a particular element name as 'belonging' to a specific vocabulary, and thus to be understood in the way that that vocabulary demands:

```
<book:title>Information Architecture with XML</book:title>
```

By whom, how and where such sets of tags, or vocabularies, are defined is the subjects of Chapter 5, *Foundations of an XML Framework*. It is sufficient here to recognize that once a particular tag has been explicitly flagged as belonging to a vocabulary, the dangers of ambiguity are greatly reduced. In addition, use of the namespace mechanism can go further and allow a user or process actually to be pointed to a definition.

Be warned however, that the use of namespaces does not in itself ensure that an otherwise conformant XML-processor will know what to make of the namespace declaration: that is a matter of programming. And that itself means that humans understand the intention of a particular label in a particular context, underlining once more the value of XML being in plain text.

Food for thought

Identifying natural language

In the examples above, I used two tags, <fruit> and <profession>. Although which *natural* language deployed would normally by evident in context, they could both still be meaningful in either English or French. I could eliminate any doubt by indicating the language of a particular content by using the XML language 'attribute' xml:lang thus:

```
<fruit xml:lang="EN">orange</fruit> or
```

```
<fruit xml:lang="FR">orange</fruit>
```

We look at the concept of attributes in more detail in the next section.

Meaning

It can be tempting to sign off XML interoperability too soon, thinking that simply creating a set of meaningful tags is enough. We have already seen how 'namespaces' make it easier to associate a particular name to a specific context, but it still makes us none the wiser as to the actual *meaning*.

In many other areas of application integration, process modelling and knowledge management, enterprises are seeing the value of establishing centrally-managed 'business vocabularies' that define certain key terminology in unambiguous terms for use consistently across the enterprise. There is both an immediate association between such efforts and the naming of XML constructs, and a longer-term benefit in defining and naming 'topics' in the context of knowledge management – as we will see in Chapter 13.

The anatomy of XML

An XML document is a continuous and sequential stream of characters. This stream is punctuated with 'markup', consisting of:

- *Elements*: the basic, labelled information container that we have seen already

- *Attributes*: reference or other control information

- *Comments*: unprocessed text that serves only human readers

- *Processing instructions* or PIs: as an 'escape mechanism' from the stream, allowing non-XML processing or manipulation of non-XML content

- *Entities*: placeholders for a block of text, set of rules, or even entire XML-documents that are defined outside the character stream

We have already encountered the first two: the following sections explain them in more detail.

Elements

At its most primitive, an XML document contains text enclosed in any number of perfectly-nested elements. Such containment within elements is indicated to human and machine processor alike with a pair of tags.

```
<recipe>
<step>Gently fry 2 finely sliced
<ingredient>onions</ingredient> in
<quantity>30g</quantity> of
<ingredient>unsalted butter</ingredient> for
<time>several minutes</time>. Add the
<ingredient>sausage meat</ingredient>,
<ingredient>chopped liver</ingredient> and
<ingredient>cooked chestnuts</ingredient>
...
<step>
...
</recipe>
```

The tag label can currently only contain only ASCII alphanumeric and a handful of other characters, while any Unicode character can be used elsewhere in an XML document. There is however an initiative under way within the W3C to change this, the 'Blueberry' initiative.

Attributes

The start tags of an element can optionally contain any number of attributes. By convention these usually store values for reference or processing purposes, or indicate specific properties of a given information content. Attributes come in 'name/value' pairs. There is often only a very fine distinction between the use of an element or an attribute – this issue is examined in detail in Chapter 5.

We could add attributes to our recipe:

```
<recipe>
<step n°="1">Gently fry 2 finely sliced
<ingredient ref="0687">onions</ingredient> in
<quantity measure="metricWeight">30</quantity>
<measure>g</measure> of
<ingredient ref="0688">unsalted butter</ingredient> for <time mea-
sure="informal">several minutes</time>. Add the
<ingredient ref="0689">sausage meat</ingredient>,
<ingredient ref="0690">chopped liver</ingredient> and
<ingredient ref="0691">cooked chestnuts</ingredient>
...
</step>
...
</recipe>
```

Here we can see that the elements are the same: the two documents are made up of the same semantic building blocks. However, the properties of some of the element content are different, hence there are different values for the attributes.

Comments

In common with many programming languages, comments allow authors and programmers to embed comments and ideas in the stream of characters without having any influence on the processing of an XML document.

```
<!--Recipe first tested out in December 1996 -->
```

There is one fundamental difference however between XML and programming languages: as the terminology in XML is extensible, it is unlikely that you will ever have to resort to the formal comment construct to express a comment. Indeed, this book argues very much against using it at all – comments, in general, are a form of human user documentation or information. XML comments are often lost – stripped away – by a properly-functioning XML parser, and it would be far better in many cases to define and use a specific <comment> element that can be stripped away only when you want, and otherwise maintained in the source document.

Processing instructions

XML is designed to allow non-XML content to be included in an XML document without problems. This is done using processing instructions and entities.

Processing instructions, or PIs, are a structured means of allowing processors to pass non-XML content to another application or process for handling in a specific manner:

```
<?process1 source="recipe.txt"?>
```

The instruction can be anything, provided that the XML application handling the document knows what to do when it encounters such an instruction – for example, launch another application or load a file.

Entities

Entities can be thought of as a type of placeholder. When an XML processor encounters an entity in a data stream, it is required to replace the placeholder with the 'target' content indicated by the entity.

Different types of entity are recognized by XML. Examples include:

- *Predefined entities*. These allow the five special characters used in XML markup, <, >, &, ', and " to be included as normal characters in content rather than as indicators of markup. For example, the symbol '<' cannot be used within content, as it would signal the beginning of the content element's end tag. Therefore its corresponding entity '<' is used instead.

  In this first example, the following:

  ```
  <example>Using the < entity in content</example>
  ```

  would cause an error, as the processor would be expecting the matching end tag label as soon as it encounters the '<' in the text. The following however, would process normally:

  ```
  <example>Using the &lt; entity in content</example>
  ```

  and the '<' be preserved and understood as representing the character '<' when needed later.

- *User-defined entities*. These, as their name suggests, permit a user to specify a 'shorthand' to signify a target piece of text, markup or mixture of both. This is particularly useful when there is much repetition within a document, such as a particularly long or oft-used name or title, or when reference needs to be made to a particular text indirectly using a reference, for example for security reasons, or to protect personal data. Supposing that the entity is defined – we'll see how and where later – we could have a document that includes:

  ```
  <proceedings>In the case against &X; little evidence has been...
  ```

  where the entity reference '&X;' would only be replaced at processing/ If the definition and resolution of the reference are kept secure, the actual value of the information referred to can be made available only when and how you wish.

- *External entities*. These can be anything from a string of characters to a whole document. In this case the placeholder 'translates' as a filename or other resource location that allows a processor to find the entity's contents, or hand them off – in the case of non-XML content – to another application.

Well-formedness

All XML documents will contain a mix of these five constituents, but the only minimum requirement is that an entire XML document is contained within a 'root' element – a matching start and end tag pair – as the first and last parts of the data stream:

```
<doc>This is a perfectly legal and complete XML document</doc>
```

Beyond that, there is a requirement that every XML document is 'well formed'. This means that all elements are properly 'nested' within each other – elements must be completely contained within their respective 'parent' without any overlap.

'Granularity'

The extent of detail or 'granularity' of the markup will be an important design consideration, as we will see in Chapters 5 and 6. For the moment, it is sufficient to note that:

• Too much markup could put off the average author, if the volume of markup required represents too much of an overhead:

```
<recipe>
<step n°="1">
<objective>First of all, prepare the <term>stuffing</term>. </objec-
tive>
<process>
<technique>Gently fry
<quantity measure="unit">2</quantity>
<preparation>finely sliced </preparation>
<ingredient ref="0687">onions</ingredient> in
<quantity measure="weight">30</quantity>
<measure>g</measure>
<ingredient ref="0688">unsalted butter</ingredient> for <time mea-
sure="informal">several minutes</time>.
<technique>Add</technique> the
<ingredient ref="0689">sausage meat</ingredient>,
<ingredient ref="0690">chopped liver</ingredient> and
<ingredient ref="0691">cooked chestnuts</ingredient>
...
</process>
</step>
...
</recipe>
```

- Too little markup, and the benefits of such markup cannot be felt, as there is insufficient detail:

```
<paragaph>First of all, prepare the stuffing. Gently fry 2 finely
sliced onions in 30g unsalted butter for several minutes. Add the
sausage meat, chopped liver and crumbled chestnuts...</paragraph>
```

Finding the right balance is essential: it will rarely be the individual programmer or project leader that can decide, precisely because their assessment will be made largely in the context of their own needs. You need a wider and higher view.

X-M-L

We cannot underline the point enough: XML is neither a technology nor a programming language – it is a data-encoding standard.

Although it can be processed or 'eaten raw', the benefits of XML will only be felt if specific uses, functions and processes are clearly defined.

'X' is for extensibility

The great advantage over HTML is that XML permits and encourages the creation of markup tags for specific purposes. The generic nature of HTML markup <TITLE>, <H1> and <P> makes processing possibilities very limited. On the other hand, the fact that XML allows *any* tagging or structure to be defined by a user means that the situation can rapidly become over-complex and out of control.

The need is for controlled vocabularies developed by communities of users working with similar documents and information types. This has been the backbone of the spectacular success of those e-businesses working in highly information-integrated environments. These controlled vocabularies are expressions of collaborative intent:

'Together, *we* intend that *this* particular markup tag be understood to mean *that*'

The 'we' in this statement can be any group of business units or enterprises working with similar information types. These vocabularies can be expressed as a specific, published markup language, or as a series of schemas or formal designs that define the semantic structure of specific XML documents

We will see, in particular in Chapters 6 and 7, that one step in this direction is to set up a process between interested parties by which agreement is sought to 'markup' and structure identified texts in a common manner.

'M' is for markup   How much or how little needs to be marked-up and identified? At its most comprehensive, an all-XML information and document management system will identify and markup every discrete 'atomic' item of information with appropriate tags and attributes.

At its most basic, markup could be limited to some types of 'packing information' – metadata or other information accompanying and describing the content of a document or information set, rather than markup of the content itself.

Given the early deployment benefits of such metadata management, this can be the ideal starting point for any XML implementation strategy, as we will investigate in Chapter 5.

'L' is for language   XML documents are marked-up for a reason: so that they can be processed, by human as well as by machine. That processing can take many forms:

- Determining the presentation of a document for different media, together with style-sheet processing instructions (using CSS, XSLT and XSL-FO – these and other processing standards are defined later in this chapter)

- Managing work processes and workflow, triggering particular actions according to values found in the markup (using XSL, SOAP, DOM and SAX or any 'bespoke' system)

- Implementing any process or function that a user community could care to define and develop particular applications for that are capable of recognizing and managing XML-conformant markup.

XML documents without applications that can use and process them, let alone create them in the first place, are therefore of limited interest. It is not normally difficult to find enough potential 'partners' that represent a sufficient user-base to make collaborative efforts not only worthwhile, but economic good sense, with rapid returns on investment and economies of scale. In the private sector, they could even be your competitors!

The biggest value of markup, however, is to make your content available to any process or application, even ones that you don't know about or have not yet been developed.

The XML family

On its own, XML is nothing more that an alphabet and a syntax. The XML standard itself merely lays down the rules needed to create compliant XML documents. As we shall see, XML schemas offer a mechanism for laying down a vocabulary and a grammar to express your particular needs as 'content models'.

We are therefore not so interested in 'raw' XML as the particular 'variety' or dialect that we establish for a particular need.

Food for thought

Beware the 'XML expert'

When it comes to garnering expertise, handle with caution any expert that declares confidently 'Yes, I know XML' – it is like saying, 'I know the alphabet' – so what?

It's having a vocabulary and being able to string sentences together that help you master a language and forward the claim to be able to communicate. XML is no different. So be sure to look for the right experience in XML deployment.

This is an important issue for managers. You can develop vocabularies and grammars that let you describe and create XML entities as diverse as blocks of text, formatting rules, complex graphics, business rules or an application interface. This explains the power that XML offers for wide-scale interoperability.

Indeed, the 'tricky bits' in any XML strategy will not be the questions relating to understanding XML itself and having sufficient users and developers high on the learning curve. The hard work will come in agreeing standards and vocabularies and in document and information design considerations. These are policy rather than technical issues and have to be handled and answered by management, not by programmers or developers.

This point serves to underline the central message of this book:

Management needs to take the lead and stay ahead.

What can XML do for me, then?

To know what 'XML can do for you', you need to be aware of the range of XML standards that are available. Although there is an ever-increasing and bewilderingly interrelated range of standards, they fall into three broad categories:

- *Infrastructure standards*: the bedrock of the family, these are the standards that offer the basic building blocks, raw materials and infrastructure of any XML strategy

- *Processing and management standards*: these are concerned with actually 'doing something' with your XML content

- *Output standards*: these are concerned with delivering or displaying XML content to a specific end format, and usually represent the end of a processing chain

In addition, there are XML 'applications' – the application of XML to a particular end using a common vocabulary, whether to meet the needs of a particular business sector (insurance, manufacturing, public administration etc.) or to enable inter-operability in one form or another.

We will now take a brief look at the members of the family. The objective is not to gain the intimate knowledge of each standard that is necessary to start a development project, but rather to gain a high-level overview of the scope of the standards and their intended application to information management problems. These family members, unless stated otherwise, are published and maintained by the World Wide Web Consortium, W3C and published in the form of *recommendations*.

Architecture and design standards

The basis for all XML work is the XML standard itself. It can be used on its own to created the so-called 'well-formed' document that we mentioned briefly before.

It can also be used with one or more Document Type Definitions, or DTDs, to 'validate' that the way XML is used in a particular document conforms to the intentions and expectations of the user or document designer. In addition, DTDs serve to inform other potential users of the structure and possible internal constraints of a document, so that those users and automated processes can know what to expect.

The structure and syntax of DTDs are unusual within the family, as DTDs themselves are not written in XML, but instead employ the syntax of XML's 'parent' standard, SGML (Standard Generalized Markup Language).

Many commentators and XML evangelists alike have been predicting the early death of DTDs, as they are considered to not 'fit the picture' of an elegant set of standards all written in XML. Such predictions have proved premature, largely because of the delays and controversies associated with the much-awaited 'schema' standard, and also the DTDs familiarity to those document-management specialists who cut their teeth on SGML.

XML schema

Although suitable for validating the structure of an XML document, the DTD has nonetheless a number of important limitations.

Firstly, although it allows validation of the required and expected structure of a document, such as the correct positioning and nesting of elements, it can say nothing about the validity of the content.

Taking a leaf from the database designer's book, the XML schema adds also the concept of 'data-typing'. This allows a designer to specify what a specified XML element should contain, for example a date, an integer within a particular range, just text. In addition, XML schemas can include user-defined datatypes, such as a Zip code specified in a particular format, a name from a predefined list or a product or reference code.

An information manager should avoid being embroiled in the details of schema design, but nonetheless maintain a high-level view of their development. What is important is to give your developers guidelines on the basis of clear and comprehensive analyses of your information and document types. We will look at this in Chapter 6.

There are ongoing debates about whether document analysts and designers should now abandon the DTD completely in favour of schemas in one form or another. Without losing ourselves in the detail, a good reason for using DTDs would if an organization already had a substantial investment in SGML and associated tools. SGML tools validate conformity of document instances to their associated types exclusively by means of the DTD.

The second limitation – now no longer valid – is that the XML Schema standard has not yet been finalized, so that developers must hedge their bets for some time to come. If your organization is coming into XML 'clean', with little or no SGML legacy, it is probably better to opt for the more powerful schema.

In this book we will not make much reference to DTDs explicitly, even if their use can still be appropriate in places where schemas are mentioned, unless specifically necessary.

Namespaces

As we saw earlier, labels can often be ambiguous when different people use the same term to signify different ideas. When processing a document, elements may well be checked against a schema. In a schema, each element's *content* could additionally be validated against a datatype. Remember the example of:

    <title>

If the schema is expecting 'Dr.', 'Ms.', or 'Prof.', but is instead presented with a book title, the processor would probably throw an error. The XML Namespace standard is a simple but powerful mechanism that allows us to use the same term in different contexts.

By declaring that XML elements belong to a specific vocabulary and identifying them as such through a namespace declaration, we eliminate any possible ambiguity.

XML Infoset

The Infoset – or XML Information Set – can be thought of as a normalized inventory of, or reference model for, the parts of an XML document. Its main use is intended for developers that require that a data model and related information – the *information items* that make up an XML document's Infoset – are made available by a conforming XML processor for use and manipulation by an XML-aware application.

It should not be confused with the 'Document Object Model' – see below.

XML base   HTML has already introduced the idea of a base reference to allow a Web page devel-
                      oper to avoid repeating the full URL everywhere it is used, but instead use addresses
                      relative to a defined 'base'. The same concept is used with XML, allowing other related
                      standards and constructs to use similar relative addressing methods.

XML fragments   A *logical* XML document can be composed of any number of *physical* components. For
                      example, a complete XML document might be broken down into, say, chapters, like this
                      book, with each fragment being maintained and stored separately. At the same time, a
                      schema might specify the overall structure. A single chapter, read alone by an XML-
                      conformant tool and checked against the schema, would possibly throw errors unless it
                      was given some clue that the fragment is part of a larger whole.

                      It is necessary, therefore, that the different parts – or *fragments* – can be distinctly iden-
                      tified and related to each other independently of their context. The XML Fragment
                      standard allows for different components to be organized or managed in separate envi-
                      ronments. The standard therefore allows developers to manage the component parts of a
                      document without fear of losing the logical connections between them.

XPath   XPath is the only member of the XML family that does not itself share XML's basic
                      syntax. XPath is a syntax intended to identify specific parts of an XML document, often
                      known as 'nodes', and then locate them by offering a path to them relative to a defined
                      point in the document. XPath is not strictly an XML application on its own, but is
                      intended for use with XSLT and XPointer.

                      These two standards use this path to point to or process a particular part of a document
                      that conforms to specified criteria. For example, an XPath expression could be
                      constructed to identify every block of information contained within a particular element
                      type, or all content contained within an element with a certain attribute value.

                      Two other standards can be considered here, although technically speaking they are
                      specific XML *applications* – SVG and MathML.

SVG   Scalable Vector Graphics (SVG) is a standard that encapsulates graphics and describes
                      them using an XML vocabulary. While initially this might seem a long-winded way of
                      encoding graphics, the programmability and transformability of XML means that
                      graphics so described can be generated, manipulated and transformed in the same way
                      as any other XML document. Further, the elements of a graphic can, like any other XML
                      element, carry valuable semantic information to describe themselves.

                      As graphics themselves are often used either to reproduce real-life objects or concepts
                      (think of the graphics in the simplest workflow diagram), the potential for SVG starts to
                      become apparent. We will examine this in later chapters.

MathML
Given the particular difficulties of representing complex mathematical equations in word-processing packages, MathML allows both the presentation of mathematical notation and the content of mathematical expressions in XML. This allows such expressions to be used in machine-to-machine transactions, which was previously impossible if the mathematical formula could not be captured other than as graphics.

Processing standards
A number of other members of the XML family are used to *process* rather than merely describe content. These standards include:

XSLT
Extensible Stylesheet Transformation Language, XSLT, is something of a misnomer, as it has little to do with document styles or presentation. It is rather concerned with transforming a source XML document into a target XML document according to a series of instructions applied to the identified parts of the document. This is of particular value when many documents of a particular type and structure are to be transformed in a standard and predetermined manner.

One immediate and popular use of this standard is to transform a complex XML document into a simpler HTML version that can then be directly displayed in a browser as a Web page.

XLink
Anyone familiar with the World Wide Web will recognize the simple hyperlink, consisting of a 'hot-spot' on a page that, when clicked, takes the user to a destination indicated in the target address embedded in the hyperlink code.

XML is not limited to use in displayed Web pages, but the linking concept is essential. Although HTML is limited to creating single-dimensional one-way links, XLink allows developers to link two or more content 'chunks' together in such a way that the links can be traversed in either direction.

This requires not only that the target is uniquely identifiable, but also the source: if a two-way link is to be created, clear 'labels' are needed at both ends of the link. This raises the need for coherent resource identification and naming conventions for all information content. This is a cornerstone of a solid information architecture and scalable XML-centred system, as we will see.

XPointer
While an Internet-accessible file can be identified and addressed by reference to its URI, use of XPointer allows a specific location or fragment *within* a file to be addressed. Using the XPath language introduced above, a pointer – either in the form of a specific fragment identifier, or expressed as a query that is resolved when addressed – allows parts of a document to be addressed by context or nature, rather than by means of an explicit static label.

DOM

The Document Object Model is not really a model, despite its name. Rather, it is a series of interfaces that allow the entire contents of a specific XML document to be presented as an application programming interface (API), allowing any conformant XML application to identify, address and perform operations on designated parts of the document.

SAX

While DOM builds a complete interface to a document, the Simple API for XML (SAX) takes the document a step at a time. It allows a processor to perform actions on particular points in the document as and when they are encountered when 'reading' the document from start to finish.

See *Processing XML* later in this chapter for further details on these two standards and their use in interfacing with XML documents.

RDF and Topic Maps

XML, properly used, allows you to identify clearly the building blocks of your content. It does not however offer much insight into the way in which the different blocks or document types might relate to each other.

For example, one document may contain a piece of draft legislation and a second a proposal for an amendment to that draft. The respective nature of the two document types may be clear and well-documented in the XML markup applied to them. What is less immediately clear is that the second document will amend the content of the first. There is no inherent way in XML to represent the relationship between them.

Two standards exist to address this sort of question. The first, the Resource Description Framework (RDF) grew out of work in the World Wide Web Consortium. The second, 'Topic Maps' emerged from the International Standards Organisation (ISO). Both offer powerful means of describing the conceptual relationships between different addressable resources.

More recently (August 2001) an XML formulation of the Topic Maps standard has emerged – 'XML for Topic Maps' or 'XTM'. It makes the strengths of both RDF and Topic Maps directly available using the same XML grammar and syntax.

SMIL

The Synchronised Multimedia Integration Language ('SMIL', pronounced 'smile') is designed to encourage the authoring and packaging of multimedia presentations, particularly where time synchronization is important. An example might be a video recording with subtitles in multiple languages and links to related texts or resources mentioned during the recording.

Presentation and publication standards

A third set of members of the XML family is concerned with getting XML out of a computer and application-centred environment and into a more human-readable one. As we saw in Chapter 2, humans like visual cues to guide their understanding of a document structure's intent. These presentation and publication standards aim to do that

Canonical XML

We mention this standard here even though its use is normally closely associated with electronic authentication issues. Canonical XML, despite its fearsome name, is a standard that provides the means of ensuring that two XML documents that are identical in *intent* are not considered as being different because of minor or otherwise irrelevant differences in their formal XML representation. This is important for example, when:

- A particular physical representation of a document is relevant – for example a text is in red, irrespective of whether the color code says 'red' or '#FF0000'

- In authentication procedures, it is necessary to assess whether any changes that a processor has made to a document have actually altered the substance – for example, irrelevant white space or a comment being stripped by a parser

XSL-FO

Originally a single draft recommendation, the Extensible Stylesheet Language (XSL) was separated into two distinct projects and subsequent recommendations. The first was concerned with the transformation of a source XML document to a target through the application of templates, the XSLT described on page 65.

The second type of transformation – and closer to other understandings of stylesheets – concerns the transformation of a source XML document into a given output or display format: XSL Formatting Objects. This recommendation is concerned with the way in which the different parts of a document are rendered to a particular presentation device or medium, such as a Web browser, DIN A4-sized paper, a PDA or a mobile phone screen. XSL-FO is therefore concerned with once-only rendering to a *terminal format* that is not destined for any further processing.

CSS

The Cascading Style Sheet recommendation was originally developed to leverage some separation between HTML content and presentation. Its principal motivation was the growing problem of maintaining visual identity in large or rapidly-evolving Web sites. It has evolved to manage quite advanced presentation issues, giving more control over how Web pages are rendered on user's browsers according to their preferences.

The CSS recommendation essentially associates a series of presentational and/or formatting styles with defined tags or attributes. As such, it is a 'low-energy' alternative to XSL-FO for formatting XML documents rendered within Web browsers.

Processing XML

In order actually to *do* anything with XML content, the source XML document has first to be *parsed*. This involves processing the source file by a software application that then 'presents' the source to an XML-aware program to work on.

The two main approaches to processing XML have come to be known as *stream* and *tree* processing. In stream (or event-based) processing, the analogy is that of a single continuous current or stream of data: the whole document is parsed from start to finish, one byte at a time. An XML processor is passed the stream of data from the parser and reacts to the content and markup as and when it encounters it in the data stream. It thus reacts to 'events' as and when they are encountered. Such processors can be very fast, as they can be very small: they only have to keep in memory a small chunk of a document at any one time. On the other hand, they have no foreknowledge of what is coming later in the stream.

Figure 12. Processing of XML

In Figure 12, think of every 'bend' in the path as representing the opening or closing tag of an element. Whilst SAX follows the path of the line, DOM gives you the whole picture.

In *tree* processing, a two-dimensional 'map' of a document is created, with each branch representing a nested element within the overall structure. Processors that handle this approach are likely to be much more complex: as a complete picture of the document is built in memory of the tree, any prior knowledge of the likely size of a document or document type allows realistic predictions to be made as to the memory requirements.

It is difficult to predict the processing power and memory required to process a particular document in this manner – it will be proportional to the size and complexity of the XML document. When complex, non-sequential manipulations and transformations are to be performed, or indeed when there is any interactivity with a user or other processes, the tree approach 'exposes' the whole document simultaneously and very efficiently.

The stream and tree approaches are closely associated with sequential and hierarchical processing. The SAX and DOM recommendations introduced above offer a standardized interface for each of the two processing approaches.

Whither XML?

There has been some concern about the stability of the basic XML standard. XML Version 1 is certainly stable and widely in use. Version 1.1 is offered as a minor update that clarifies a couple of compatibility issues and makes XML fully international. There is an ongoing debate within the World Wide Web Consortium, however, about updating XML more radically.

A particular concern is to break off its cumbersome links with SGML – notably the DTD – and to incorporate within the core standard other members of the family that many consider an indispensable part of XML itself. One approach that has been broached would be to drop DTDs and references to entities, add XML Base, Namespaces and the Infoset and re-baptize the whole as a new XML version. There is clearly a strong desire by many to drop the dependency on SGML that is responsible for the 'foreign' syntax found in parts of the XML standard.

The Consortium has established a Technical Architecture Group (TAG) with a mission to address and hopefully resolve these issues. Together with issues regarding referencing of resources – increasingly important given the growing area of Web services – this promises to be a rocky ride, but should be followed with attention.

XML applications

In addition to the 'standards' as such, there is a whole range of specific XML vocabularies that have been developed as a response to particular sectoral or other interoperability needs. In formal terms these are called *XML applications*, and should not be confused with applications that process or use XML. For the latter, to avoid a terminological jungle, favour the use of 'XML Tools' or 'XML-aware programs'.

Where (not) to use XML

XML is about encapsulating data with semantic wrappers, and as such can be used in a whole range of areas to store and process:

- *Information content* (data, text or a mixture of both). XML 'constrains' text into semantic building blocks and maintains the importance, for text, of 'sequence' – something completely absent from database systems. At the same time, XML can constrain content through database style data-typing and enforcing conformity to permissible value ranges for particular content elements, by using XML schemas.

XML thus offers advantages to both text-processing tools and database management systems. It also means that XML-centred systems can use the strengths of both: the efficiency of queries, sorting, filtering, search and retrieve of a database paradigm, coupled with the read and writeability, sequencing, flow and humanly-manageable features of the word processing paradigm. It dissolves the artificial barrier between the two.

- *Business rules*. XML can be used to encapsulate your information workflow and can be a central part of a business process management strategy.

- *Massaging between systems*. You can think of XML schemas as contractual agreements on the meaning of content in a particular context. With information flowing in an enterprise between disparate systems, it is critical that messages do not deteriorate in quality at each step.

- *Transformation, presentation and display rules*. This is the 'workhorse' area of XML, with content repurposing supporting the principle of 'single source, multiple use' and the possibilities of content reuse.

- *Knowledge management*. A well thought-through XML architecture and use of controlled vocabularies for semantic structures will help the development of intelligent search and discovery, 'rot-free' link management and dynamic content delivery. XML can help in extract meaning from text and, together with RDF and/or Topic Maps, can help express meaning and relationships between concepts.

XML would seem for the above to be usable everywhere, particularly with complex, textual structures and high-volume information exchange between heterogeneous systems. XML can capture any information in Unicode, metadata, containment, order of content, hierarchical relations and processing information – whether using XML-based processing or simple 'escapes' to proprietary applications.

However, it is less usable in some areas, notably:

- *Programming*. XML is not a programming language. The nearest it comes to it is the XSLT standard, but even this is only a declarative language, relying on example rather than programming logic to achieve its transformation processes.

- *Modelling*. XML is not in itself a modelling language, although models can be expressed in XML, something we will return to in more detail in Chapter 6.

Conclusions

In this chapter, we have not only looked at XML and the family of standards that had grown around it, but have started to build of picture of how it is used, processed and presented.

By now, we should start to understand some of the risks of plunging right in, as XML is not, on its own, a guarantee of inter-operability or understanding between systems.

Taken with the first two chapters, this chapter rounds off the introductory part of the book that has attempted to put XML in the context of information management concerns in general. In the following chapters, we will start to build a deeper understanding and set out a management strategy for introducing XML to the enterprise.

But what is it about XML that seems to require such an upheaval in IT and management? As we will see, there is a need to keep a 'holistic' view of XML's deployment, and there are serious and deep management implications that must be taken on board. Y2K highlighted all too clearly how many 'all-in-one' information systems did not adapt easily to change.

XML wants to go even further and forces a number of important changes in roles and responsibilities within the enterprise, including:

- *Authors*, whether bringing them into the world of structured composition of text, with an emphasis on representation and not presentation, or in the *ex post facto* restructuring of content downstream.

- *Documentalists*. Specialists in documentation and document classification, often tucked away in documentation centres and archive services, their skills are being called for upstream as XML allows encapsulation of valuable metadata and other information at document creation time.

- *Disintermediation*, or 'cutting out the middle man': XML promotes the automatic and seamless transformation of content between systems and formats – which is fine as long as you know what to do with all those staff who have built their skills-base on precisely that.

- *Editors and designers* will be drawn into XML issues, despite seeing these as questions exclusively for IT staff.

Shortage of IT professionals requires non-IT managers to understand the concepts and importance of XML and information management, and to keep their management focus while encouraging scarce IT professionals to concentrate on their core competences.

4 Developing a Management Strategy

Introduction

In the first three chapters we looked at the main concerns of information management and what the XML family of standards can offer to address them. We have floated some ideas of where this should be taking us, but we need to develop a clear and comprehensive work plan to keep them afloat and see them through into something practical.

In the following chapters, we will outline a strategy for introducing and implementing XML in a way that keeps a focus on your important information assets. We will *not* be looking at how to develop XML tools or specific applications, but rather how to build what I call an *XML framework*. This framework will be a combination of rules, guidelines and best practices brought together and managed as an accessible point of reference for any XML developer or analyst. It will be your information architecture for an XML-centred, information-rich enterprise.

When starting out, we need to think a little about two key questions regarding our proposed management strategy:

- What is the nature of the work?

- What is the scope of the work?

Regarding the nature of the work that we are about to undertake, we might wonder: is it a project? Or is it a long-term and possibly permanent fixture of our organization's work in the future? Is it about management? Is it a complex coordination job?

Regarding the scope of our work, we might wonder: do we aim to 'XML-ize' every-thing? Will a standardized bit of labelling be sufficient? How far do we need to go to ensure maximum interoperability between systems before the law of diminishing returns kicks in?

The nature of the strategy

An IT development team may be set up to design, develop and put into production a specific XML-based tool or information system. If undertaken professionally, the venture will be a well-thought through, scoped and resourced *project*. It will have a start and a finish, a project manager and a project team with clear responsibilities.

On the other hand, our considerations of XML until now have stressed that the central concern should not be about the technology associated with a particular application or project. It is rather about a broader, management-centred approach to the use of XML throughout an enterprise.

The scope of XML's use is too wide and potentially slippery for it to be limited to a series of unconnected IT development efforts. Delicate internal politics within and between business units must be addressed and resolved and clear relationships estab-lished between them.

What we are setting out to develop does not seem therefore to be the stuff of 'classic' project management. But in many ways it is. Putting the ideas into practice will take hard work. Building your target XML-centred information architecture will be a project – it will need vision, scope, objectives, sponsors, resources, targets, evaluation and success criteria.

Encouraging overworked and highly-focussed IT professionals to let you into their domain may not be easy. They may feel that certain of their projects – new applications or tools and the funding and staffing that go with them – are under threat. It will take not just patience, but clear demonstrations of the benefits for them of a coordinated XML framework.

It will not be for the fainthearted. In this and the following three chapters, we look at the questions related to planning a strategy, building the basic infrastructure and building a momentum for change towards an XML-centred system.

The scope of the strategy

It is common to want to dismantle current but imperfect systems and rebuild a perfect, integrated information architecture from scratch. In practice, it is nearly always impos-sible to halt an entire enterprise for a major overhaul: it is necessary to build upon the existing infrastructure and try to introduce, step by step, a more coherent architecture.

If we examine and identify the different parts of an enterprise's information architecture, it should be possible to target the introduction of XML to parts of that architecture one at a time. This has the triple advantage of introducing XML in a 'bite-sized' manner, offer immediate benefits for the overall architecture and – most importantly – not bring the existing edifice tumbling down.

We start in this chapter by looking at why a management-driven strategy is so vital to the success and long-term stability of XML-centred systems, and what that strategy should involve. Then we take an 'holistic approach' that demonstrates that we can move towards XML on a step-by-step basis, provided that we keep an enterprise-level view in mind.

Making the business case

In the previous chapter we looked at some of the arguments for using XML. You may be convinced already, but it is highly unlikely that you alone will be able to switch an entire enterprise to the idea and reality of an XML-centred information management strategy.

In order to stimulate discussion, gain momentum and, more importantly, release resources and develop an implementation strategy, it is vitally important to develop a business case *appropriate to your organization*. This needs to be built from a good understanding of all of your enterprise's main functional units.

Food for thought

IT is not for me...

Two information systems that businesses now run side by side –computer based data processing and the accounting system – increasingly overlap. They also increasingly come up with what look like conflicting – or at least incompatible – data about the same event; for the two look at the same event quite differently.

Until now, this has created little confusion. Companies tended to pay attention to what their accountants told them and to disregard the data of their information system, at least for top management. But this is changing as computer-literate executives are moving into decision-making positions.

Peter Drucker *Wall Street Journal* 1st December 1992

Convincing management

A key concern you will have to keep to the fore, particularly in the early days of discussions, is how to put forward convincing arguments for and to middle and senior management.

The intelligent use of metaphors can be invaluable: your objective is to sow the idea of what XML could offer, but leave your target audience to mull over the metaphor and extrapolate for themselves. Senior management time is scarce, and you can't afford to squander a hard fought-for half-hour of attention on a detailed presentation attempting to get to the heart of XML schemas.

Here are some examples of the type of metaphor that you could be using:

- *Urban planning and architecture*. You wouldn't let electricians design your house any more than you would expect them to announce that they were ignorant of standards regarding voltage or wiring. Building permits are issued not only on the basis of the aesthetics of a new construction, but the building's ability to fit into a particular local environment and infrastructure.

- *The EU single currency, the Euro*. Replacing twelve national currencies involved painstaking planning and a thorough preparation for the changeover, but the gains are obvious: elimination of costly conversions, greater transparency in pricing across different countries, economies of scale and so on.

- *Interpretation regime*. With each addition to the working languages of the European Parliament, there is an exponential increase in the number of possible language combinations needed to ensure conference interpretation and written translation of work. As it becomes increasingly complex and difficult to meet every language combination directly, recourse is needed to a 'hub and spoke' system that limits the increase to a single pair of combinations for every language added.

Issues in the business case

There are a range of issues that need to be underlined when developing your business case for XML adoption:

- XML offers the potential for major cost reductions: publication costs, shortened turn-around times for application development, low entry costs.

- XML helps reduce and even eliminate errors when transferring data between different systems (remember the fated Mars Orbiter).

- XML maximizes training investment, with a high reusability of skills acquired. A high level of motivation is possible by keeping well-qualified staff moving between interesting projects, an approach of immense value in times of professional IT shortages.

- XML is standardized and stable, is developed by consensus, is non-proprietary, open source, free and in synergy with other standards and applications also all written in

XML. It is a well-tried and tested technical syntax and is very well supported by a wide range of vendors, service and solution providers.

- XML is a professional and determined response to planned obsolescence and is, if used properly, future-proof. It explodes the myth in management folklore that IT always moves forward on the basis of upgrades and migrations.

- XML promotes transparency, interoperability and accessibility, at the same time as offering security, encryption and protection of digital resources. In a world of mergers, out-sourcing and brain drain, XML offers a way of encapsulating knowledge that would otherwise be lost from an enterprise on the departure of key knowledge workers.

- XML is vendor-independent.

- XML is evolutionary. Remember that Darwin's theory of evolution was based not on survival of the fittest, but of the most adaptable: as such it is ideal for change-management scenarios. It is of immense value in mergers and acquisitions, joint ventures and cooperation, as it offers much easier integration and inter-operability between otherwise incompatible information systems.

In summary, XML must be seen as a business tool designed to manage a vital business asset: information. In the same way that UML has become a *lingua franca* for modelling in application development, XML can be the *lingua franca* between business units intent on promoting inter-operability. It is a common currency both for management and for information content itself.

XML must be understood and treated as a business asset: independently of the information content it encapsulates, XML elements, attributes and schemas are themselves reusable, transformable, stable and future-proofed.

There are, however some arguments against XML, which must be understood and not underestimated when developing your business case:

- '*Tag bloat*'. XML-encoded information flows more slowly than binary, proprietary data formats. XML files are in most cases much larger than corresponding proprietary formats. In an era of relatively cheap data storage and ever increasing bandwidth, this should not be a long-term worry or an excuse not to act, but it may well be a performance-limiting issue that some enterprises will have to address.

In response, we can argue that data quality, in the form of explicitly and detailed descriptive tagging of content, is more important than poorly-descriptive code. Remember Y2K? It is easy to give in to the temptation to be terse, whereas XML offers you the opportunity to be more expressive. In many cases, the real danger is *application* bloat – hundreds of new functions that you might not really need – rather than bloat in your actual data.

In XML-centred systems, servers spend more time delivering and less time processing, and clients use more of their time processing than laying idle with unused clock cycles. This is an important issue when you consider the increasing pressure on many Web and departmental servers, when compared with the relatively low activity of the average, but costly, desktop computer.

- *'The standards are not finalized'*. There have been a couple of 'wobbles' with the Namespaces and Schema standards, and new standards will always be issued to meet new information management challenges, but XML *is* finalized and stable. What are far from finalized are the reflections that enterprises need to make regarding the specific uses of XML. These require the production of problem-specific agreements in the form of schemas, preferably developed from a common, agreed, vocabulary of semantic building blocks. Until those sorts of standards for the specific needs of a given enterprise are agreed, little can be shared or developed.

It is true that XML requires additional effort and investment – it's as much 'minds on' as 'hands on'. It may be necessary to negotiate and win support for sharing the cost of the investment across business units and departments. Convince your financial department to consider the costs of introducing XML as infrastructure investment and business assets, not just cost centres.

Unpicking the complex interdependencies of current systems will probably be a daunting task and there may be no visible short-term payback. What's more, even in seemingly non-mission-critical systems, it is often impossible to stop the system for a refit. Coupled with business units' reluctance to forego the comfort and familiarity of *ad hoc* and heavily proprietary local applications, there is a high risk of failure.

Finally, XML projects are already proving extremely difficult to scope in many businesses, often precisely because of problems of vocabulary and definitions of business terminology. As we see below, XML can cover just about anything, which is why it is essential to keep a sharp management focus.

Not just XML   It is true that many of this book's proposals may not be considered exclusive to an XML-centred strategy. However, the nature of XML means that its consistent use can provide a *lingua franca* across all aspects of information architecture and management. Information architecture is a subtle and complex mix of management, technology and information science. The value of XML is that it can express the concerns and policies of all these disciplines.

It is important to remember that it is not technology that will drive the change, but management. XML is very good at expressing business issues in a way that can be immediately exploited by technology. This allows for very powerful management-driven use of technology.

If you do not feel that your enterprise is ready for a full-blown XML-centred strategy, none of the steps in investment in information architecture that are outlined in the next two chapters will be wasted. If you haven't done so already, you should be planning to identify your information assets and resources, and structuring and naming your content more coherently and comprehensively.

You could engineer an entire strategy merely around making the most of your current office suite of desktop applications. Care should however be exercised over the eternal problem of lock-in to a vendor-specific functionality or solution – you can always open the door to later XML developments.

Most so-called 'off the shelf' tools are rarely useful 'out-of-the-box'. They cannot be exploited immediately, and need to be configured to meet your precise needs. You are forced to think for yourself and invest time rather than merely accepting the defaults proposed by the manufacturer. Such an investment is not wasted in a vendor-specific environment, however. 'Upstream' reflection on configuration enables an easier migration of all or part of your systems and content when you do choose to invest in XML.

The main message must be: doing nothing is not an option. It may not be leaping straight into explicit XML solutions, but rather an approach based on long-term thinking on your information architecture.

A holistic approach

The so-called 'stovepipe' approach to application development is notorious. It might seem to be efficient to maintain focus on the specific requirements that an application development is intended to address. However, an application developed in this manner is unlikely to integrate easily with other applications and systems unless:

- There is already a high degree of interdependency, so changing one will necessarily involve changes to others

- They are all developed by the same design team and according to the same methodology and conventions

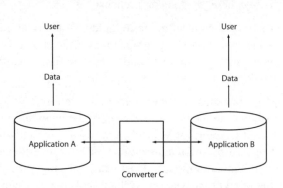

Figure 13. The 'stovepipe' model of application architecture

In the 'stovepipe' model, all the content is 'locked' into specific applications. To use it elsewhere involves proprietary 'middleware' that converts it from one application's format to another.

In reality, very few applications can claim to be genuine islands unto themselves. If they are, it is often at great cost in data replication and overlap. We live in the era of interoperability. 'System islands', where non-interoperable systems sit side by side, pose particular problems, as they are notoriously unresponsive to change:

- Dependencies that are identified between such islands act as inertia to change

- Ignorance of the overall picture acts as an inertia to even *desire* change

XML, as a ubiquitous data format, can and will reach into every part of an organization's information infrastructure and resources. Do not believe for one moment that, because XML has its origins in document management and text markup, it will not penetrate into all areas of electronic data representation and management.

For this reason, it is important from the outset to establish and maintain a holistic view and approach. You must not become locked into the tunnel vision that is so often a part of the development of individual information systems in isolation from the wider canvas.

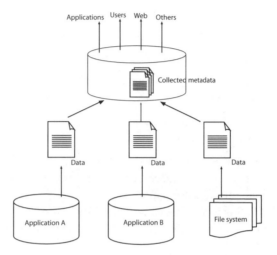

Figure 14. A different approach that keeps content available across applications

In Figure 14 the content – or at the very least, the metadata about the content – is managed 'above' the application and can be 'virtually' regrouped for reuse anywhere.

Compare this approach with that illustrated by Figure 13. We have introduced a new layer above the 'data layer' that provides a standard set of metadata for each object below it, whatever the nature or structure of the data it describes. In this way, we are providing a first level of interoperability.

Even if the data is not directly interoperable – whether sets of documents produced in different word-processing packages and/or stored on different platforms, information sets in different database management systems, and so on – the information about them, the metadata, is.

By introducing this new layer, an additional task initially, we are making valuable packing and labelling information available across applications. Whether they can use this metadata directly depends on the applications, but adding this layer makes the task simpler and more likely to succeed and be used than the one-off and proprietary approaches used in Figure 13.

In many cases 'adding a new layer' may be something of a misnomer: often it will rather be a case of separating out and standardizing this layer of metadata. Many applications and information management systems generate their own metadata. What we are concerned with is making that metadata available and useful beyond the application and platform that originally created it.

This will involve a number of distinct steps:

- Identifying the semantic information you want to make available

- Agreeing on a common vocabulary by which to refer to these semantically-discreet data elements

- Providing a 'translation' or 'mapping' mechanism to convert the in-application data to an external metadata set

This process does need to be restricted to extracting metadata about your information *content*. As we will see, the exercise is equally valuable whenever you want to build a standardized information set about any aspect of your information architecture, including your applications, business processes, user profiles and target audiences or house rules regarding information design and presentation.

Deciding on a strategy

Your strategy should be developed according to the specific requirements and context of your enterprise. An aspect common to all, however, is that an XML strategy is likely to be as much about change management as it is about technology. It will be all encompassing, it will affect everyone and it is likely to step on a lot of toes before being operational. So plan with care and attention to detail.

Bearing that in mind, it is invaluable to reflect on the type of strategy that you need according to a number of criteria:

- Strategy by *type of enterprise*. Whether public or private sector, profit or nonprofit making, it is important to identify the main business drivers of your enterprise. If XML is about adding value to your information management, you need to focus – particularly in the early stages – on those aspects of an XML strategy that are going to deliver the best value in the most responsive areas.

- Strategy by *size of enterprise*. Large organizations can probably generate the economies of scale needed for investing in XML standards development to meet their specific needs on their own. Smaller ones can more easily maintain an overview of all enterprise operations that allow sophisticated and complex XML integration to be undertaken in an easily-manageable fashion.

- Strategy by *type of infrastructure*. If you have an infrastructure predominantly composed of desktop personal computers, the approach you should take to XML developments will be radically different to that which you would pursue if your infrastructure is centred on bespoke, server-based enterprise applications with 'green screen' terminals.

- Strategy by *type of information use*. If you are mainly concerned with providing better interoperability and data exchange between heterogeneous information systems, your focus of attention and concerns will be different than if you are concerned about integrating business processes to information transformation and access, or publishing to different output formats from a single data source.

This reconnaissance work will inevitably involve:

- Gleaning information from human resource, development and finance departments about who uses what information and how

- Determining what relationships there are between internal users and external clients, customers and suppliers

- Identifying who has the background and capacity to manage specific XML developments

- Deciding your time constraints or related project deadlines

In summary, all the classic project management considerations.

There is one important additional point to remember, however, when considering your strategy that will help you avoid losing yourself in unnecessary detail. We can't always know when, where or how information may be used or reused downstream of its original purpose. That is why we tend to content ourselves with developing information systems for a particular and exclusive end purpose. A well-thought through and developed XML strategy is precisely one that allows you to develop an 'information architecture' irrespective of data's possible uses in specific contexts. It is this 'future proof' aspect that will be the lasting legacy of well-defined XML-centred architectures.

A final word of caution and advice for outlining your strategy: don't go it alone. A large proportion of the issues that you will face have already been (or are being) faced by others, friend and foe alike. Don't launch yourself or your enterprise into costly standardization efforts before assessing the work that might have already been done by someone else. Remember that proprietary solutions and standards cut you off from the rest of the world and make comparisons impossible that might be to your advantage.

You may need to discover what development initiatives are under way within your enterprise (you might be surprised) and build a consensus that a common infrastructure is to everybody's advantage.

Decision-making

The most depressing and frustrating part of the development of your management strategy is likely to be everyone's contention that they or their business unit are 'already responsible for XML'.

We encountered this phenomenon already in the introduction when considering the complex questions of responsibilities that surround the title 'Webmaster'. Here, the problem is little different. The first question to ask again is 'what do you mean by "responsible for XML"?' As with the Webmaster, we will see that there are many aspects to this generic claim. One of the centerpieces of your management strategy should be to ensure that the different areas of involvement are clearly identified and assigned explicitly-scoped responsibilities.

This may not be easy, but it is a bull that has to be taken by the horns. You need to be sure of senior management backing and 'buy-in' to the strategy you are developing, and to be sure that they are prepared to impose their authority should it be required.

There are two main approaches that can be taken to decision-making in this area: you will have to decide which is the most appropriate to your enterprise and work culture.

The 'Republic'   You may need to expend considerable effort in explaining the distinct aspects of the work to be identified and undertaken and build a consensus around the division of responsibilities. Conflicts of interest and interpretation of responsibility cannot always be avoided, but they can be handled diplomatically and resolved, particularly if all involved feel that they have a stake in positive cooperation.

This approach will be most appropriate in working environments that are less hierarchical, reward innovation and have a keen culture of enterprise, or in large parts of the public sector where, despite formal hierarchies, informal corridor politics are likely to carry more weight.

The 'Monarchy'   In centralized management systems, with strong hierarchies and line management, it may be sufficient to have the ear of top management and a handful of executive decisions. This may not always work, however. We all come across staff and business units who are stubbornly convinced that they have the monopoly of wisdom in a particular project.

Although they will certainly have something to contribute, there is no room for 'prima donnas' that are incapable of cooperation with others. As in many fields of conflict, the threat of force can often be as powerful a weapon as the force itself. The threat of a return to absolute monarchy can be enough to ensure the success of the republic!

There will need to be agreement on a whole range of issues and standards as part of the XML framework to be developed. The decision-making process that leads to issues being agreed and included in this framework must be known and shared. Someone, or some business unit, must become – or take responsibility for – being the central reference authority to which anyone involved in XML issues will turn. This involves building trust, confidence, a sense of cooperation and a solid, reliable and professional reference base.

Food for thought

"We will if they will"

It shouldn't matter what standard is agreed, provided that it *is* agreed, that it is adequate for all business units' needs and that everyone is willing to follow it. As a vendor- and platform-independent, neutral format, XML-encoded data offers a standard free of any department's own 'baggage'.

It should be the responsibility of this reference authority to ensure that decisions are made and standards set. Most of all, there must be mechanisms to assess conformance and offer a combination of 'carrot' and 'stick' to all business units to follow the agreed standards and conform to the proposed information architecture.

Roles and responsibilities

If possible, engage your senior management by inviting them to adopt some general principles for information management that will serve as objectives for the different business units concerned. This can be achieved either as a result of a single initiative or of some consensus building beforehand. If you have a weak information management culture – poorly documented or nonexistent classification schemes, filenaming and scoring conventions, etc. – suggest the establishment of a cross-service task force or other working party charged with putting meat on the bones of such high-level principles.

Cultivate a sense that everyone has a contribution to make and should concentrate on their core competencies. A database manager will be responsible for application infrastructure and performance, while specific business units are responsible for the actual data, and should be heavily involved in data modelling. An IT user support business unit will be responsible for word-processing software but not for filenaming conventions, document design or file storage. A computer centre will be responsible for ensuring 24/7 performance of Web servers, but not for the Web page design, site navigation or content.

You are in the process of identifying, clarifying and agreeing function and responsibilities. For every area of competence in information management questions, you should assess which of the increasingly complex set of XML standards needs to be understood and applied and by whom. This is why the newspaper paradigm introduced in the first chapter is so valuable. Not only does it underline the importance of clear division of responsibilities, but it highlights the need to keep a holistic view of the enterprise.

Remember that the number of people who *really* need to know the innards of the XML standards is probably very few. What is really important is the detailed knowledge implicit in many people's work of what data is used, how it is defined, where used and how it interacts between different information systems. This cannot just be bought in as XML expertise: it is intrinsic to your organization.

You may be lucky, working in an enterprise in which areas of responsibility for all information management issues are clearly defined. Most of us however will need to enforce the following guidelines for all business units:

- Make business units responsible for the management of information content that they produce, but in accordance with centrally-agreed guidelines.

- Base information organization on simple principles of identification and classification of content, and *never* allow them to be tied to the proprietary designs of a single application.

- If a type of information is described formally somewhere as a 'business term', make it known and find out who else is using the same terminology. This will be the key to identifying your 'semantic building blocks'.

- Ensure that management rules are top-down, management-driven and imposed, but drawn up in cooperation with as wide a range of business units as possible, and drawing on existing good practice.

- Centralize your 'house rules', make them visible and well-known, with someone clearly in charge and seen as an acceptable 'honest broker', preferably without any stake in the choices of any particular standard or technology. In this, use the time-worn 'federalist' principle: decentralize as much as possible, centralize as much as necessary.

- Only bring technologies to bear to implement house rules after the rules are established.

- Agree and publish the process by which anyone can influence the design of the overall framework and the standards used. It must be responsive to new needs, or it will fossilize.

- Consider the specific function of 'data steward', responsible for ensuring data quality within particular business units. A group of such people will provide a valuable network of contacts and encourage the harmonious development of your framework.

Food for thought

Starting the ball rolling

From the outset, it is critical to involve non-IT staff from across the enterprise who are faced with the day-to-day realities of information management shortcomings. An XML-based vocabulary developed for an enterprise will only be used as the reference if it reflects the needs of different users adequately. A holistic view of those needs is therefore essential.

Certain current responsibilities and functions may need re-scoping or redefining in preparation for, or as part of, the introduction of an XML-centred strategy. This can be painful, but firm management is needed, as we see in the following examples.

Data modelling   This is often the preserve of application developers and database designers. If particular content is to be tagged in XML, with defined and named elements, it is important that those involved in data modelling understand that the names they attribute to database tables or modelling objects can carry valuable semantic information. This information can be built into an agreed vocabulary that has value beyond immediately foreseen uses, so users of this information must be involved in the process. It is important that they develop an instinctive response to consult and use a central reference 'dictionary' of agreed names or follow the naming conventions laid down.

Consider as an analogy the problem of designing forms and form interfaces: it is difficult to master and involves communicators and authors beyond the analyst, whose only concern is that users enter data in the right places. Equally, the laborious process of document structure analysis that is the key to good XML schema design requires input from beyond data modelers, including authors, business process managers, editors and publishers. Good design will always pay off, so don't skimp: make sure that everyone who has something to contribute does so.

Authors   The masters of unstructured text, authors are the bane of a database designers' life, particularly when let loose with sophisticated WYSIWYG word processors. They must be convinced that their central role is producing well-structured and labelled content and less so presentation or clever page layouts.

Old skills need to be broadened and redefined. The conventions governing the structure and placing of citations, familiar to academic authors, need to be broadened to a more general understanding of the importance and use of information linking. Many authors balk at the idea of being 'sausage machined' into producing text that fits neatly into crude database forms. Using *knowledge moulds*, which we explore in Chapter 10, *Content Management*, can sharpen thinking and force authors to reflect, particularly if their texts are governed by formal house rules.

Equally, however, authors need to contribute to XML schema design – the rulebook that determines what text structures are valid in what context – if they are to ensure that the constraining model does actually reflect their specific needs.

Desktop publishing   Desktop publishing has certainly proved its worth in the Web revolution. Few would dare challenge the artistic freedom of Web designers, but their designs may have to be reigned in as much as anybody else's to ensure that valuable information is not locked up in presentation issues. Information structures must be kept clearly separate.

On the other hand, if designers are responsible for creating and proposing visual identity guidelines and house style, XML can help them automate the integration and generalization of those rules across all types of information content. You must therefore ensure that they are brought on board and shown how the separation of responsibilities can help them impose those standards on others.

XML experts   Be very wary. If expertise is called upon, make sure that they know what they are being asked to do and, equally important, what they are not to do. Many XML consultants come from data analysis and application development backgrounds. They are therefore familiar with information design *within* a particular system, and will tend to create data variables to meet specific needs within that system.

They will often transpose that same thinking and model to their perception of XML: 'just another programming language', with XML element names acting as variables or objects and XML attributes acting as properties. As such, they may not be sensitive to the value that element and attribute naming can have in XML. They are often concerned only with developing solutions for a specific need – which, to be fair, is what is usually asked of them!

Make sure that they understand the need to fit their work into a wider information architecture including, for example, a common vocabulary. In all of these areas, you will need to be clear in the division of responsibilities and where an XML expert fits in. Ensure that their qualifications match the specific aspects of your overall strategy for which they have been engaged.

Pulling together all the different players and encouraging cooperation is clearly, therefore, a critical factor for success.

Team and relations management

It is important that everyone knows why they are involved in the project. Knowing all the players and their respective roles is clearly important, as in any major project. Whether the driving force is hierarchy or teamwork, communication is critical. It is not sufficient for participants to be asked to send their contributions into a black box and to be automatically satisfied by the outcome.

In this project, the 'stakeholders' need to buy in, not just to the objectives, but to all stages of the development and realization. There must be continuous dialogue and exchange of ideas, with all participants seeing what their contributions are leading towards. There should not just be newsletters or information bulletins, but real opportunities for dialogue with online discussion forums.

There are clear benefits to this approach: clearer lines of responsibility, a transparent and predictable process for advancing and resolving issues, improved chances of information sharing. Most of all, though, it underlines the upstream role of management, as distinct from the role of IT.

There will be internal politics issues that must be resolved:

- The department that has too much 'baggage' may be loath to cooperate in developing a common XML strategy, because it will expose the limitations and cost of bespoke systems.

- Inter-service coordination and arbitration are both needed. The more there is of the first, the less you will need the second. But both will be necessary to a greater or lesser degree, and you must ensure that the rule book and mechanisms are in place to handle them when the need arises.

- The actual 'processability' of XML may be seen as a direct threat by those whose jobs and financial resources depend solely on the need to convert data between different systems. Their ignorance of progress and improvements must not be confused with legitimate and valid concerns about work profile and job satisfaction. Unnecessary tasks can never be defended on the basis of saving a work profile. But neither can simply abolishing posts to cut short-term costs, thus losing human capital and knowledge that are invaluable for your strategy.

- The project sponsor should not be someone who is likely to use the project to extend an empire and use it to attack others. The project will only succeed if there is a strong sense of cooperation and trust. This may mean going all the way to the top and involving the CEO.

Workplan and timetable

As with any project, it is useful to develop a timeline and establish clear milestones. No off-the-shelf magic formula is available to calculate this your enterprise. It is clear that you should not be attempting to do everything at once. You should focus your XML deployment efforts on those areas likely to offer the easiest and quickest returns, if only to demonstrate the proof of the approach, and try to balance this with a focus on the most urgent information management questions for you.

Preceding specific application developments, however, there should be a logical progression of activities that enable you to build the consensus and momentum needed, without becoming caught up in specific technologies or systems. This is not always easy. You might find yourself the victim of your own success, with business units clamoring to implement XML-centred systems *now* and not taking kindly to being told to hold on while others catch up, particularly if there are internal business incentives to do so.

Establish a rough project timeline that keeps all the initial issues on board and in view as a development process, and that gives everyone visibility of the sequencing of some areas of work. These are the issues to tackle *before* any XML developments even take place.

There should nevertheless be an attempt to develop a project timeline that can provide for the logical progression of these important steps. Some parts may be concertina'd and others skimped by pressures to move forward. Play 'catch up' where you can, because it is important that this infrastructure is developed.

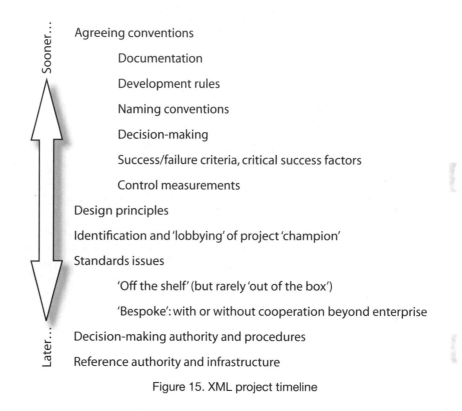

Figure 15. XML project timeline

Conclusions

This chapter has attempted to underline some of the urgency of bringing management issues to the fore. Doing nothing is clearly not an option. If you as a manager do not take the initiative, the hype surrounding XML could cause technologists to take the lead and start to impose XML standards based on their own understanding and needs.

Three key messages are important here:

- *Avoid quick fixes*, such as using XML merely as an interesting Web-document production technology, in isolation from other thinking and potentially valuable applications throughout the business.

- *Provide early and simple solutions* that offer some clear added value to your enterprise. For example, providing a standardized approach to metadata, more and more in demand from all quarters of information management, to markup in XML and to the use of a standard vocabulary.

- *Commit for the 'long haul'*, and start to see that XML's real benefit cannot come from simply transposing current applications one by one to XML, an approach to which resistance would be understandable. Rather, build momentum patiently and let managers start to see that the advantages of future interoperability will not just fall into their laps, but must be planned and organized.

Having nurtured and established management authority, you now need to be seen to take the lead: all those business units that you have been holding back will now want to see whether it has been worth it. Now you have to 'walk the walk', and actually ensure that the XML framework is developed and delivered. We turn to this in the next chapter.

5 Foundations of an XML Framework

In theory, theory and practice are the same thing. In practice, they never are.

Anon

Introduction

In the last chapter, we addressed the need for a management strategy for the introduction of XML. In the light of the main concerns addressed in the introductory chapters, there is an urgency in bringing management issues to the fore, and keeping them there within a coherent framework.

That's the theory, now we need to start building something. The underlying principle that will drive our development effort is:

For information to circulate freely, it requires a common currency to establish a common understanding of the terms and entities that will be used by others building specific XML-centred systems.

If you have a common currency, you need a central bank. That is where the idea of a Framework comes from. In this chapter, we start looking at the foundations and architecture through the development of such a XML framework.

XML project and road-map

What is the project that we are undertaking? I call it the development of an 'XML framework', a term I have already used earlier in the book.

Other analysts and practitioners have their own definitions and idea of what an XML framework is. In the context of this book, it is:

> *The set of reference information, procedures and infrastructure that are put in place and managed by a respected and reliable central authority to direct and advise on the introduction of XML standards in a given enterprise.*

Defined like this, it is clearly an infrastructure investment, and should be considered as an asset to the enterprise, rather than as a cost centre. It has however to be built and maintained using basic project management principles, including:

- Defining the *scope of the project*. This project is not about any XML application or tool development. It will not offer miracle solutions for XML content models, for user working environments and XML tools, or ensure that all future text editing conforms to structured models. But it is intended to provide the ways and means for these things to be achieved. It is about standards, procedures, reference data, best practices and infrastructure. Certainly, some business units will be champing at the bit to move into particular implementations as soon as possible. Let them. But at the same time, flag up the potential dangers of moving too far too fast. Engaging such business units constructively may well help to build the momentum needed to act cooperatively and even liberate resources to make the framework a success.

- Assessing *constraints*. 'Cheap, fast and professional – choose two'. The budget-time-table-quality triangle is ever-present in all projects. This is an infrastructure project, the reliability of which will have a direct impact on all developments and implementations of XML. As such, the quality criterion should not be compromised. The resolution will therefore have to be on the budget-timetable axis: pressure on both of these criteria should be identified from the outset as a critical risk factor requiring notification to, and intervention by, senior management.

- Developing a *project plan and road map*. Even if subject to revision, outline a road map so that everyone can see where you are intending to go and what you hope to achieve. This also helps to underline the progression of activities in developing the framework in a way that business units can prepare themselves for the inputs that are expected of them.

- Quantifying, mobilizing and managing *resources*. As this is an infrastructure project, you should be attempting to convince your IT and financial departments to consider the work as capital investment, and the outcome as an enterprise asset. Exceptional – that is, nonrecurring – budgetary resources should be allocated. If that is not possible, it will be necessary to badger those business units considering XML development efforts to commit a part of their resources to the initial effort in order to reduce their costs at a later stage.

- *Building support* and 'buy in' to the project. You should capitalize on offers of support by bringing in motivated business units as part of the project team, giving them a stake in the outcome. You should commit sufficient resources, and certainly energy, to explaining the nature and benefits of the project, and to researching the issues that are likely to be brought up by business units.

- *Communication* and progress reporting. You should organize information meetings, not just for management, but for the business units most likely to benefit, and keep all the discussions and evolution of the framework in the open. Business units need to be able to trust that what you are doing has momentum and support from business units.

Background research

As we have already seen, XML is by nature evolutionary, and keeping track of its evolutions and use is the key to keeping management ahead. You need not only to keep an eye on new standards and evolutions being developed and proposed in the outside world, but also be able to manage a growing collection of knowledge on XML's introduction and use within your enterprise.

Keeping up with the standards

Keeping up with the rapid evolution of the XML family of standards is one thing, and could turn into a full-time job, but there are valuable reference sites on the Internet that do this for you. More important is the need to digest and understand the relevance of these standards to your particular environment. This area needs to be permanently monitored, because issues that start out as problems can suddenly acquire solutions when a new standard is added.

You should make a distinction between standards bodies, consortia and specific application-centred initiatives. The standards bodies themselves can be the *de jure* standards authorities, such as:

- The International Standards Organisation (ISO) world-wide

- The American National Standards Institute (ANSI) for the USA

- The European Standards Committee (CEN) in Europe

or *de facto* authorities such as:

- The World Wide Web Consortium (W3C)

- The Internet Engineering Task Force (IETF)

These are the bodies responsible for the reference standards themselves. They are often not the most readable of technical material, but by definition need to be accurate, complete, stable and unambiguous. By their nature, standards emerge on the back of wide consensus building, a process that is often time-consuming, but that provides reliable building blocks for a stable information architecture.

Consortia and sectorial initiatives aim at specific implementations of the standards in a particular context, or add an additional layer of functionality or standardization beyond the core standards themselves. They will often work to much tighter time-frames than the standards bodies and be driven by the most active member organizations. These include, amongst others:

- The Organisation for the Advancement of Structured Information Standards (OASIS), whose focus is largely on specific sectorial applications of the XML standards, and now includes the heavyweight ebXML standard, developed together with UN/CEFACT

- The Dublin Core Metadata Initiative (DCMI), which is concerned with providing standardized metadata structure and content for all types of Internet-addressable resources

- The Object Management Group (OMG), an industry consortium seeking to promote open standards in object-oriented programming, and the body responsible for the increasingly popular Unified Modeling Language (UML)

However much you decide to respect vendor-independent open standards, you may often need to look at *application-centred* initiatives that address specific objectives within a particular user community. You will need a dose of realism when transposing XML standards into a specific information architecture, and such initiatives may provide you with a solution. If the solution proposed meets your needs, check nevertheless that its use will not compromise the rest of the framework.

Probably the most comprehensive overview of XML-related developments is provided by the so-called 'Cover Pages' and now hosted by OASIS. This and other references are included in the further reading references at the end of the book.

Developing in-house knowledge

You need to assess what mixture of these categories is right for your enterprise. There will be no shortage of opinions and points of view within the enterprise, let alone on public discussion forums and opinion columns of the specialized press. Keep yourself informed, scout widely for information and opinions and make sure that you feel able to defend any choices that are made. There are plenty of on-line resources available offering opinions and advice on most aspects of XML and its use. Some are seeking to sell you software or a solution; others are more objective.

The 'normative' references – the W3C Web site for example – are fail-safe if you need to refer a developer and/or contractor to the specific standards that you want them to follow. On their own, they make for dry reading and offer little to reassure you on the conformance of one solution or product or another, but that it is not their function.

As a starting point in building a reference base of useful information and sources, it can be helpful to let your enterprise know what *you* have seen and have found useful in your initial research. It could be nothing more sophisticated than a lightly organized set of links visited, but it serves to give developers and contractors a feel for the sort of approaches and ideas that have informed your policies for XML developments in general, and the development of your XML framework in particular.

Managing XML content

Little attention is paid in many guides to how and where you should store your XML content. There are many XML content repositories that store your XML documents in native character-based files, or are internally 'optimized' to save space and boost performance by 'hashing' or otherwise reducing the verbose markup into binary code. The humble hierarchical file system has also been brought to bear in some systems, more comfortably fitting the hierarchical nature of XML element and document nesting than, for example, relational database systems.

In developing an XML framework, however, attention should not be restricted to the storage and management of your XML documents only, whether actual content, processes, transformations or 'meta-content' such as the framework reference information itself. Due attention should also be paid to the storage and management of fragments, entities, DTDs (if you use them), schemas, vocabulary entries, encoding schemes and interfaces.

Remember that XML is chosen and promoted as a vendor-independent, future-proof and open format. Be careful, therefore, of committing your entire XML content to a proprietary system that stores the data in a native binary format, even if it guarantees 'XIXO' ('XML-in, XML-out'). There is nothing wrong with this approach *per se*, and it will almost certainly boost performance and storage. But watch out for 'additives' over which you have no control, such as proprietary XML elements and markup applied by the content management system itself.

Further, be sure that whatever infrastructure you choose, there are sufficient mechanisms to avoid lock-in. You do not want to find that in order to migrate your entire XML content to another platform, you will need a whole new set of proprietary filters!

Stability in logical structure

Remember that the XML standards have been developed in order to develop information management systems that *last*. Although the *physical* location of your XML content can obviously be located and moved as necessary, the *logical* location – in other words where users and applications 'see' and point to that content – should be stable over the long term. There is a strong link here to your approach to conventions for identifying and addressing your information content and other objects. When deciding on your content repository, you should ensure that the software will submit to your policies in this matter and not the other way around.

Repository management

Security, security, security: it really can't be stressed too much. Even a simple intrusion, such as changing the value expected of an attribute in a source DTD or schema, could have catastrophic effects downstream. Your repository must be tightly secured and managed with all the care that you would for other valuable business assets and critical information systems. This should be laid down as an essential requirement at the beginning of the work on the framework, with whoever is responsible for system security in your IT business unit.

Security is one important aspect of repository management, but there are others. There will have to be very clear rules governing maintenance, additions and update of the XML framework, as well as responsibilities and agreed processes for it. This should cover all aspects of versioning and status as well as quality control: anyone using the framework will want some guarantees that what they use is reliable. If it isn't reliable, people will lose faith in the process and simply bypass it.

Best practices and baseline recommendations

You need to establish some baseline rules that anybody should respect in any context. The scope of this book is not to elaborate on what these specific rules might be, but rather to underline the fact that they are necessary. Nevertheless, here is a sample that should give your technical analysts a flavor of what is needed. These could include:

- Agreeing on the *character-encoding scheme* to use. UTF-8 and UTF-16 are to be favoured above more restricted character sets such as ASCII or ISO 8859/1. You will need to ensure that all applications in use can handle these encoding schemes, but using them will offer you greater flexibility. With increasing globalization, enterprises need to keep open to the management of information in different languages. The more restricted the encoding scheme, such as ASCII, the more difficult the task.

- Using the xml:lang attribute consistently and as comprehensively as necessary. That does not mean placing a language attribute on every tag. It could mean making users and developers aware that if particular content is transformed or reused in another context, each new context may make the attribute valuable or essential. Rules should therefore be laid down as to what those transformations should include.

- Always using the XML Prolog, even if a specific processor or application does not require it. Given XML's success, no one can guarantee that there will not be future versions, and one minor update, V1.1, is already in the pipeline. The information contained in the Prolog, such as the XML version, is a valuable maintenance indicator. For the sake of the single line of code that is required, it will pay dividends.

- Always creating and using *element and attribute names* with reference to the Framework. As <element> and <Element> would be seen as two distinct elements by any conformant XML processor, it is vital that you obtain agreement to use only approved names.

- Always storing *metadata* associated with any document or object externally to the document itself. Even if a document production application creates and embeds metadata within the document itself, it will prove invaluable and improve accessibility immensely if that data is also available externally. If it exists both internally and externally, however, the maintenance of the parallel data sets could represent an additional burden and provoke integrity issues. If you don't have a reliable solution, avoid the problem and only use external metadata.

- Proscribing the use of *general entities* and limiting any development to the five predefined entities that come with the basic XML standard.

It may be some time before you have an XML framework up and running as a service to your developers and project managers. In the meantime, to be able to provide some basic guidelines from the start will put everyone on the same 'wavelength' over the way forward.

Content management

When deciding on your XML content management solution, there are a number of criteria you should bear in mind, as for any content management system. Some of these issues will be addressed when we look at content analysis, and the solutions to particular problems handled with various transformation and management questions. They should also be borne in mind, however, when considering your management software and infrastructure.

Your criteria will depend on your needs and attitude to a series of business requirements, including:

- *Content access*. Will access be generally public? Will certain content only be available to certain categories or audiences? Will access sometimes be restricted to parts of a document while other parts are not accessible? Do access policies mean that access to certain content will change over time (for example, in public records disclosure policies)? Does certain content have to conform to personal data protection policies?

- *Infrastructure access*. Who will need to access what infrastructure elements, such as schemas, reference data and vocabularies, APIs, style sheets and templates? From where? With what levels of authentication and security?

- *Version control*. Do you need to keep thorough audit trails of all document version histories? Do you want to do this by managing distinct versions of documents, or by including document changes and history ('this bit deleted on…', 'this added by …') within your document's markup?

- *Complete or canonical integrity*. Is it more important that the XML content is maintained *exactly* as it is created, down to the detail of the appearance of 'whitespace', the order in which attributes appear, etc? Or is it sufficient that the integrity of the content is *functionally* or *canonically* respected? Some processors and storage systems that optimize content management may output your XML content in a slightly different manner to that in which it was originally created or stored. The Canonical XML standard offers a means of checking whether such changes are significant or not, and whether the differences are insignificant from the point of view of authentication and certification. But you should not leave this issue to chance – have it checked out and tested.

- *Legal constraints*. If any of your content serves as a normative or legal reference for third parties, you need to ensure that the content is identifiable, 'referenceable' and accessible according to standard and stable conventions. This must not be compromised by any content management system.

- *Fragments*. Is your content normally used as distinct separate files, or are you likely to be making heavy reference to internal structures and fragments? Are some fragments heavily reused, for example as boilerplate text? Managing individual fragments, particularly large numbers of small fragments, can have a major impact on your storage and management infrastructure, but can also offer greater flexibility for composing larger documents dynamically from content blocks.

- *Typology management*. Do you need, and will you have, complete control over the management of your different document and information typologies?

- *Comprehensive management*. It is not sufficient to think only in terms of managing documents as you would in a 'classic' file system or document repository. The nature of XML is such that content – whether text, processes, transformations and so on – may need to be accessed by multiple processes or users, in a many-to-many or peer-to-peer architecture.

The content management infrastructure must be robust enough to handle complex object lifecycles including 'non-linear' ones. Built into the logic of 'traditional' workflow systems is the idea that there are a finite number of options at each decision point, and access and process rules can be applied accordingly. In peer-to-peer processing (a paradigm to which XML is probably uniquely suited), that 'flow' model breaks down and more attention thus needs to be paid to ensuring that – for example – access rights information is associated with the (XML) content and not hard-coded in the workflow processes.

Repositories

Whatever the physical and software infrastructure put in place, we need to be able to manage different types of 'meta-content' as well as our actual information content itself. As we have seen, this includes our vocabulary elements and definitions, XML elements and attributes, tag sets or common vocabularies, thesauri, schemas and documentation.

Arguing the business case

How these are managed will be critical to the whole undertaking: it is the reference hub of your target information system. The repository – where you store and manage all aspects of the XML framework – is the key to the whole. If you are going to develop a coherent strategy, there can be no skimping on this infrastructure. You may need to build in costs for the 'retro-conversion' of developments already underway at the time that the framework becomes operational.

An XML repository is a major exercise in asset management: the assets are valuable, and you can put a specific value on them, as we see in the next chapter. As such they represent an important initial investment aimed at downstream cost-cutting. You should be prepared to demonstrate return on investment (RoI) to your financial department as well as to your senior management, both as an estimate and as actually achieved. The repository will be the key to easing the exchange and interoperability of information at the earliest possible stage, aiming also to reduce long-term development costs and improve economies of scale through systematic reuse of common building blocks.

Types of repository content

For each of the types of content that our repository will need to manage, specific issues will need to be addressed. Remember that this is part of a reference resource, so the information is essentially targeted at information system developers, rather than end users directly.

Both the language used in the descriptions and the manner of interfacing with the information sources should reflect this. There is a case for keeping the language as clear and as unambiguous as possible, however, in order to avoid the need to 'interpret' every issue that is referenced.

- *Namespaces*. At the very, for the purposes of the Framework and for human readers, you need a brief description to explain the intended scope of each information 'territory' that individual namespaces are intended to scope. How these namespaces relate to each other and to other information territories beyond your own should also be documented.

- *Business terms*. It is remarkable how easy it is to build large parts of systems on poorly-interpreted or understood terminology. In IT project management, for example, the difference between a 'prototype' and a 'pilot' can be critical. This underlines the need to keep a good reference dictionary of your business terms – whether unique to you, used in a particular manner by you, or using publicly accepted definitions. This can be used not only to arbitrate on meaning where necessary to avoid ambiguity, but also to n help you build your XML-specific vocabulary.

- *Subject indicators and PSIs*. As we will see in the context of 'Topic Maps' and the specific XTM standard, subject indicators can serve as unambiguous references to a particular subject or topic, in the same way that a Namespace does for a particular information territory. Published Subject Identifiers (PSIs) allow you go one step further, by declaring and publishing the indicators, making them available and known to the outside world.

- *Metadata*. In terms of naming conventions, the same issues arise with metadata as with elements. If you use a standard set of metadata, whether based on existing standards or your own, you should indicate not only the metadata elements being used but also the mandatory or recommended 'encoding schemes' (see below).

- *Elements*. You want your repository to provide the main dictionary and definitions for the semantic building blocks of your information content. Think of this as your reference list of allowable and recognized ingredients or dictionary of terms. This is possibly the most important part of your complete naming convention. The keyword with naming policies is *consistency*.

- *Attributes*. In terms of management, there are similar considerations as for elements. If your attributes are used with pre-determined allowable values, these should be indicated and referenced also.

- *Datatypes*. You should reference the datatypes you are using, particularly if they are custom types that can be applied beyond the context of a single schema, as well as details of the allowable values or value range and value structure (for example: 'two letters followed by five digits'). This information will be of particular value for the development of user interfaces, offering users pick-lists or structured data entry means to ensure valid content.

- *Controlled vocabularies*. The fact that certain elements and attributes have been assigned explicitly to a particular vocabulary should serve as an indication to developers that they are there for a reason. This can help in schema design, providing another valuable pointer for coherent development, and situating particular constructs *ontologically* alongside others (for example: 'element x is always a child of element y', 'element y contains the name of a physical person, who can be a member of an authority expressed in element z').

- *Schemas*. These should be well and transparently documented and managed, whether you are using the XML Schema standard, RelaxNG or any other.

- *Encoding schemes*. You should keep track of and make available the lists of allowable values for metadata entries or any other controlled value set. These encoding schemes can be public and highly formalized (such as the ISO-approved structures for, and lists of, country and language codes) or 'home made'. In all cases when a particular value from one or other encoding scheme is used, it is of immense value to indicate the encoding scheme to which it belongs. If there are no formally-agreed encoding schemes, at least you should be maintaining user guides or 'best practice' information to avoid values for metadata entries, elements or attributes being allocated arbitrarily.

Developing standards policies

'I believe in using standards, so let's use mine' is a common-enough refrain in the IT world. All too often, the 'stovepipe' tradition of applications development means that a particular team will, through tunnel vision, concentrate on the sole objectives of their own project, defining and creating standards according to their needs.

For as long as one application works in blissful isolation from any other, this is not a problem: the resolution of any situation is to be found, by design, within the application. If it isn't, you can just add it as a new feature.

XML encourages a healthier approach: to see an enterprise's IT infrastructure from the point of view of what is produced and managed, the information and data that collectively form the knowledge base of the enterprise, rather than seeing it from the point of view of the applications themselves.

A common reference point

An important starting point for an XML-based strategy is the development of a sense that standards provide a reference point for everyone, and that they do not need to be either arbitrary or proprietary.

The problem with XML however, unlike HTML, is that it is in reality only a *metalanguage*. In other words, it does not impose a particular vocabulary – HTML markup is limited to the 50 or so valid elements – but only a standardized *method* for developing a vocabulary. Everyone is free to develop their own vocabulary.

In some ways, XML can make the situation even worse than with the proprietary data standards used in, say, word processing or database management systems. These 'standards' – however heavily tied to a particular vendor or application – will usually have a very substantial user base. If conversion questions arise, there are incentives to develop exchange and transformation filters through large economies of scale.

A particular XML vocabulary, on the other hand, can be developed for a single, very specific use. There is therefore a danger of hundreds of proprietary formats spawning from the uncontrolled and over-zealous introduction of XML. Until there is high-level agreement over the scope of a common approach and reference vocabulary from which any developer can 'pick and mix', little can be guaranteed as interoperable.

As we have repeated before, XML is a standard, not a technology or a computing language. There is thus an expectation that it will, once and for all, offer the solution regarding document structure, formats, production and management.

The need for a vocabulary

Taken on its own, XML is about as useful as an alphabet is on its own: it is fine having an agreed set of letters, but by itself that set does not constitute a language. To communicate you need:

- Words, to identify objects, actions, descriptions
- Grammar and syntax, the rules that define permitted structures and relationships
- Semantics to establish common understanding and meaning

XML 'as is' offers the user only an 'alphabet' and some syntax. Industry-specific vocabularies, on the other hand, offer a dictionary – at least the set of words that are to be 'understood' in that vocabulary, if not their meaning. Specific XML schemas add grammar and syntax to the vocabulary.

It is very tempting to launch straight into XML by developing prototypes and small applications that actually do something. Certainly do this, but don't commit large-scale to a specific project before assessing how the project fits within your overall information territory. It will be very costly to convert retrospectively all the tags of half a million documents to a common vocabulary because it was agreed too late.

There is a conundrum to be addressed, by establishing a balance between:

• The need for strategic reflection and detailed study of how XML should be used in an enterprise, before anything passes into the hands of programmers

• The need to gain management support through tangible and demonstrable benefits for the enterprise

This book attempts some solutions: from the outset, it is vital to understand that the greatest benefit is to be wrought from XML if certain enterprise-wide norms and standards are discussed, agreed and imposed. This is only possible if all business units that have, or are likely to develop, an interest in deploying XML agreed to contribute to and abide by the rules.

Agreeing responsibilities for standards

This raises the question: who sets the standards? There is no avoiding the fact that standards have to be imposed and respected, preferably by a 'top-down' approach. This is not to say that they must be imposed without any thought behind them, or in the face of major opposition from users or developers. The standards that are most likely to be respected are those in which users find some benefit.

Getting such a process of the ground can often be achieved as a side-effect, such as:

• Opportunism: a chance comment in an inter-service meeting trying to resolve data transfer problems between two bespoke applications

• Part of an unrelated effort to organize any aspect of information management, such as a new file classification or document management system

• A need to produce HTML and PDF rapidly from a single word-processed source

These can all be opportunities to start the ball rolling and start talking about the need for a common approach, and for exposing the inherent advantages of every application referring to the same block of information in the same manner.

You might get one or more business units to involve themselves by such means, but there will still be battles over whether to use 'your' description of a particular type of information or 'theirs', or someone else's. In some ways, it doesn't matter what is agreed upon, as long as there is agreement. It is essential to avoid turf wars: the key to intelligent adoption of XML is an approach that is acceptable to all parties.

It is up to the parties to decide whether they opt for the 'republic' or the 'monarchy' – whether to adopt a process by which they can agree the standards amongst themselves, or whether to agree to submit themselves to a higher or external authority that will impose a solution. Both are excellent approaches, and there should be no sense of failure if one is preferred over the other. The important factor in both is that there *is* a central authority – elected or imposed – that all actors are prepared to accept.

Establishing such an authority is however another matter. Your CEO has to be brought in at some stage. Even if it is possible to agree the central authority by consensus, it should always be signed off at the highest level, as this authority will have the main function of ensuring that standards and norms are agreed and followed.

The most difficult part of this exercise may be gaining an IT department's acceptance of the need for:

- A specific and separate responsibility for an XML framework in particular

- Data standards in general

It must be achieved, however, otherwise each XML development effort will see application-specific standards bloom. Be absolutely clear about the limits of this authority. If you are setting up a reference authority through a framework, do not be tempted to start down the road of tools development. Certainly, you should be able to offer advice to developers on the criteria they should apply in choosing software, development methodology and application scope, but you will build greater respect for your work if you keep off turf that is specifically theirs.

Process and management

As well as establishing authority, you need to ensure that you agree the rules for the resolution of doubt and arbitration of disagreement. Do not underestimate the value of establishing such rules and conventions, and agree them as early as possible and before too many individual projects get under way. Take heart, however, that it is never too late: attempts at any stage all help to reduce the dangers of dispersal across too many different formats and data standards, or convergence on tightly locked-in vendor-specific solutions.

The establishment and maintenance of the framework itself should be the subject of an agreed process:

- To develop the framework in the first place

- To update and maintain it

- To build and maintain relations with similar initiatives beyond the enterprise, linking with other standards where appropriate

- To guarantee the traceability of all decisions, progress and extensions made

Agreeing and enforcing conventions

To keep everyone 'on board' you need to have a clear and comprehensive rule-book. Once an authority has been established as being responsible for the XML framework, make sure that an early priority is establishing the rule-book, keeping it up to date and if necessary indicating enforcement mechanisms.

The objective of the framework is to offer an infrastructure and process by which all business units can develop specific XML initiatives with the greatest opportunities of system interoperability, reuse of existing infrastructure, and expertise. This is the carrot you should be offering.

Enterprises often condition the funding of major projects on the basis of respect for certain standards. But if carrots don't work – offering support and advice on, say, use of XML elements or attribute values – use a stick.

Guidelines

Users and business units need guidelines as to when and how XML should be used, and when *not* to use XML, an issue too often overlooked in the zeal of the moment. Everyone should be left in no doubt about the types of information and information system that would best benefit from a move to XML and the priorities of the enterprise.

For example, compare these two situations:

- You have a reasonably well-functioning relational database that 'talks' coherently to a limited number of other systems with little overhead or problems. The database administrator has followed the specialist press and specific training and has become a dab hand in XML (allegedly) and is awaiting a decision to mobilize considerable resources for an XML-centred solution.

- A small spreadsheet which sits on the desktop computer of a colleague in the accounts department and – for reasons nobody really understands – maintains a list of reference data on product codes. Nobody has tinkered with it much, as a whole series of downstream applications replicate the data through a range of transformations and filters that are hard-coded into different systems and uploaded from the accounts department desktop. The administrator who maintains the spreadsheet knows her job and the codings well. She is worried about a move to another application, not so much because of the data but because the prototype that a database analyst showed her looked completely unfamiliar.

There is a whole series of issues here, and it should be the job of a good systems analyst to separate the functional, presentational, interface and management questions raised.

The first situation may be clamoring for attention, and have a high chance of success if the claims of experience, understanding and available resources are all correct. This is missing the point, however. From the perspective of potential gain, the second situation ought to be given far greater attention. This would mean not only dealing with the objective data integration and reuse questions, but bringing the user on board and demonstrating that her preferences of user interface are not a stumbling block.

Scope

XML standards are important in transactions between information systems, but are not at the time of writing fully mature in one key aspect.

Much attention has been paid to exchanges and/or transformations of data between pairs of information systems, and to 'hub and spoke' approaches that have XML at the centre as the 'common currency'. Where more effort is required is in the field of 'many-to-many' transactions: complex information webs containing no single lines of transaction. While traditional data modelling and relational database systems can handle such complexities for many-to-many data exchanges, this is not true for information and document exchanges. Take a look at many large-scale Web sites: navigation is still largely hierarchical, with often very little 'transversality' unless added by complex and powerful link-management tools.

The linking possibilities are a function of the application infrastructure that supports and manages the content, not an inherent feature of the content itself. In the future, intelligent use of the XLink and XPointer standards should enable such linking 'intelligence' to accompany the content and maintain a further level of application and format independence.

This highlights once again that the 'standards' we need to set may well be used by XML, but can be defined independently of it, as part of a more generic document-management strategy. In the coming chapters we will take into account the needs of these standards, so that such functionality can be built in as the standards stabilize and technologies become available to implement them.

Security

It is vital to scope security questions explicitly as part of XML framework development. Security and access management, both of the framework infrastructure and your XML content, are issues that must be handled from the start. To use a well-worn commandment: if you think about security at implementation time, you have already lost.

These issues must be scoped not just in terms of the best technological infrastructure, but in terms of management policies. It is not a technical decision that allows a junior programmer to 'hack' the schema repository in order to solve a tricky implementation issue – it is a management oversight. Every issue of access rights, by human, process or machine, and to whatever resource – schemas, external entities, XML content or XSLT templates and the like – has to be clearly and explicitly addressed and managed.

Documentation

Best use of XML will be as much a management issue as a technological one. Although there are strong traditions of project and application development documentation, there is rarely any written record suitable for senior management. The nature of the XML framework is that user-oriented and readable documentation will need to be available for all.

A word about comments

It is vitally important to fully documentation your naming conventions, as well as all aspects of the XML framework being developed. The syntax of HTML and SGML allowed designers to use a 'comment statement' to create *ad hoc* documentation in document instances:

```
<!-- This is a comment -->
```

Such portions of a document are ignored by any processor and are intended for the human reader. Comments using the above SGML-based 'comment statement' syntax *can* be made in XML documents and, as they are XML documents themselves, into XML schemas employing this standard structure. In doing so however, once 'parsed', the comment content will be lost permanently.

If you are tempted to insert comments this way, a simple word of advice: *don't*.

You should of course encourage the extensive use of comments, but such information should be considered as *marked-up content*, even if for a very restricted audience. One person's comment is another person's valuable resource, and almost always valuable reference documentation. So ensure that comments are made explicitly within purpose-built elements.

Remember that any element or element content can be deliberately filtered during transformations, as and where required. The same is true for comments. The comment statement, however, may be stripped out at any stage of parsing or processing, and you have no control over where they appear and disappear.

The <annotation> element is also available for use in an XML Schema, and offers a legal set of child elements including <documentation>. You may need to use more than this, however, and aim to build a 'knowledge mould' specifically for managing reference information gathered according to document types. 'Knowledge moulds' are described in Chapter 10.

If all the documentation you create is clearly and *semantically* structured, for example by using consistent word-processing templates, it will not be such a major effort to convert into XML, if desired, at a later stage.

Building your reference dictionary

We have talked several times about developing a 'common vocabulary'. The set of namespaces, schemas, elements and attributes largely constitute that vocabulary. A vocabulary without a dictionary to maintain it is going to fall into disuse quickly. As with any dictionary, each and every entry should explain, in a consistent and readable manner:

- The exact construction (spelling, case, special characters, etc.)

- Optionally, a unique identifier for the dictionary entry

- The intended meaning

- The relationship to and dependencies on other entries, and known downstream effects

- The origin, creator and person/business unit responsible for any questions or to whom update requests should be addressed

- Its intended use

You need to determine the best computing and application infrastructure within which to maintain all the documentation and reference information you will accumulate during the development of your XML framework. It could be in XML itself: after all, the information collected and managed is clearly structured and defined and can itself be reused in other contexts. Alternatively, you could adopt the approach proposed by ebXML, both in its proposal for a 'Core Components' model to help build specific vocabularies and its 'Registry Information Model'.

Meaning

Names of elements, attributes and so on should strike a compromise between conciseness and clarity. The actual names are not important to computers – they are arbitrary strings of characters as far as parsers are concerned. It is important not to argue inordinately over element and attribute names – computers only recognize them as a distinct string of characters to be compared with others.

Human readability is, however, important, and if element names cannot be made entirely meaningful, it is important that you document the intended meaning of each entity very clearly. When the same element name is used in different namespaces within your information territory, or namespaces defined elsewhere, make reference to all and fully cross-reference them. This will give hints and pointers to developers, ensure that the correct namespaces are indicated, to avoid element name clashes and highlight potential danger areas:

```
<title>1. In the /legislation namespace, indicates the formal title
of an item of EU legislation. Has equivalents in other EU languages,
see …
2. In the /administration namespace, indicates the official name of
an administrative unit. Has equivalents in other EU languages, see ….
Administrative unit code should be used in the optional 'Code'
attribute…
3. …
```

See also the question of naming conventions, discussed in Chapter 6.

Dependencies It is important to indicate all dependencies on a particular structure and where it fits within a larger picture:

```
<member> A child element of <assembly>, <executive>, <organ>,
<politicalGroup>, <delegation> or <administrativeUnit>. Is used also
in <action> ('tabling', 'voting', 'joining', etc) and ...
```

The ISO 'Topic Map' standard and the W3C's RDF are both ideal means for representing this information in a machine- and human-readable manner.

You may have no idea why a particular attribute is required within a particular element, and be tempted to remove it when reviewing or 'tweaking' a particular schema. Good, clear documentation can help:

```
Duration (XML Schema primitive datatype, see definition) Used as an
attribute to the <intervention> element to indicate the time dura-
tion of a speech. Required for SMIL application managing synchroni-
zation of sub-titled text to video stream of plenary sittings…
```

If you are building schemas from common building blocks, this question of dependencies is vital and requires careful documentation.

Project management

Information should be documented describing the life history of any structure, including indications of origin, ownership, date and/or period of validity and procedures for updating or changing dependencies:

```
<elementDefinition>
<elementName>
legCode
</elementName>
<dc:Author scheme="EU:EP" authorityCode="01C">
DG1-Legislative Coordination Service
<contact>
E-Mail: DG1C
</contact>
</dc:Author>
<dc:Date.Created>
1987-05-12
</dc:Date.Created>
<dc:Date.Valid>
1987-09-17
</dc:Date.Valid>
<dc:Creator scheme="EU:EP" authorityCode="01D">
Directorate for Information Technologies
</dc:Creator>
<managedBy authorityCode="IILC">
Inter-Institutional Legislative Co-ordination Working Group
</managedBy>
<businessTerm>
Inter-Institutional Legislative Code
</businessTerm>
<dc:Description.Abstract>
This code, created by the European Commission at the beginning of a
legislative procedure, is used to identify all documents relating to
the procedure and the advance of the legislative dossier
</dc:Description.Abstract>
</elementDefinition>
```

In this example, we have taken that extra step of coding the reference information itself in XML.

Rather than invent elements ourselves, we have used part of a standard set proposed by the Dublin Core Metadata Initiative. To indicate that these elements belong to the Dublin Core 'namespace', we use a namespace prefix dc: which – in a separate and earlier declaration – we must associate with a specific namespace, as we will see in Chapter 6 in the section *Namespaces*.

Reading through the example, we should see that the XML element to be named legCode is being documented, with information about who was responsible for creating it, when it was created, when it comes into effect and so on. By standardizing the way in which this reference information is maintained, we are ensuring that information kept here is always usable elsewhere.

Multilingualism   By providing comprehensive documentation, you lessen the risks of misunderstanding of the intended use of a particular structure.

If you are working in a multilingual environment and you can't translate all your element names and attributes, or do not think it advisable to, then at least attempt to translate the documentation. From this you should at a later stage be able to derive a multilingual dictionary of terms, particularly if your element names and attributes correspond to common terminology that you use in your business.

Check with the database administrators responsible for localization-specific systems: they will almost certainly use different display labels and values to render information more understandable in a particular context. The quality of work done here will reap immense benefits later on, particularly in the domains of 'knowledge management' and information navigation. We investigate these in Chapter 13.

Best practices   One of the weakest areas of application development is the problem of documenting and learning from the development process itself. You should ensure that all aspects of an application's development are fully documented – including requirements documents, analyses and development progress reports. Use standard document templates if you do not yet use a formal XML document structure and, as ever, markup in a consistent, structured and semantically-relevant manner.

This should be done with documentation relating to the development of the XML framework itself, and will prove a valuable 'proof of concept' to show to other developers.

Technical documentation should be thoroughly and semantically 'tagged', so that references – for example – to important vocabulary or blocks of text can be identified, picked up and later processed and linked to. You should ensure therefore that references to any key terms within documentation are marked up. This should include references to the XML elements, attributes and entities used from the common vocabulary in a particular development, references to other applications or tools and references to standards. Even if you do not have the infrastructure today to manage, process or analyze this information, by doing so you have made the information immediately accessible from the moment that you do have such an infrastructure in place.

Readability   XML is designed to be human-readable as well as machine-processable. By thinking very carefully how you intend to document and manage the information you will construct, you will make the entirety of your XML framework much more readable, accessible and thus understandable to all.

Users and developers, contractors and business partners alike will then be able to understand the origins, purpose and design principles of your XML strategy, saving you costs, effort and a lot of misunderstanding and aggravation. Use Topic Maps and RDF to make your framework more navigable and understandable.

Rolling your own standards

If you do decide to follow a path to the definition of your own standards, be sure to do so according to a clearly-established process. You need to have a clear idea of the scope of what you are attempting to cover, your success criteria, how you intend to manage the development and how to address 'governance' questions, for example those regarding decision-making, responsibility and arbitration.

Help is on hand in the shape of various consortia, as we will see in the next chapter, but you must be sure that their processes and objectives can be used in a way that adequately reflects your needs.

You should concentrate at the outset on identifying your distinct, common vocabulary, rather than launching into full-blown schema development or specific transactions or processes. Once you have a 'big picture' and have created some momentum within your business and beyond for your particular vision, others will bring their hands to bear and fill in the detailed landscape.

Conclusions

Having built solid foundations for your XML framework, you now have to start to build it and give it some substance. This is the subject of the next chapter.

6 Building on the Foundations

I say: take no thought of the harvest,
But only of proper sowing.

T. S. Eliot, *Choruses from The Rock*, I

Introduction

Now that we have agreed the infrastructure, rules and procedures for our XML framework, we have to start adding some content. Unlike any other content management system, the content of the framework is reference data that can be reliably used by any subsequent development as a stable point of reference for the best use of XML and its family of standards in a particular enterprise.

It may be difficult to draw a line in the sand at the outset of the project, but it must be a clearly defined and early objective to do this. Everyone needs to know exactly the boundaries of the information territory whose management you are scoping within your framework. These boundaries must consider both the vocabulary and its use.

Vocabulary

We must understand that an XML framework seeks to define a common 'vocabulary' and lay down how and where its vocabulary elements are used – in other words, what are the semantic building blocks that we identify and want to name and label?

Vocabulary definition

The big challenge offered by the XML Namespace standard is precisely to be able to declare: 'These are *our* definitions – what are yours?' A large part of the framework will consist of this identification, naming and management of the building blocks that business units will be able to use for specific XML implementation.

Vocabulary scope – the use of Namespaces

The intention is not that you should use only the vocabulary that the framework defines. On the contrary, using existing vocabularies that have been developed elsewhere is a practice to be encouraged. Your framework should concentrate on what is not defined elsewhere and/or needs to be implemented in a specific manner within your enterprise.

In Figure 16, territory A is explicitly excluded from the scope of your attention. B and C have some aspects useful to you which you could use (rather than 'import') and refer to by means of the Namespaces standard. Your territory covers D and E completely, but that doesn't mean that you need to import them into your Namespace, just be more careful about duplication and properly assigning and using Namespaces.

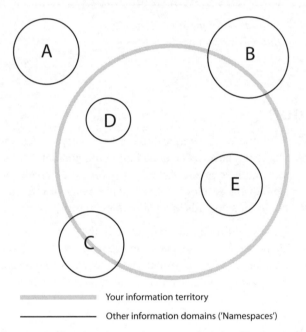

 Your information territory

———————————— Other information domains ('Namespaces')

Figure 16. Overlapping and non-overlapping Namespaces

Using a combination of XML Namespaces allows you to direct your tools to a correct understanding of a particular XML element as part of a recognized 'dictionary', without any confusion or conflict in meaning.

As a checklist, be sure to:

• Cover your whole information territory, even if by doing so you are able to refer to other 'namespaces' and vocabularies already defined elsewhere.

- Keep your eyes open – look around you and see what other enterprises in your field are doing. If a standard seems close to your needs, ask yourself if you can live without the 'extra bits': many buyers are rarely completely satisfied with all of the features of a car that they buy, but few people customize them once bought. Tinkering around can be fun, but once you start, you are on your own and it can be very costly to come 'back to the fold'.

- Keep a clear focus on your objectives and on reality. You want to ease the exchange of information within a particular information community, so be sure to include the current costs of conversion between different formats when undertaking a cost-benefit analysis.

Vocabulary use   Without too much effort, it is possible to imagine marking up and 'XML-ising' pretty much anything and everything. As well as content markup, we can imagine marking up metadata, or the 'wrapping and labelling' of our content, marking up the processes that manage our content, marking up the manner in which the content is stored, rendered and displayed in different ways, or even marking up your office plans and layout.

Planning ahead

It would be a very brave enterprise that embarked on marking up everything in XML. What is probably most important is to capture an early 'high level' view of the extent of your XML work and decide in consequence not only *what* should be your main areas of concern, but also if there is a logical progression that could be followed.

Even if your explicit objective is not a shift to 'all-XML', you can lay very valuable groundwork by thoroughly analyzing your information types. Consider the following example:

> To facilitate the exchange of documents, three organizations agree to standardize around the document format of a single word-processing package. They recognize that ultimately there is sense in developing a common vocabulary to structure and mark up the content of their documents in XML. In the short term, being able to work on each other's documents already and without conversion makes the exchanges easier.

The more they look at the question of common structure, however, the more they realize that in fact the issues are more complex. They may share the same word-processing base, but within that, they each use hundreds of different types of document, and there are no common rules governing their *internal* structure. Identifying structures, automating routines to identify, extract and manipulate particular content 'chunks' is not actually so easy.

They could conclude that the gains to be made from a shift to XML are too costly or complicated to implement, certainly in the short term.

On the other hand, they could step back a little from the document itself and at least agree to standardize the documents' *metadata* in XML. In this way, irrespective of the heterogeneous nature of the content, at least every document can be 'wrapped' or packaged and labelled in the same manner. This would be much less ambitious, but nonetheless a very valuable starting point. It would allow information about a document's content to be exchanged in a standardized manner, information that could shape expectations of a document's content, the processes associated with it, instructions or warnings. It is the sort of thing we do already with electronic mail, as we saw in the introductory chapters.

Accompanying this exercise, it should be possible to at least make a first-cut analysis of the main 'semantic building blocks' of the documents used. This way – as we will investigate in more detail in the next chapter – we can start the process of 'mapping' current content building blocks onto formal XML schemas, and in a manner that ensures that management and users stay in control.

So, initial reflection should be as much about how and in which order you can make progress as it is about how far to go. The nature of the XML standards is such that they encourage this. You can embark on a modest project, knowing that your investment in analysis and development is safe, as future developments can build on and use the same standards.

An evolving framework

The job of an XML framework is not only to determine what should be in your sights, but also to agree a process by which to widen its scope as time progresses, technologies develop and the XML family grows. Agreement on such procedures may be as important in some enterprises as agreement on a common vocabulary.

It is your decision whether you intend to limit your XML investment to content markup or are already mapping out a path to using XML for business processes, user interface design or content repurposing. It is not important as far as developing an XML framework is concerned. As far as developing an XML framework is concerned, it is unimportant. The objective of the framework is not to develop a global implementation plan for all of your XML projects, but to agree:

- Who is responsible for what

- How the standards are used

- How reference standards are agreed and how they are managed and maintained

- What terminology to use, where and with what constraints

Developing initial standards

You want your framework to offer a clear set of vocabulary, reference data and best practices to any developer or project manager that intends to use XML and who is required to follow your enterprise's rules and standards.

Opportunities Before taking the step to develop your own standards – a step that should not be taken lightly – take a look around to see what else exists first. There are many publicly available vocabularies, specific markup languages, schemas and related namespaces already. Do not add to these valuable Web standards by developing something that is not strictly necessary.

Vocabularies and formal XML repositories are available that are developed and maintained by consortia, by commercial ventures or by industry associations. Do not be put off by the fact that a potentially useful markup language is maintained by a competitor. When they see that others are using it, it will become rapidly apparent that it is in everyone's interest that further developments take place cooperatively.

The role of the public sector cannot be underestimated. Many companies and organizations look for guidance from us, as a stable and legitimate reference upon which they can depend. Not only are public sector organizations often the ultimate repositories of legislation they are also concerned with interoperability and cost reduction without having their own commercial interests or profit motive to drive any standardization work.

The last resort is that if nothing appears suitable, you can develop your own standards. That is the essence of the 'X' in XML.

Dangers There are obvious advantages to cooperating with others in the development of a common standard for the use of XML within a given 'information territory'. You all benefit from economies of scale in the shared development effort by pooling knowledge and resources: you will benefit from the use of the common vocabulary, once developed, to encapsulate and express your information content.

Since 2000, however, there has been an explosion in the number of initiatives that fall short of their objectives, although worthy in intent, because they are not sufficiently representative of all those involved in the use and/or production of a particular content type.

Imagine a handful of grocers collaborating with a single supermarket to define a global vocabulary to describe the ingredients of the products they stock. You can appreciate the potentials for danger. If key actors who collectively have a global view are not party to such definition exercises, the resultant vocabulary is not going to be representative, and thus of limited use beyond the small group that developed it.

Key actors working in the same 'information territory' must be offered the opportunity to take part in such development work.

Solutions

There is no single, approved approach to developing common vocabularies, but there are three starting points that you should consider.

UN/CEFACT

The United Nations Center for Trade Facilitation and Electronic Business (UN/ CEFACT) seeks to encourage trade through the standardized use of information that relates to trade, for example, orders, invoicing and so on. Its precursor, EDIFACT, was the authority behind the Electronic Data Interchange (EDI) standard that offered a powerful, if cumbersome, infrastructure for managing information flows between businesses. UN/CEFACT has been responsible for developing a successor to EDI, more agile yet still robust. It is now being superseded by ebXML.

These UN-based bodies are criticized for being slow, but boast wide participation. UN/ CEFACT's decision-making procedures are sufficiently robust to ensure that any decision taken has wide consensus and a high chance of being widely used. The proposed Core Components Technical Specification has been heralded as a major step forward in building business-specific vocabularies from common core building blocks while offering the design flexibility demanded by many.

OASIS

This membership consortium has established a standard decision-making process that allows its member organizations to concentrate their effort and resources on getting things done rather than agreeing procedures. It is criticized for not having strong 'user-community' input, being driven rather by vendors and industry, and for allowing new 'standards' to develop too easily without sufficient attention to redundancy. This is unjust when one considers 'heavyweight' projects such as eBXML, now co-hosted by OASIS with the UN, and the more recent Universal Business Language, UBL.

Maintenance and implementation

It is important to distinguish between the roles that UN/CEFACT, OASI and other bodies play. On one hand, there are the important functions for developing and maintain standards. On the other, however, there is the work of proselytizing and implementing the standards that are developed.

The World Wide Web Consortium, together with the Internet Engineering Task Force for infrastructure standards issues, assumes responsibility for maintaining the standards it has developed. In this, it follows the model for many ISO standards: it ensures that the standards are up to date and in conformity with each other and has a process for agreeing updates.

However, the ISO is generally not concerned with how a standard is used or implemented – that is not its job. It is merely a reference against which implementations can be checked and validated by appropriate authorities. Those authorities, often national standards bodies such as ANSI in the USA or CEN in Europe, have rules and procedures for ensuring conformance and implementation of particular standards.

The W3C, on the other hand, although it promotes conformance and best practices in the use of their standards, has no role in guiding or enforcing implementation or indeed any interlocutors with whom to achieve this. There are no authorities that could regulate on the development of, say, particular XML schemas or vocabularies.

The whole area of implementation is therefore completely 'up for grabs'. This is why many seek safety in numbers through agencies like UN/CEFACT and OASIS. Keeping a high-level overview of all the XML applications developed is becoming an increasingly difficult task. There is as yet no initiative to tackle such a tricky but potentially valuable exercise, to 'map' the semantic intent of the component building blocks of publicly-registered schemas and vocabularies to all others that share the same semantics. If redundancy cannot be avoided, it should at least be known and visible. This is a task for the Topic Maps standards that we will see in more detail in Chapter 13, *Navigation Strategies*.

We are going to develop our XML framework step by step, using standards that do exist, best practices where they don't and common sense throughout. Our main concern for the use of XML is interoperability, and this principle should apply to all aspects of the framework design and development. As well as content, terminology can be reused and standardized to good effect, as we will see.

Naming conventions

Many tools are appearing on the market that allow an XML schema to be generated from data modelling environments. In many ways, the actual names of formal structures may seem to be arbitrary and of little consequence, whether they are the 'machine' names given to database tables or to XML element tags. As long as applications and machines know what is supposed to link with what, so the argument goes, names are just arbitrary tags. That argument, however, is potentially dangerous for XML, and is a hangover from application-centric systems development, rather than the information-centric model that XML favors. Let's explore why.

Can names be arbitrary?

One of the strong points of XML is precisely that it doesn't limit itself to immediate needs or a specific context, but keeps the door open to interoperability. Leaving naming conventions to tools, only seeing the names proposed when you generate specific schemas, is probably leaving the issue too late. It is already too far downstream in the development process and likely to be limited to a specific production, rather like developing a human language using phrases with a specific context, without learning the meanings of the individual words.

It is important to think both extensively and exhaustively about how all the building blocks themselves are going to be stored and labelled. In the process you should be able to glean all the information you need to know about each building block – who designed it, who 'owns' it, what is its worth, etc. This is why starting your 'XML-ization' with metadata can be so valuable, as we see in the next chapter. Consider the following example:

> Two development teams within the same enterprise are each producing a small application, both use many of the same information types and the same development methodology, for example UML. But each creates its own data and information model and automatically generates a set of XML tags. It will be little surprise, therefore to discover that the XML tags do not necessarily correspond.

Two IT reactions to this are typical:

- '*Retroconversion*'. This viewpoint can be stated as follows: 'The idea of having a common vocabulary is fine in theory, but until you can put it together, we have to get on with our work. We can reconvert what we have produced at a later date and catch up again easily'.

  This approach may need to be considered in some cases, but if you have development teams anxious to proceed with an XML implementation, get them at the very least to cooperate in defining common XML elements and attributes before progressing too far. The idea of retroconversion sounds fine in theory, but by the time you have half a million documents, several hundred DTDs and schemas to align, it is different matter – expect large contractor's bills.

• *'On-the-fly' conversion.* This viewpoint can be stated as: 'There is nothing to worry about. The whole beauty of XSLT is that you can precisely use it to convert one source XML document to a target with a set of simple transformation rules. You could use it on the fly to convert the two sets of tag names as and when you need them.'

This sounds more convincing and seems to offer some of the power that XML is already famed for. However, if there is one common criticism of XML, it is that it is verbose compared to proprietary and binary data encapsulation formats. Adding another layer of transformation imposes a further potential processing burden. Just because XSLT lets you repair your mistakes later is not an excuse to make them if they could be avoided in the first place.

Upstream coordination

In both the cases above, the responses seem to miss the point: just because you can transform XML content easily should not allow you to be less disciplined where it counts. If two information objects are semantically identical, call them the same thing. The name you give them can either be arbitrary, or conform to a naming convention determined as part of your framework, to maintain clarity and transparency.

A consistent approach to naming removes any shadow of doubt regarding interoperability. If errors or problems do arise in information exchanges between different systems, it ensures that you have already eliminated one possible culprit from your inquiries.

Case-sensitivity

Element, attribute and other names in XML are case sensitive, so you should be consistent about how you mix upper and lower case. Sooner or later, someone is going to develop an application with a schema that confuses a single letter and unwittingly creates two functionally different elements, even if the *intent* is that they are semantically equivalent. Consider:

```
<legCode>COD(2001)2365<legCode>
<LegProcedure>Co-Decision</LegProcedure>
```

compared with:

```
<legCode>COS(2002)2512<legCode>
<legProcedure>Consultation</legProcedure>
```

It is easily done, but is the different so easily spotted? In the second example, the `<legProcedure>` tag starts with a lower case letter. A minor difference, but a real one nevertheless, one that a processor would consider as two completely distinct element names.

Multilingualism

If working in a multinational and/or multilingual environment, in which language should element tag names and attribute names be written?

It is best to have element names in the language of the content, unless the volume of documents in one language is so small and occasional as not to merit such specific attention. If you produce documents of the same type in different languages, you should ensure absolute one-to-one correspondence between each part of the schemas in each language version. You could create 'meta-schemas' to define your overall document structures in a language-neutral manner, then provide a mapping mechanism to language-specific schemas. Or you can simply maintain parallel sets of schemas and propose XSLT transformations using the one-to-one mapping of language specific elements.

The Blueberry Requirements initiative at the World Wide Web Consortium is currently considering an update to the XML standard to allow most Unicode characters to be used within element names, allowing markup to be made in any language. At the time of its original adoption, XML accepted any Unicode Version 2.0 character, whereas a number of languages with complex character sets, such as Japanese, were only fully coded in the later Unicode Version 3.1.

Terseness versus clarity

All XML documents are plain text documents: as such, every character counts, both information content and markup. Long element tag names or attribute names, particularly if repeated often within the same document, take up a lot of space. On the other hand, one of the design principles of XML is to favour descriptiveness over terseness, so element names should not be so short as to be cryptic. You need to strike a balance between the two.

What should you cover?

A consistent and complete naming convention does not necessarily mean having to control and approve every element or attribute created in every project. It does mean however that you must ensure that the mechanisms in place within your XML framework can ensure that each element created is unique for the semantic content it identifies, and is available for use beyond the project that created it.

This is exactly idea behind public and private XML registries. Often, however, they concentrate at the document type level – the DTD or schema – as this is the operational unit that business units intend to use 'off the shelf'. Coordinating at the higher level, that of a common vocabulary, is less common, but offers greater security and freedom for developers. By doing so, you are allowing anyone to build their needs-specific schemas from a common set of semantic building blocks, while at the same time offering a guarantee of interoperability because the structures so defined are part of a wider common model.

Having laid down some general rules for naming conventions, let us now look at each of the main component types of our planned repository: namespaces, elements and attributes.

Namespaces

Namespaces are not just valuable as shorthand to signal use of a part of a vocabulary, but help systems and users to recognize that elements may come from different territories, including the XML standards themselves. When scoping your namespaces, you should also consider links and references to any public namespaces that are used and referenced, either in your own schema or schemas that your enterprise uses.

This will help developers obtain a high-level picture of where your namespace 'fits' and better understand the proposed use of other namespaces where these are proposed.

Establishing a namespace sets a default territory for your work and ensures that any vocabulary you define is unique within that declared namespace. The mere 'creation' of a namespace itself has no practical consequences or implications, and is only needed when you want schemas and elements to refer to it. In this sense a namespace is implied from the moment you intend to develop a context-specific vocabulary of elements and attributes.

Namespace declaration

The namespace itself is an arbitrary URI and does not actually need to point to anything. It is important however that it is *stable*. Once defined and used you should not change it. It is arbitrary in the sense that only specific applications are expected to 'know' what is implied by such an indicator. It does not actually have to resolve or point to anything when processed.

In making a namespace declaration, current practice seems to favour using a URI based on the DNS name of the organization responsible for the particular schema, or vocabulary using that namespace. But care should be taken that the DNS name itself is stable.

For example, the European Union institutions currently use Internet domain names under the top-level domain for international organizations – .int – with all the Union's institutions and agencies using a single second-level domain, `eu.int`. It would be tempting to use this as a 'root' for any XML namespaces that are declared, such as:

```
xmlns="http://europa.eu.int/xml/"
```

However, the European Union received approved in 2002 for its own ICANN-registered top-level domain, `.eu`.

The 'old' domain could certainly be used without problems as the declared XML namespace – even after the shift of domains, nobody else would be using the old domain, so as an arbitrary pointer its continued use would be 'safe' and stable. However, as we know it is a policy that will come into force, it would probably be better to use the new domain, even if it is not yet operational:

```
xmlns="http://union.eu/xml/"
```

Another approach is to use a 'Uniform Resource Name' (URN) rather than a URI. This is based on the assumption that the Namespace is only an arbitrary label and does not need to point to anything. Our above example could therefore be expressed as:

```
xmlns="urn:union-eu:xml"
```

The namespace itself is arbitrary, but it can be helpful for understanding the origin of a particular schema or who is responsible for maintaining it. It can also be the location where XML schemas themselves are stored, or indeed any information or resources that are concerned with that particular namespace, including who is responsible for it, maintenance processes, etc. This is one convention that is encouraged and proposed in the Resource Directory Description Language, RDDL. It would also be the ideal starting point for pointing to your XML framework.

Namespace prefix

In some documents, all XML elements used will refer to the same XML namespace. If elements refer to different namespaces, however, the different uses need to be identifiable. One way to do this is to refer to the referenced namespace in every such element:

```
<title xmlns="http://union.eu/xml/">
```

This is clumsy and prone to errors and maintenance problems over time. The XML namespace standard offers a solution. The second aspect of the standard is the *prefix*, a 'token' used as a form of shorthand to replace the full namespace:

```
xmlns:eu="http://union.eu/xml/"
```

When an element is used that has to be referenced to this namespace, it would then be sufficient to use the prefix `eu:` as a 'placeholder' for the full URI:

```
...EU <eu:legType>Directive</eu:legType> on Data Protection...
```

Again, the token is arbitrary and of use only to the human reader, as any parser or tool will replace the token with the full namespace in the same way that a program resolves variables before processing. Prefixes that we do see in XML documents, such as xslt: or fo:, are used consistently to point to a consistent namespace. This is a convention only, but a convention worth following, as it helps human 'debuggers' to access the code more easily and understand the meaning of any particular namespace.

Remember that the namespace prefix is only of any programmable significance as a prefix to an element or attribute name: it serves as a placeholder or variable for the whole namespace URI. Unlike the more familiar HTML <base> tag, the namespace is *not* a device for resolving any other issue, such as relative or 'base' URIs or multiple namespaces.

If you are developing a common vocabulary, your namespace should declare a name that identifies the information territory it intends to cover. Within that common vocabulary, however, you may be confronted with the need to use the same element or attribute name to identify two or more information object types. It is possible in this situation to use several namespaces for the different fields of work in which there might be confusion, assigning a unique namespace prefix to each:

```
xmlns:l="http://union.eu/xml/legislation/"
xmlns:p="http://union.eu/xml/programs/"
xmlns:a="http://union.eu/xml/administration/"
```

In the above example, we have simply created three arbitrary prefixes for three distinct namespaces, all of which are still however part of our wider information territory. To avoid confusion, we can make it clear that although there are different namespaces in use, they are all grounded in the same territory.

```
xmlns:eu_l="http://union.eu/xml/legislation/"
xmlns:eu_p="http://union.eu/xml/programs/"
xmlns:dc="http://purl.org/elements/1.1/"
```

Although the namespace prefix should be kept as simple as possible, we must remember that terseness can be costly, so always err on the side of caution. Here at least we have spelled out the issue a little by giving two pieces of information in the prefix for the eu namespaces, and indicating them clearly and differently from the final Dublin Core namespace declaration.

Elements

The main building blocks of our XML documents are elements. These can be classified into two broad categories:

- Block

- In-line

Block elements represent distinct content chunks:

```
<intervention>
Mr. Speaker, I rise here on a point of order. (Laughter) Are you
aware that...
</intervention>
```

Such blocks can be assembled sequentially, as a series of the same element type, of different element types or a mix. They can also be nested following the 'well-formedness rules'. The schema lays down the arrangement of content building blocks.

In-line elements appear arbitrarily within content, particularly in text rather than data-intensive information:

```
<intervention>
Mr. Speaker, I rise here on a point of order.
<interruption>
(Laughter)
</interruption>
Are you aware that...
</intervention>
```

These elements serve to pick out or highlight, within a flow of text, a section of content for particular treatment.

As a rule of thumb, the contents of a block element can be meaningful on its own, even if only fully understood within the context that it is written. An in-line element, on the other hand, as it picks out a chunk or marks a spot within an otherwise continual flow, is less likely to be used or reused on its own, but is 'highlighted' for particular treatment in its context.

In the example above, the short speech in Parliament can exist as a separate entity, could even be quoted wholesale elsewhere, for example a press communiqué. The reference to the interruption however is tagged as an in-line element for potential further treatment, say by presenting the text in another manner, to be picked up and ignored by an indexing agent, and so on. On its own it has little meaning.

Giving an element a value

As an aid to understanding, XML is sometimes portrayed as a common currency, akin to the Euro or US Dollar. We can extend the analogy further: if XML is a currency, then we should give a 'monetary' value to each XML element that is created.

We can put a 'price' on each element used by a system according to the 'market value' that business units are prepared to give it as a reflection of its usefulness and value. In this way, you are not only considering your XML elements as business assets with an intrinsic value. You are also able to make some interesting cost-benefit and return on investment calculations. These can be used to compare different application developments that use those elements. Furthermore, managing such values should be part of a coherent XML asset-management strategy.

We can imagine a situation where such an asset-management approach would be useful: project arbitration. When senior management is confronted with a decision to allocate scarce resources between competing projects, it useful to be able to highlight the relative costs and benefits of the different proposals. If an expensive-to-develop tool is nevertheless creating, using and maintaining XML elements that are agreed as being of high value to the enterprise, it might secure funding against an equally costly tool that handles or manages more marginal assets.

Identifying elements

Deciding what is and what is not an element may not always be simple. The rule of thumb should be that an element must identify and thus 'tag' a unique content 'chunk'. This raises the question of how fine you want sieve your content: what level of granularity you are looking for.

We will take an earlier example and work on it in more detail for the following sections. Imagine that we are preparing a report of proceedings in Parliament that currently is prepared for print as follows:

> Friday, 15th November 2002
> Hon. Vice President Dupont presiding
>
> (1) The **President** declared the sitting open.
> (2) **Hon. Mr. Bloggs**: Mr. Speaker, I rise here on a point of order.
> *(laughter)*
> Are you aware that…

We could consider the proceedings for a particular one-day sitting as an element. We have left out the introductory text and all formatting at this stage, for reasons that we will see later:

```
<proceedings>
(1) The President declared the sitting open. (2) Hon. Mr. Bloggs: Mr.
Speaker, I rise here on a point of order. (Laughter) Are you aware
that...
</proceedings>
```

In reality, of course, the sitting is made up of a number of events, including speeches, points of order, votes, interruptions, procedural declarations, questions and so forth. Each of these represents a semantically-distinct event and as such should be treated as separate elements:

```
<proceedings>
<procedural>
The President declared the sitting open.
</procedural>
<speech>
Hon. Mr. Bloggs: Mr. Speaker, I rise here on a point of order.
<interruption>
Laughter
</interruption>
Are you aware that...
</speech>
...
</proceedings>
```

It is probably best to head first for the finest level of granularity when identifying your elemental content building blocks:

```
<proceedings>
<date>
2002-11-15
</date>
<sittingPresident>
<member>
Hon. Vice President Dupont
</member>
 presiding
</sittingPresident>
<intervention>
001
<procedural>
The President declared the sitting open.
</procedural>
</intervention>
<intervention>
002
<speech>
<member>
Hon. Mr. Bloggs
</member>
: Mr. Speaker, I rise here on a point of order.
<interruption>
Laughter
</interruption>
Are you aware that...
</speech>
</intervention>
...
</proceedings>
```

You can always remove overly-detailed tags and merge the content back into the parent element at a later stage if that should prove necessary. Further refining a coarsely-defined element, on the other hand, if a far more tricky task.

Order and use of elements

In deciding your use of elements, you need to address the following questions: do blocks of text have to appear in a particular order in a text, are they are optional or conditional on other elements or rules, can they can be repeated or need to be unique in a particular context? When identifying your elements, this information is also valuable and will help you to develop coherent and workable schema.

Attributes

The use of attributes is likely to be affected by the publication of the XML Schema standard exists, and in other ways some earlier and clearer distinctions between elements and attributes are fading. This issue is discussed in more detail in the next section, *Datatyping and constraints*.

Uniquely identifying an instance – object identification

A 'classic' use of attributes is to associate a particular value, often a reference, to a particular *instance* of an element. We could thus refine our example above:

```
<proceedings date="2002-11-15"
docUID="P5_CRE(2002)11-15">
<sittingPresident>
<member>
Hon. Vice President Dupont
</member>
 presiding
</sittingPresident>
<intervention id="001">
<procedural>
The President declared the sitting open.
</procedural>
<intervention>
<intervention id="002">
<speech>
<member>
Hon. Mr. Bloggs
</member>
: Mr. Speaker, I rise here on a point of order.
<interruption>Laughter</interruption>
Are you aware that...
</speech>
</intervention>
...
</proceedings>
```

In this example we have given a unique identifier to both the document, with root element <proceedings>, and to the individual interventions. This is of particular value when using the reference as a marker for a block that you might want to point to at a later stage using XPath and XPointer.

Alternately, it offers greater flexibility for text output, if you decide that you wish to replace the code with specific text. Compare the above with the functionally-equivalent example below, but in which the reference values are included as elements:

```
<proceedings>
<date>
2002-11-15
</date>
<docUID>
P5_CRE(2002)11-15
</docUID>
<sittingPresident>
<member>
Hon. Vice President Dupont
</member>
presiding
</sittingPresident>
<intervention>
<id>001</id>
<procedural>
The President declared the sitting open.
</procedural>
</intervention>
<intervention>
<id>002</id>
<speech>
<member>
Hon. Mr. Bloggs
</member>
: Mr. Speaker, I rise here on a point of order.
<interruption>
Laughter
</interruption>
Are you aware that...
</speech>
</intervention>
...
</proceedings>
```

The first is arguably clearer, and keeps a useful distinction between *machine-process-able* data being included as attribute values and *human-readable* data within element content.

As well as uniquely identifying an element as part of a series – in our example, the identification of a particular intervention – we might want to attribute a code to the value of a particular element. This is useful for:

- Repetitive text blocks, such as the opening procedural text or interruptions in our example,

- Occasions when we might want to process or validate a particular block further and reduce the risk of spelling mistakes, etc., such as might be achieved by using a code to represent a particular referenced Member:

```
<proceedings date="2002-11-15"
docUID="P5_CRE(2002)11-15">
<sittingPresident memberID="0298"/>
<intervention id="001">
<procedural type="01"/>
<intervention>
<intervention id="002">
<speech memberID="0678">
Mr. Speaker, I rise here on a point of order.
<interruption type="04"/>
Are you aware that...
</speech>
</intervention>
...
</proceedings>
```

Facilitating processing

In the example, we have removed the name of the Member speaking from the flow of text. This would allow us to have more flexibility over the presentation of this information – the name of a Member – possibly associating other information with it, provided from a reference database. This could include the Member's political affiliation or area represented, or even how the name should be displayed – there are different conventions in different countries and for different languages, for example. Additionally, we now have a ready-made set of metadata that could be extracted and reused in an external metadata record of the document.

What must be remembered is that labels are very important and are central to the use of the XPointer standard. These labels should serve their purpose: identifying a type of content when that required, such as an element name, or a specific content instance, such as an attribute. Plan this carefully and you will reap the dividends in later content and link management strategies.

Building an accessible information architecture

Imagine that at a later stage you wish to be able to point to 'all interventions by Honourable Member Bloggs during the month of May 2002' through a combination of queries and links. This is possible using the XLink, XPath and XPointer standards, as we will see in Chapter 12. For such queries to work, we have to provide the appropriate hooks to link to the relevant content.

Our example could now be rendered in a printed verbatim report, with the identifiers processed using the XSLT transformation language to provide appropriate substitute text, as:

> Friday, 15th November 2002
> Hon. Vice President Dupont presiding
>
> (1) The **President** declared the sitting open.
> (2) **Hon. Mr. Bloggs**: Mr. Speaker, I rise here on a point of order.
> *(laughter)*
> Are you aware that…

In other words, exactly as the initial printed text. Now, however, as the original is in XML, we also have access to various codes and reference information that can be processed further without touching this original.

Of course, if the value of the attribute id in the intervention element, or the content of the memberID element, are incorrectly coded, one of two problems may occur:

- Where the value indicated corresponds to an incorrect value, the output presentation will be valid but will not be correct

- Where the value indicated does not correspond to *any* value in the reference set known to the processor, the 'hook' that the reference represents is not going to be picked up by any correctly-formulated query, and the processor rendering the output will throw an error

No amount of sophistication in tools and automated processing is going to solve human error such as giving memberID an incorrect value. However, powerful validation mechanisms exist in XML to deal with the second situation.

Validation

It is already possible to indicate a list of attribute values that are permissible within the start tag of a given element by using DTDs.

In our example above, however, this will not be of much use. In the case of the element <intervention>, we cannot predict the full range of values. It is in the nature of this example, in fact, that each new intervention would give a new identifier value. We would need to keep updating the referenced DTD to add to the list of permissible values, clearly of little benefit. We do at least have an idea of the structure and nature of the value foreseen – in this case a code made up of a date followed by a serial number.

In the case of the element <memberID> or <member>,we cannot predict the value either, but do know that the value must reflect a valid code, for example, codes representing all the current Members or a name in a list.

We need two extra functions to make the use of attributes worthwhile in these and many similar cases, both provided by XML:

- A means of validating the structure of the attribute's value. This provides a first level of security that the value being indicated conforms to an expected model. In our example, this would be valuable for creating the unique identifier for that particular content 'chunk', the <intervention>.

- A means of accessing either a list or a defined range of allowable values. In our examples, we need either to pick a name from the list of current Members or provide a corresponding code. If any list is itself maintained as an XML document, then of course the query composed to return such information to a user or application interface can be done also in XML.

The XML standard that allows us to perform such validating mechanisms is the W3C recommendation for XML Schema: Datatypes.

Datatyping and constraints

New with XML Schema, the purpose of datatyping is to apply some constraint to what a user may input at a particular point in an XML document. It is analogous to the 'data entry mask' common in database design and data-input forms. The standard database form implements this function, with varying acceptance from users, depending on how well the form is designed and how consistently the information can be coded.

The database record analogy is obvious in the examples used by many XML books, many of which use a standard invoice as their first example of a text to be 'XML-ized'. Even an office memo or an e-mail can be seen as a structured form with predefined fields, as we saw in Chapter 1. In free-flowing text, however, it may be less obvious how datatyping could be used. As we will see, however, it offers great power when it comes to identifying reference information within a block of content and providing appropriate markup for it.

Built-in datatypes

When developing your schema, you may want to limit or structure allowable content in a particular element content or attribute value. You do this by specifying the datatype to which that content or value must conform.

Building on existing work in database design, the XML Schema standard includes a wide set of predefined datatypes that includes:

* A set of *primitive* datatypes such as date, time, string, decimal

* *Derived* datatypes, such as integer, derived from decimal, or language, derived from string.

In our examples above, we could add an indication of duration by using the primitive datatype duration directly to constrain the value of an attribute of the same name used with the <intervention> element:

```
<intervention id="001" duration="PT3M25S">
```

or to tag the language of the intervention:

```
<intervention id="002" xml:lang="EN">
```

On the other hand, look at the structure of our unique document identifier attribute docUID in our root element. There is no predefined datatype suitable for this. However, the XML Schema standard allows us to define our own datatypes based on the primitive structures by using *complex* datatypes.

Complex datatypes

Our identifier attribute, docUID, shown in the example on page 134, is clearly a string of characters, so it would appear that we could use the primitive datatype string. But this string itself is made up of a number of constituent elements:

* An initial code P5, which in this 'information territory' indicates a parliamentary authority

* An underscore

* A further code, CRE, a document typology code

* A year value in brackets

* The month and day in digits, separated by a hyphen

So our attribute is made up of a number of primitive elements, strings, decimals, each of which has different characteristics.

With a complex datatype, we define first the built-in datatypes that make it up. In addition, we can indicate in the schema that the use of a datatype is restricted to a specific pattern, for example:

- 'The authority code shall be a series of alphanumeric characters terminating with an underscore'

- 'The document type shall be a series of uppercase letters terminating in an open bracket'

- 'The year shall be expressed as four digits'

- 'The chronological code shall be expressed as the month and day separated by a hyphen and expressed as digits with leading zero'

Each of these patterns is declared by writing your schema using a formal notation known as *regular expressions*. The regular expression syntax used in the XML Schema would give us, for the first element of our attribute above:

```
<pattern value="[\p{Lu}]?_">
```

meaning 'one or more uppercase characters, followed by an underscore'.

Care with user-defined types

We started out to structure the allowable value to be included in an attribute. We have seen that in analyzing this problem, however, we have managed to extract valuable information, such as a code representing the authority responsible for the text, a code for a document type and a date. This information and other like could be used elsewhere or to derive and include information automatically, as we did by converting a memberID code into an actual name.

You need to exercise caution when considering whether to develop proprietary datatypes. As with other information building blocks, the key is to keep interoperability at the forefront of our mind. If parts of a complex, user-defined datatype can be used elsewhere, generalize their definition so that this is possible. In the examples we used two such re-usable components – the codes to designate a parliamentary authority and a document type – in the course of defining just one attribute value.

Common vocabularies

In the rush to develop individual, project-specific schema, reference back to already-defined and re-usable components may get overlooked. You can think of a controlled vocabulary as a sort of generic schema, and it can be encoded as such, covering all the possible elements, attributes and datatype information for a given use domain. This allows the development of context-specific schema that will always conform to the master design, and ensures that all elements and structures created are validated against the overall vocabulary.

Schemas

After developing a common vocabulary, the next stage is to develop individual schema, which are XML documents in their own right. These need to be named and saved using a formalized file-naming notation, for example:

```
../P5_CRE.xsd
```

Note that we have used parts of the attribute value from the earlier example as part of such a filenaming convention, here suggesting the authority and document type to which the schema refers.

Schemas will also be referenced from within document instances that are to be validated against them. They are your rulebooks for the creation of instances of a particular document type. The elements, attributes and datatypes are the individual 'rules' that can be used to compose a particular rulebook.

Every schema carries the potential danger of becoming a proprietary format, capable of being used and understood only in the context of a specific application or by a particular development team, with all the dangers that represents for a later, unwary, developer. Try to design and use schemas with as much general application as possible and as much specificity as necessary. Remember that namespaces exist to allow you to reuse an element or other structure from another domain without having to import and reinvent it in a specific 'one-off' application.

Version control However well you plan, it is advisable to assume that schema will need to be updated from time to time. You may therefore want to include versioning information in the schema's filename, for example:

```
../P5_CRE_v1-0.xsd
../P5_CRE_v2-1.xsd
```

You should use a versioning convention that suits your needs for validation. More information and ideas on versioning policies can be found in Chapter 12, *Delivery Management*.

Language versions

If you produce different (human) language versions of otherwise semantically-identical schemas, you should establish a naming convention that indicates the language in a consistent manner, for example:

```
P5_CRE_v1-0_FR.xsd
P5_CRE_v1-0_SV.xsd
```

Maintaining the parallelism of otherwise semantically-identical schemas across languages requires a thorough analysis of your content, to ensure consistency of their semantic building blocks across the different languages.

You approach this in a number of ways. You could build, for example:

- A schema from a single language, which then acts as the authentic, reference version and from which all other languages are derived

- A 'metaschema' that uses language-neutral element names and attributes, to which you associate extensive documentation for each language, or at least a minimum number of reference languages. Language-specific schema could then be derived from this.

If you have a common reference vocabulary for all your elements, attributes and datatypes, it is easier to start by establishing a translation of the dictionary entries and their descriptions into the target languages.

This would be an invaluable resource for your designers and give them more freedom. They could then develop specific schemas using tools and methodologies with which they are familiar. However, by being required to refer back to a standard vocabulary available across all languages, there is a guarantee of one-to-one conformance between different language versions of the same elements.

Conclusions

Establishing an XML framework allows you to map existing information typologies into a target XML-based infrastructure irrespective of how they are currently organized. This allows you to discover:

- What you have

- What it is worth for your enterprise

- Where and how to find it

- How the different content 'chunks' relate to each other

- Who can access what, under what conditions and constraints

- What you do with it

- What you might do with it

The workload and plan for this information audit is the subject of the next chapter, *Mapping the Old to the New*.

7 Mapping the Old to the New

Beware of people who know the answer before understanding the question.

Anon

Introduction

Managers get less than a third of the information that is valuable to them from company documents. Many will admit that how information is organized and captured is beyond them – 'it just sort of comes together' – but at the same time never seems to be at their fingertips just when they want to cite something specific.

We unconsciously filter the mass of data we receive every minute of the day. In the 'village store' analogy introduced in Chapter 1, we saw that the human-centred model for information organization and management is workable as long as it is relatively small-scale, personal and with sufficient staffing to meet the needs of your clients.

We are now working in enterprises with millions of information objects, stored away as data in distinct files, work processes, forms and databases. Data becomes *information* if it can be encapsulated or encoded, put in context and understood by humans. Information in turn can become *knowledge* if it is organized, accessible and usable to solve a particular problem. Knowledge is an essentially human undertaking, relying on organized information.

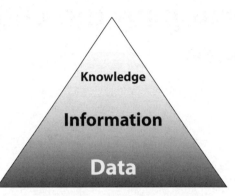

Figure 17. The Knowledge Pyramid

The 'Knowledge Pyramid' in Figure 17 reflects our desire to rise from undifferentiated data, through more structured information – data structured with a purpose – to knowledge. Knowledge however is essentially captured by humans. So, how are we going to transpose the 'village store' model, that emphasizes human involvement so strongly, to the 'supermarket' model that is necessary to handle vast information loads? More importantly, how do we do it without losing the ability to work upwards through this knowledge pyramid?

Our objective must therefore be to 'expose' content in such a way that it can be accessed and used by humans. This is all the more difficult if the content is scattered across different applications and platforms, as we saw in *A holistic approach* in Chapter 4.

To do this, you need to organize our information firstly by its nature – represented by an information or document typology – then move to a detailed process of identifying the different types of semantic building blocks that hold that information. By organizing and making information content accessible, you can make it usable to knowledge advantage. You probably cannot achieve this in one go, so there is a case for a step by step approach, starting with metadata.

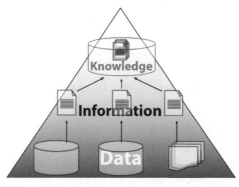

Figure 18. An information architecture

As with the knowledge pyramid, we want an information architecture that helps us move from data up to knowledge, but not within the confines of a single application.

Metadata

A starting point for building our target information architecture must be to work with what we have. While keeping in mind the ultimate objective, an XML-centred information system, it is useful to at least have some uniform information about contents. Like the library record of old, or most food labeling, we have at least some valuable and standard information about our contents, irrespective of their nature, format or source.

Why start with metadata?

Agreeing an early standard for metadata allows basic reference information on all information objects to be standardized before the content itself. Think of it as your packaging and labelling standard. It is the key to content mobility and the first currency of exchange.

An analogy illustrates the value of standardized metadata. The EU passport, although issued under the auspices of the national member states, is now of a standard physical format. The information, although entered in different languages, seems to conform to a standard pro-forma design. Despite this, the numbered data fields in different passports, that would have been so easy to standardize, do *not* correspond. Item 5 on a UK passport indicates how many children the passport holder has, while the same item on a French passport indicates the sex of the passport holder. In a blind transfer of data, it is difficult to imagine what would be deduced from an apparent value of Sex=3.

Standardizing metadata involves two distinct steps:

- Agreeing the information items to be used.

- Agreeing the allowed values for each item, where necessary or useful.

Standardize metadata and you have an immediate and tangible benefit in interoperability. A library record card, for example, is a standard set of metadata describing widely diverse information artefacts.

Why encapsulate metadata in XML?

We saw in Chapter 2 the arguments for using metadata as a guardian against 'digital rot', but what are the arguments for making metadata available in XML, rather than some more efficient database system? At its simplest, a metadata record in XML, created for and associated with each information object in conformity with a straightforward DTD or schema, can be generated by and maintained with any type of object. As XML is written in plain text, any application that produces *content* can also produce such an XML metadata record in a standard way, accessible to any human or information system.

Many information management systems maintain metadata independently of the information itself. If XML documents are to be considered as 'self-describing', however, surely the metadata itself can also be included as part of the XML document? Both approaches have strengths and weaknesses:

- Keeping it separate allows you to manage and run an efficient and fast reference information base, rather than having to query the whole content of each XML document.

- Keeping within the relevant document makes the document portable and self-referencing. A basic principle of XML is that the XML document is complete and authoritative. This is certainly a strong argument for the metadata to be maintained completely as part of the document.

Some have argued the case for using both approaches, supplying tools to maintain and update metadata by transferring it between the document and an external record as needed. This requires care in design to maintain synchronization between the internal and external metadata information sets.

Whichever approach is chosen, it is essential that your metadata elements and encoding scheme are common across all information types. Even if one particular application or information type requires metadata that others do not, the elements used should be part of your agreed vocabulary, as with all other XML elements.

One use of metadata mentioned above is the need for enabling programmatic access to documents. If metadata is expressed in XML, the metadata content is immediately available as a programmatic interface through XML's basic programmatic interfaces (APIs), the Document Object Model (DOM) and Simple API for XML (SAX). The metadata can thus be queried, manipulated and updated programmatically, irrespective of the nature of the document it describes.

Metadata can be used to describe the characteristics of particular document typologies and thus allow default values to be passed to new instances of a specific document type upon creation. This approach can provide a high-value, low-cost starting point for introducing XML. As each document is created, most of the metadata can be created from information inherited from the document class and stored externally in XML, irrespective of the format of the information object that the metadata is describing.

This approach is also important for a long-term strategy. As more and more of the actual information content is encapsulated in XML, then many if not all metadata elements will figure as markup within the content itself. When that stage is reached, sooner or later depending on the complexity of your information systems, the need for externally-managed metadata records may well disappear: the metadata will be generated dynamically from within the document's content. It would also remove what some analysts consider to be an artificial distinction between metadata and information content, and in any case would be the approach favoured in more sophisticated knowledge management systems based, for example, on the Topic Maps standard introduced in Chapter 13.

Preparing to move shop

The objective at this stage is to attempt to switch from an old application-centred information architecture to a new one centred on XML and with a focus on actual content. At this stage we are not actually changing any information systems as such, but rather changing the architectural principals on which they are based.

Returning to our shop analogy, we now want to move to a new and hopefully well-organized supermarket model, without initially changing the actual content on offer or the means by which it is produced and managed. The principal focus of the move is to make our information content more accessible through clearer labelling, 'addressing' and complete and relevant metadata.

To do this, we need to prepare well – as with any house or business move – with a series of clear and distinct steps:

- Packing up and labelling

- Identifying where everything will go in its new home, while checking there is space for everything

- Agreeing a timetable for the move

- Informing people of the move and warning them of possible interruptions in service

- Removing any 'junk' that has accumulated that won't be needed in the new home

- Making the move

- Installing and 'setting up shop' in the new home

Capturing knowledge – a road map

We will progress through a series of steps in this chapter that will enable us to construct:

- A *description* of your information types, what they represent for your enterprise, how to find them and how they relate to each other. This 'information audit' is a descriptive analysis and process aiming to gather information about how content is currently managed.

- A *prescription* for how that information should be handled, managed, accessed or otherwise manipulated. Agreeing what you want to do with your information is often less clear once you start investigating. We will show how 'Use Cases', a methodology offered by the Unified Modeling Language, can help this analysis.

- A *declaration* that formalizes the information gathered and maps the validated results to target structures such as schemas.

- A *process* that enables us to keep this map up to date and thus pertinent to the overall XML framework.

Mapping your existing systems – the types of documents and information for which different business units are responsible, the processes that manage them and their interdependencies – gives an overall corporate view shared by all. Duplication of effort can be identified and eliminated, and information types and processes re-engineered to maximum advantage.

Setting up an information typology audit

In the descriptive part of this exercise, you must play the role of auditors. Everyone hates auditors, yet when they have gone, there is a sigh of relief that your business unit has passed a test. Information auditing is no different. It is a painful and sometimes long-winded process, but the benefits are enormous.

The information auditors

Agree a common set of information that is required to be mapped for each type of document or information resource, but have the mapping done by people in the respective business units responsible for those information types.

This not only ensures that a more complete picture is drawn by the people who actually handle the data and texts, but strengthens the whole XML project by being inclusive and democratic.

Remember that the information audit itself can be formulated, and the results stored, in XML. This offers greater flexibility over how the data can be subsequently used.

In this audit, your objectives should be to:

- Identify and give a value to the various information assets of the enterprise
- Map out the current information flows through business units
- Identify how knowledge is 'captured', supported, shared and managed
- Identify whether and how users document and 'encode' their own knowledge
- Propose and agree best practices for encapsulating information that is difficult to classify
- Describe the work that has been undertaken in an analytical report

This is a big undertaking, so we should set out by establishing a clear process by which to proceed.

Preparing for the audit

To staff your audit and start the process, you should undertake a number of preparatory steps:

- To promote the project and gain visibility and understanding
- To bring people into the project who know the main information types produced within the business units of the enterprise
- To identify the main production sources and information types
- To ensure and formalize the backing of the IT department and business units

You need to be realistic over scope, timing and available resources.

Promoting and scoping the project It will not be productive to assemble a group of managers and state 'We are going to create some XML schemas for our documents', even if that is what they end up doing in practice.

Your approach should rather be a statement of objectives couched in the language they will understand, such as 'The demands of information and document management are becoming a great burden on everyone. It is increasingly complex and costly. We need to have a clearer view of the types of information and documents we produce and manage, and a clear and agreed terminology. As such, we are launching a small project aimed at identifying and cataloguing the important types of information and document we use. We are not concerned here with the contents – that remains the responsibility of each business unit – but with types of information, how it is structured and managed and what rules govern its use. The technologies available today are mature enough to respect and reflect the needs of management. As mangers, therefore, we need to indicate what is important for us...'

It's not the sort of stirring stuff that gets pulses racing, but it needs to be clear and leave managers in no doubt that the ball is in their court. They need to know why it is important for them, what is expected as an outcome of the audit and what is expected of them personally.

The concept of a 'data steward' is recognized as one that describes the functions of a knowledgeable manager responsible for managing access to databases or administering user rights over particular data domains. For an information typology audit, you need a slightly broader concept: an 'information resources steward', or 'IR steward'. The IR steward is not responsible for administering information or document content, but rather the administration of information typologies.

In addition to identifying managers with responsibility for content, therefore, you should also be seeking to involve:

- Secretaries who have experience in producing and using word-processing templates, as they should have a good grasp of document users' view and understanding of documents produced for various information types

- Documentalists or a manager responsible for corporate archives and filing systems, who should have a strong understanding of classification schemes and records management

- An Organization and Methods unit, if your enterprise has one

- The Finance department, as its staff are normally competent in process and methodology, and fully understand the importance of data validation and authorization procedures

- Communications or advertising departments. They are valuable allies in promoting the project, but are also potential major beneficiaries: if a strict separation of content and presentation is undertaken – as proper use of XML dictates – then these departments will benefit with greater control over, for example, corporate house style.

Ensuring IT backing

The work you are undertaking in an information typology audit can easily be interpreted by IT systems analysts as an incursion on their domain, so delicacy may be required. Avoid 'turf wars' – be practical, clear and firm. You need the backing of the IT staff, but only for the IT aspects of the project – the first part of this typology audit is a management exercise that will have organizational as well as IT implications.

Your Chief Information Officer (CIO), if you have one, will understand this: their job is enabling rather than defining business objectives. What you are undertaking will require considerable management investment, but will offer major dividends for IT. You should not need to explain the strategic position that XML standards play, nor the consequences of failing to adopt them. Many IT project leaders, on the other hand, may see the shift to XML for their own projects as straightforward migration exercises, whereas the difficulty consists precisely in maintaining a holistic enterprise-wide approach.

You need a robust information model for your XML framework, as well as reliable and stable IT environment to support it, whether for managing reference and process documents or for building an information typology registry. Your IR stewards can be helped in their work on the information resources audit by providing them with questionnaires and structured forms. This not only guides their work, but allows the information gathered to be encoded within a future XML framework repository, with data entry to this repository and subsequent validation being made easier. This makes such information immediately reusable, for example for generating the production of XML schemas.

The backing of your IT department should itself be formalized as a project, with clear objectives to provide:

- A repository for your typology audit data

- A reference point (for example, a Web site) for the whole XML framework

- A toolkit for entry, validation and maintenance of the audit's data

Your XML framework may need to be publicly accessible, available via a secured extranet to external suppliers, subcontractors and others who will follow the guidelines laid down. If this is the case, the architecture of the framework site needs to be constructed carefully to control all aspects of security and access.

Scope

The 'big bang' approach in IT projects often turns out to be a small snivel. The development of your XML framework, and the information typology audit itself, is a process and needs to be handled progressively as momentum builds up. Lead by example, taking one document family at a time, gradually bringing more and more users and business units into the project to follow the methodology of the resources audit and the examination of document types through analytical eyes.

If your current content management approach does not scale well to the proposed target information architecture, or is becoming too difficult to manage, consider migrating a domain at a time, particularly if you can identify areas that do not have a high level of interdependency between information systems. A payroll and personnel management system, for example, may have less connection with document management systems than other parts of your enterprise.

When choosing where to start, choose tactically on the basis of one or more of the following criteria:

- *Importance*. The CEO or Director General's mail, legal and financial regulations are more important than internal office memos. By proposing to work on high profile document families, you are putting your project in the limelight of senior management. This is a high-risk strategy, but also high reward if you succeed.

- *Relevance*. Target a document family that currently presents problems. Showing that your strategy can be of immediate use is critical to developing user 'buy in' to the project.

- *Simplicity*. Starting with a manageable, simple document type allows you to gain confidence that the project is realistic and its result capable of being validated. This approach also allows users with little understanding or knowledge of document analysis to follow the process through and gain an understanding.

- *Complexity*. At the other extreme, it may be precisely because some document types are extremely complex that an XML-centred approach is needed. In such cases, the users and business units that work with these documents will have a detailed understanding of their complexity, even if they are not always easily explained. Breaking down a complex document into its component semantic building blocks, necessary for the deployment of XML, also helps to give a better picture of the whole and how it works together.

Objectives

The information typology audit is a central part of the development of your XML framework, and as such it must be extensive, inclusive and conclusive.

Don't start writing DTDs or schema or get bogged down in detail – the audit is upstream of such considerations. However, when handled carefully, it ensures that the maximum of business knowledge is captured and made available for the explicit XML coding to come.

Keep an open mind to change, particularly if users involved in document production and management are concerned, as they are likely to have a clearer view of their work than you. The project is about transposing their understanding and knowledge of document types, processes and management into a form that can be exploited within the XML framework.

It is important to separate:

- Descriptions of the *current* document types

- Prescriptions of how they *ought* to be

You need to capture information about both analysis and needs. When working with users, you and they must be clear about the distinction. Do think about the infrastructure needs of the framework itself, and in particular the job functions and roles that need to be identified and played, including a coordinator of the project and the framework more generally, a secretariat, Web designer, data, metadata and document analysts and the physical infrastructure.

The information typology audit should conclude with a report. This should describe the structure, types of content, logical organization and processes associated with each document type analyzed. It should be readable and understandable to managers as well as IT professionals. Finally, this report should allow a formalization of the audit information collected – to be used for developing target schemas – and provide sufficient information about the scale of the undertaking to move to the target information architecture – to quantify resources needed, for example.

Process

To make the most of the information audit, a standard approach should be used by all the IR stewards. This will include a shared understanding and use of metadata, document typologies and classification.

Metadata

We saw at the beginning of the chapter that metadata can be a useful starting point for moving to an XML-centred information architecture, when metadata itself is encapsulated in XML. Such standardized metadata will also provide a common denominator of reference information about and across all document types and information resources.

The basic metadata set proposed by the Dublin Core Metadata Initiative represents a standardized 'off-the-shelf' set of metadata that reflects the key types of reference information, including:

- Document title
- Reference
- Author(s)
- Language
- Subject

Beyond the Dublin Core metadata elements, you might decide that you need more enterprise-specific elements.

If you are able to agree a common set of metadata elements, the next task should be to establish common sets or ranges of metadata values where this can be done. Provide guidelines to users and business units where it cannot. For example:

- 'For language, use the standard ISO coding contained in ISO 639/1'
- 'For title, give a short descriptive title in less than ten words'
- 'For authors, indicate the user identify in the corporate directory business unit'

These encoding schemes can be less or more formally expressed according to their nature and the level of application support that your enterprise can offer. The more precisely that can define the legitimate values or structure of the values (using datatyping, for example), the more easily this information can be integrated into automated information management applications.

Typologies and instances

We are concerned here with document typologies and not with specific document instances. It is important that this is clear to you as well as for the business units. Your aim is to understand the structure and logic of document creation, management and use, the typologies' distinguishing features or characteristics. You are not concerned with the content, with what actually goes into the documents.

This is important for business units involved in managing sensitive or confidential information. You should make it clear to them that the object of the information typology audit is to reinforce their role as being responsible for the content types that they originate.

For each typology, you should also be prepared to offer guidance for the specification of metadata:

- For metadata elements common to all documents, to indicate the default value(s) that might apply for all instances of a given typology

- To indicate which additional metadata elements should be used with a particular typology and their values, constraints or encoding schemes.

This information will be valuable in document instantiation and metadata inheritance, as described later.

Sampling and classification

It is important to identify and select representative documents for analysis. Although managing exceptions is a challenge in any project involving a system of classification, it is important to identify a representative cross-section of document types used and drawn from business units active in their production. Relevance to your business activity is the key. If in doubt, test, evaluate and iterate until you have a representative selection.

One approach uses focus groups of users asked to identify the sorts of document that they use routinely or upon which they rely heavily. Through discussion, they can probably come up with a list of the twenty or so document and information types they consider most important. Keep clear about which business objectives are served through good management of which types of information, checking your assumptions with senior management if necessary. Ask the question: which documents and information types drive your enterprise?

A potential stumbling block for cooperation is the sensitivity and confidentiality of document content. You need diplomacy and clarity in explaining the scope of the project and building user confidence.

Food for thought

"What's it to you?"

Many business units can be wary over divulging information about documents and information sets under their responsibility. It is important at a very early stage to gain the trust of all parties.

Layers of analysis

There are three main layers in the analysis you need to undertake:

- *Data layer* or content analysis: how the content is structured for different information types, and what are the distinct semantic building blocks

- *Process layer* or use analysis: how the content is used, by whom and why

- *Interaction layer* or ontological and presentation analysis: how different content types inter-relate and interact, how they are presented to, and exchanged between, users and other information systems

Content analysis

The first layer of analysis to be undertaken aims at:

- Understanding and agreeing what is meant by a 'document' or 'information typology'

- Examining the content structure, organization and logic of different document and information types

- Isolating the distinct semantic building blocks

- Identifying commonalties and differences

- Assigning attributes and values to these blocks

- Assessing how these blocks are used in combination to create formal structures for managing our content – our future 'knowledge moulds'

- Understanding the implications of content ownership

What is a document?

It used to be reasonably easy to define a document – a sequential organization of text, committed to paper. Desktop publishing, cheaper printing, the World Wide Web and electronic forms have now made it less easy.

A starting point could be to consider anything that contains a distinct set of information, whatever the medium used to represent it, as a document. Focus on the *logical* document – that is, the content that seems to go together as a document, wherever or however it is stored – rather than the *physical* file: remember a single 'document' could be stored across several files, or a single file could contain several 'logical' documents.

You should not get caught up in the detail of individual files – the objective at this stage is to compile an inventory of content *types* and not a comprehensive audit of all content. Neither should you limit your scope to text-only or text-dominant content:

- Focus on document types that are important for your business

- Do not be side-tracked by how individual departments might categorize and describe document types – keep a focus on semantic structures

- If non-text output – images, process and organization charts, audio documents and so on – is an important part of your information repertoire, do not limit your analysis to what you find on paper, but be sure to study all relevant information systems

What is a typology?

The human mind subconsciously classifies to learn from experience. When two objects belong to the same category, we expect them to share certain characteristics, to behave in a similar manner. The same is true for documents and information. If we are able to classify according to common characteristics, we can build important elements of predictability into our information systems.

The information typology audit needs to work systematically. It cannot make an analysis of every document that an organization or enterprise has produced, hence the importance of identifying typology classes and document families rather than instances.

The idea behind an information or document typology therefore is to recognize that certain documents and information sets share characteristics and can thus be considered as belonging to the same typology or family:

- Documents do not necessarily belong to the same document family because they are authored or typed by the same person, are presented in the same manner or using the same media or language

- Documents are more likely to belong to the same document family if the internal structure and presentation is the same or similar

- Document families on the other hand belong to the same *typology class* if their nature and purpose are similar

The first exercise of the information typology audit is therefore to identify and classify document families. One approach that has been used in some public administrations is to establish a 'master matrix' along two axes, representing:

- Authorities responsible for creating a document

- Generic typology classes

A part of such a matrix might look something like Table 3.

Table 3. A matrix of document typology and authoring classes

	Working Document	Report	Minutes	Decision	...
Board of Directors		X	X	X	
CIO	X	X			
Finance Department				X	
Shareholders Meeting	X	X	X	X	
Personnel Dept					
...					

An X indicates that a specific document family has been identified as fitting a particular intersection of classes during the typology audit. Several families of document can be present at a single intersection, as the typology classes are intended to be rough high-level categories.

The master matrix is built up through a series of iterations, as business units indicate where their document families belong. The first objective is to identify broadly the distinct columns and rows in the matrix, not to list exhaustively every document family that can be placed upon it.

Never assume that a particular document family is unique: check whether it shares characteristics with other families that have already been placed on the matrix. One useful method is to compare the types of metadata or other reference information that could describe instances of two different document families: if the metadata types are the same, then they can probably be grouped together as belonging to the same typology class.

A number of important points should be borne in mind during this analysis:

• The objective is not to complete every cell in the matrix – not all authorities have document types that fit all typology classes – but it is an attempt to find a place on the matrix for every document family that *is* identified.

• Matrix cells can contain several document families. Certain families may have distinguishing characteristics but nevertheless be able to coexist with others, if their essential characteristics are the same.

- Classification schemes deprecate catch-all 'others' or 'general' category. By all means create such a typology class, but be very sure that any document family doesn't actually fit better into another and more clearly-identified class.

Your IR stewards should organize their analysis on the basis of this primary classification and collect information on document families thus identified.

Content structure

Identifying common semantic structures within documents is important, irrespective of the authorities responsible or the tools used for originating them, their specific format or medium.

What is relevant

When analyzing the content structure of a given document family, you may experience a few surprises. We think we have an idea based on what we see, but no two business units see a document the same way. They might be able to agree to which document family a particular document does belong. They may not agree however on what such a classification implies. But your objective should be aimed at exposing implied understanding and making it an explicit statement of a document family's nature.

The result of this exercise may be to highlight legitimately different visions of the nature and function of a particular document family. The conclusion could be that in fact they should be considered as two different families, even if they belong to the same typology class. Such a conclusion is helpful in the development of specific and formal representations such as schema, and can avoid misunderstandings caused by leaving issues implicit.

Same content, different presentation

It is one thing to identify functional differences between documents so as to identify distinct document families. It is another to recognize differences in presentation of otherwise identical content.

Consider the example of a set of presentational slides based on the content in a word-processed document. In this situation we have the same *logical* document, belonging to a given document family, but two different *models* for the presentation of identical content.

Isolating the building blocks

In the parable of the blind men and the elephant, made famous in the poem by John Godfrey Saxe, each blind man has a different picture of an elephant, determined by which part of the elephant he touches. This is equally true for your analysis of document types.

Your IR steward will establish a set of document families to analyze, together with users from the business units that produce them. The next exercise involves breaking the document structure apart and identifying its component parts.

Identify commonalties and differences

We want to isolate the distinct semantic building blocks so that we can identify two distinct but complementary groups:

- What is common across more than one typology, and can thus be reused

- What is unique to a particular typology

Some will be easy:

- Document reference

- Date

- Author

Each of these may well apply to every typology, but others are more slippery:

- 'The text paragraph is a common structure.' Is it? As a presentational construct, it certainly crops up everywhere, but is it a semantically-useful building block, or just a lowest common denominator?

- 'A table is an identifiable structure.' Or is it just a two-dimensional data matrix with column and row labels, a title and values for individual cell elements that are referenced according to their position on the matrix? If you think of the information in this way, you can free yourself from looking only at two dimensions of data.

In both these examples you need to look further. You need to recognize that there are different ways to identify and label a document's building blocks, which will in part be a reflection of the uses made of the document by different users.

Choose a level of granularity

Deciding how deep you go – how small should be your individual data 'chunk' – can be a fine balancing act.

Too little detail, or 'coarse granularity' and you are likely to encounter problems later with the association of different elements and document validity. In our example of meeting minutes:

- Is it sufficient to mark out the block of text that lists the participants at a meeting?

- What if you need to indicate members and observers, people with and without voting rights?

- Do you include absentees, with the risk that they are included as participants?

Marking the whole block of names as an indivisible block could cause problems and misunderstanding elsewhere.

At the other extreme, too much detail, fine granularity creates more work. Not only must a much larger number of structures be identified and defined, but they may need to be recombined in more complex ways to create specific models for different situations. Using the same example of meeting minutes, we have seen that the list of participants is made up of a set of individuals:

- Does each person need to be identified and tagged separately?

- Should a unique identity code be associated with each person?

- Should their affiliation and/or responsibility be indicated distinctly (chair, secretary, member, observer, invitee from… and so on)?

- Should their family, forenames, and title be tagged separately? One listing may be ordered alphabetically by surname, another by affiliation.

All of these questions are arguments for a finer granularity.

As a rule, as we saw in the previous chapter's initial examination of XML elements, you should aim first for the lowest level of granularity and merge together chunks as needed. There may be grey areas at the boundary between one chunk and another. The solution might be to subdivide further. For example, there may three distinct 'chunks', A, B and C that exist only as the combinations A+B and B+C.

Group similar structures

Early identification of common structures avoids later repetition.

Suppose that you have identified a numbered 'Article' in a document family that contains structured decisions. You can start grouping similar elements in a broad classification: 'preamble', 'article', 'date of entry into force', 'legal basis' etc. They may not all be used in every type of document containing decisions, but where there are decisions, they use or reuse from this common pool.

You should start to see that certain structures tend to appear as part of, or associated with, other structures.

Understand datatypes

A particular content structure might be associated and constrained by a specific datatype with datatype pattern rules, then expressed formally at a design stage as an XML element, possibly with attributes. In this situation, part of the granularity problem disappears.

Take the example of a document reference, constructed from a concatenation of authority, document types, year and serial number:

```
<docRef>P5_CRE(2002)05-21(045)</docRef>
```

What if we wanted to expose the different parts of the reference structure for processing:

```
<docRef>
<authorityCode>P5</authorityCode>
<docType>CRE</docType>
<year>2002<year>
<chronoNum type='mm-dd'>
<mm>05</mm><dd>21</dd>
</chronoNo>
<fragmentNo>045</fragmentNo>
<docRef>
```

Although verbose, this approach gives programmatic access to every possible item of information.

Use structural constraints

Using datatyping, such a complex and verbose approach is no longer necessary. It would be sufficient to tag the entire reference as a single element, but to define the structure that needs to be respected as a custom datatype. The parts within it are then defined and constrained externally to the specific document instance.

Such a reference, placed within a particular document instance, would therefore be created in conformity with a predefined constraint defined and could be interpreted subsequently with equal precision, precisely because it conforms.

An alternative to fine granularity therefore is to allow elements to be more broadly defined and used, but constrained using datatyping. This is an example of a shift in analysis from the descriptive to the prescriptive. This is a useful exercise to follow that contributes, with each example, to a growing body of understanding of your content structures. The arguments – whether for grinding more finely or building up larger chunks constrained by datatyping – need to be well documented if these structures are going to be used intelligently later.

Identify relationships between building blocks

As you start to build up a catalogue of different building blocks, you want to see how they work together:

- Which blocks are always contained in some larger structure?

- In what circumstances does a particular block appear? Is it always the case?

- Is there a particular sequence that must be respected when a certain set of blocks is used?

- Does a particular block, if used, appear just once? A fixed number of times? Any number of times? Is its appearance optional even?

All of these questions help to build a clearer picture of the implicit rules that govern the use of your building blocks.

Problem areas Some information types that you identify as important for your business may be more difficult to analyze. Dynamic content such as external includes from databases, or form letters containing dynamically-generated content is more difficult to pin down.

However, such content is usually generated very precisely and according to a predefined set of rules. If you know the rules, you will know much about the structural logic of such documents.

The audit you are performing is by its nature a snapshot of the existing situation. It is clear that your enterprise's data domain will evolve over time. You should ensure therefore that this evolution is managed and not left to chance. Your XML framework should include procedures by which the overall information territory is mapped and kept up to date.

This will help create positive feedback – or a 'virtuous circle' – if planned and implemented correctly. Developers will help to keep the XML framework up to date if they see that it represents a reliable reference point for their work.

Assigning names and values

It is not sufficient to identify the building blocks of your documents. You need names for them, you need to be able to describe characteristics associated with them and you need verification that they are what they claim to be.

Names and labels It is a truism of management that you cannot manage what you cannot measure. Equally, you cannot measure what you cannot identify: 'add one teaspoonful of harissa' is clearer that 'add a squirt of thingummy'. To use the terminology of object oriented programming, you need to be able to address your objects – content chunks – and access their properties – the content itself and any attributes in the enclosing element tag. It is a common phenomenon to see the impact of a very well-prepared and well-documented analysis of a document structure weakened or ruined because the design program or analyst generates the labels for content mechanically or automatically.

If you are lucky, the labels might mean something, but likely only to mean something in the context of a particular project. You may later find another project that has identified semantically-identical content types and automatically generated a different set of labels.

The answer is often 'Well, yes, but it's OK. XSLT allows us to do a global transform and interchange the labels, as we need'. This is not good enough. The XML standards are about eliminating wasteful duplication of effort and redundancy. They are not about creating duplication because it is possible or because the upstream design is flawed. Establishing and using a clear naming convention and implementing it is an essential part of our overall strategy and a key to easy interoperability.

Link management   Another important reason for clarity is the identification of link targets.

To understand the full import of this, we need to run through a few HTML concepts to see how XML differs. With HTML the hyperlink allows a user's browser to point to a destination by means of the target embedded in the link:

```
<a href="http://www.example.org/newpage.html">
Go to the new page by clicking here...
</a>
```

This can be complemented with an instruction to the browser to seek out a particular marked point within a page that has just been fetched:

```
<a href="http://www.example.org/newpage.html#here">...
```

The #here tells the browser to look for a marker in the downloaded page that contains the corresponding HTML code attribute 'here':

```
<a name="here">You are now here...
```

If the link target is found, the browser will scroll to this point in the page. Two issues are relevant for us:

- The whole target page is downloaded and the internal pointer is then used 'locally' by the browser – the #name part of the URI is not actually sent to the server as part of the page request.

- The #name pointer indicates the start point of the target. It is not obliged to indicate the end of a block – indeed HTML has no mechanism for marking or handling a target 'block' as such.

In XML, however, linking mechanisms are far more feature-rich:

- Firstly, the identified target is not 'open ended' as in HTML, but indicates a 'block' of content, using the element tag as a block delimiter.

- Secondly, links can be two-way, so that a target document 'knows' which source document has called it, permitting a link to be traversed in the opposite direction. This requires that the point of departure is also clearly labelled.

- Thirdly, a whole range of dynamically-resolved queries can be embedded in a link that enables a browser to propose different actions and different targets to the user according to the result of a query. For this to work the blocks to be included in potential targets need to be identified clearly and distinctly.

For such reasons, granularity is an important means of ensuring discrete identification of content chunks within a document, itself essential to XML-based hyperlink mechanisms.

We can never be 100% sure how a particular document might be later processed or accessed. It is therefore in the interests of clarity and transparency that labels are as unambiguous as possible, so that they can support the use of your documents in ways that you might not yet have envisaged.

Metadata

Metadata is usually thought of as a set of data describing a discrete information object, often a complete document. However, a document can be chopped and changed, transformed and its parts reused elsewhere. As such, you need to think whether:

- Metadata should accompany the discrete chunks

- Metadata can be inferred or deduced from its new context

- Metadata is only relevant to the 'master' document and not to the individual content chunks

What you choose will depend upon:

- The likely relevance of a particular chunk to its surrounding original context

- How the metadata itself is encoded – as distinct element content or as attribute values

- Whether the metadata takes on a different significance in a different context

From the moment you grant programmatic access to an entire document you are no longer in control of what is done with it. In these circumstances, you need to think about how different chunks will behave outside their original context and whether it matters.

A few examples illustrate the sort of circumstances that might arise. You may need:

- To apply access policies to particular parts of a document that are different to the whole

- To ensure that the status of the part – draft, final and so on – is inherited from the status of the whole original document

- To know a value for each of the component parts, perhaps if you charge for access to a document and if documents can be accessed separately

- To maintain details of author, publisher or copyright holder for each part

Quality control   Labelling or packaging information is not usually an indication in itself of the quality of the contents. Having identified the type of information you are looking for, metadata allows you to examine further a document to ensure you are getting what you expect.

Food for thought

Caveat emptor

If you live in a consumer-protected market, a list of ingredients for foodstuffs may be required by law and be backed up by standards that enforce agreed descriptions. As well as labelling, the consumer has some guarantee regarding the contents. As with food, think of what might be useful for your business units as a 'quality guarantee' label.

When looking at metadata questions, you should consider whether it is sufficient to indicate simply what metadata might be required, or whether, in addition, you should indicate:

- Whether specific values must be indicated, known as 'encoding schemes'

- If only certain users and/or processes may add or amend metadata values in accordance with agreed procedures

The use of datatyping helps here. However, you may also want to ensure that a new element or attribute being added to the corporate XML framework dictionary, for example, has been identified, proposed and added according to an agreed process.

Use-analysis and process modelling

In addition to modelling the 'static' representation of relationships between different information concepts using ontologies, you also need an understanding of processes and workflow: how particular information content is generated, evolves, is approved, transformed and managed throughout its lifecycle.

The whole area of business process modelling is an art in itself. You need to be aware that it is an additional and important part of your overall picture, and you should establish some minimum means of formal representation.

Specific XML vocabularies are being developed for process modelling, including the Business Process Modelling Initiative and the more ambitious Universal Business

Language initiative of the OASIS consortium. Their objectives are to offer a standardized notation for modelling workflow and business rules.

Use-cases and the Unified Modeling Language (UML)

UML is the platform- and vendor-independent methodology for representing and modeling requirements and target architectures in an application development cycle. It also has powerful and expressive tools that can be used to visualize and validate processes and workflow. One of its central mechanisms involves the development of 'use cases' to capture and model user requirements, whether the user is a human or a system interface.

In your information resources audit, you need to learn about the action and interactions of different 'users' in the lifecycle of our identified information and document typologies:

- The 'producer' – human users, whether authors, editors, translators, involved in the creation and subsequent manipulation of your content

- The 'consumer' – human users in front their Web browser or other terminal presentation of your content

- System users – content repositories, transformation or formatting engines and so on

It is important to know about the different lifecycle stages of your document types and see the content from the viewpoints of these different users.

Markup focus

Your analysis will influence the way that some of your metadata and other building blocks are used. Your focus will be different depending on the role of the different users.

This is potentially a 'blind man and the elephant' conundrum. Some users are focussed on content. Other will be focussed on process. Yet others will be focussed on presentation. Any use cases that are developed will help you identify these issues and thus give you direction for the focus of subsequent markup.

UML: a one way street?

Some analysts have tried to model processes entirely in XML. It seems clear however that UML provides all that is needed to complete a full and proper process analysis. It is also relatively straightforward to transform UML diagrams and models into XML, while the reverse is far more difficult.

If you choose to use UML for your process modelling and workflow, take care at the transformation stage. Avoid using automated UML to XML transformation tools 'out of the box'. As we saw earlier for naming and labelling, it is vital to avoid lock-in to a particular XML naming convention over which you have no subsequent control.

Presentation analysis and ontology

We have so far analyzed both our information content and the way in which it is used and processed. How different types of content relate to each other and to presentational constructs such as logos or design remains to be examined,

Presentation problems

The advent of WYSIWYG ('what you see is what you get') word processors has led to a document's content becoming inseparable from its on-screen and on-page layout and presentation. XML forces us to reflect again on the proper separation of content and presentation.

In addition to the extensive content analysis carried out above, you need to separate and identify presentational elements. These will be part of your enterprise's visual identity, such as your corporate logo, standard typefaces, colors, signatures and layout.

In the same way that you established a dictionary of labels to be used, corresponding to identified semantic building blocks, you can also build a library of presentation elements. This library allows you to 'map' particular source content elements to specific presentational elements, setting the basis for developing style sheets and XSL formatting objects.

Ontologies

An ontology is a formal description of a set of ideas and the relationships between them that can be understood and used in a particular context. Your context is Internet/Web-based information systems, and we are looking at the set of ideas that our semantic building blocks represent. The concern is to create a representation, a picture, of the way in which the different content chunks fit together on your information map.

What do ontologies offer?

An ontology allows you to draw a conceptual model, not only of the bounds of your information territory, but also of the relationships between the semantic elements that you have defined within it.

Why is this important? After all, your analysis so far has looked at the building blocks and some aspects of 'belonging' and relationships. You may have identified the fact that element x only exists as a nested element within element y, for example, or always follows element z.

Let us look again at a part of our parliamentary information territory:

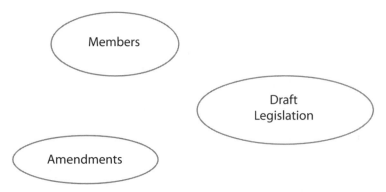

Figure 19. Part of an information territory

We know that within this territory, there are 'Members' (of Parliament, for example), that there is something called 'Draft Legislation', and that there are often 'Amendments' to that legislation

We could have already identified a number of semantic building blocks for each of these:

- *Members of Parliament*. An individual document – a single Member's 'ID card' – could include name, official contact details, nationality and political affiliation, membership of committees and so forth. This is likely to resemble a classic database record.

- Documents containing *draft legislation*. Such documents could be made up of a preamble or explanation (without legislative effect), individual Articles of a proposed new law or act, implementing measures, references to previous legislation rendered null or amended, appendices and so forth.

- *Proposals to amend* this draft legislation. Such documents will indicate who is tabling them, which aspects of the original they seek to amend, what new text is proposed.

- *Rules of procedure* that detail how this is all done, and so on.

Each of these are distinct information types made up of sets of semantic building blocks. We would have already noted them in our earlier content analysis work, but this will not have told us anything about the relationships between them, or whether there is any.

Our ontology analysis sets out to do this. We could thus add to our diagram:

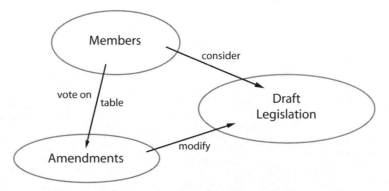

Figure 20. The same territory with associations now added

To the initial set of information types identified, we have now added associations. We now show some of the relationships between these different concepts. This can help us, for example, if we want to develop a semantic navigation layer to a Web site, permitting users to navigate the information territory concepts when investigating particular documents or document collections.

These relationships can be passed down from the general to the specific, in the same way that document typologies offer us the knowledge mould for the creation of a document instance. They can be 'instantiated':

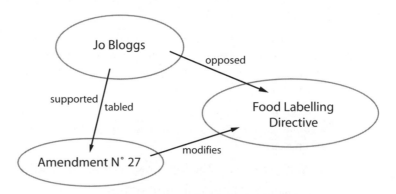

Figure 21. ...and now, with instances

Rather than dealing with general cases, we now have specific instances with values for the subjects as well as for the associations.

We can start to imagine how information linking can become far more rich and predictable. On the basis of a particular starting point, our processors could construct predetermined link sets according to the ontology. If these relationships are expressed in XML, which is possible, then we would have a new and immediately accessible and interoperable information set.

Notation We have used visual examples to illustrate relationships. Such relationships can also be expressed formally according to agreed syntaxes and grammars, and if possible in XML.

Two vocabularies in particular are available to encapsulate this ontological information in such a way as to make it accessible and usable, the Resource Description Framework (RDF) and the more recently-adopted ISO standard, Topic Maps, and its XML representation, XTM.

Because relationships are often easy to visualize, it can be relatively easy to activate this part of your XML strategy. There will however often be complex relationships between such concepts, or even between lower-level building blocks. In the example above, an 'amendment' might only be able to modify a particular type of element within a legislative document and not others. Or the relationship of a Member voting on an amendment might itself generate another document type, such as a rollcall vote result.

Do not become too dependent on visual metaphors, particularly if the relationships become very complex. The importance in ontology is to establish a coherent and consistent picture of relationships that applications can rely upon when they are attempting to understand a concept within a particular context.

Recording the results of the audit

You should be thinking about how and where you will store all the valuable data the audit will produce. Your IT stewards should be coordinating the audit work within their respective business units, rather than necessarily doing the number and data crunching themselves.

The staff who are collecting and collating the information, however, will be greatly helped by a structured questionnaire. This can serve both as a checklist for information to be gathered and as a coding sheet that a resource management tool can rapidly assimilate. An example is shown on the following pages.

Information Architecture Service
Information Resources Audit
Questionnaire

Please complete one form for each *type* of document

Document Management		
Brief description of document type		
Business Unit responsible for approving/publishing		
Business Unit responsible for managing		
Naming & storing conventions:	How could the document type be classified (agenda, minutes, mail, report, CV, "too occasional to classify", etc.)	
	How do you reference each document in a series: sequential?, date code? other?	
	Do you indicate the language of the document content in the filename?	
	Do you (need to) indicate a status (draft/final) or version n° in the filename?	
	Where are the documents stored? (give an absolute network filepath)	\\
	Comments	

Production process		
Is the production subject to an agreed and documented procedure (give references if possible)?		
Who makes initial drafts?		
What tool/application is used to produce the document, **at source**	Commercial tool (specify)	
	In-House tool (specify)	
Is any template or other "model" used to help? On PC or server ?		
How frequently are new "instances" (individual documents for the particular document type) produced? (x/per day, per week, per month)		
Is approval required before document can be published or distributed? By whom?		

Authoring procedures		
Is document "logically" structured in any way? How (Use of DTDs, schema or other set of rules)?		
Are footnotes, citations or other references used in the documents? Are public, electronic references available ("URLs")		
Which of these elements are available, or can easily be made available, when a document is initially created? (Tick)	Document title	
	Author	
	Originating service	
	Language of document	
	Keywords	
Is the content subject to change and updating ?		
If so: how frequently ?		
is there a limited duration for the validity of the information/document ?		

Editorial procedures	
Are there specific target groups identified for the document type? (management team; specific business unit; general public, journalists, researchers, etc)? Does this change according to the status of the document (draft, final, etc.). If so, how?	
What rules determine/restrict to whom the documents are made available.	
Are the documents produced already in any other format than that used for the source text (.pdf, .html, .sgml, etc)	

Link Management	
Where is this document type situated in relation to other types ("is part of", "has parts", "is same as", etc.)	

"Birds of a feather"	
Are there other types of document, produced by other services, that are comparable in structure, design, etc ?	Where? \\
Or that could serve as a model of how this document type *should* look, be structured, etc. ?	

Figure 22. Example of a possible audit questionnaire

Such questionnaires can be used by your IR stewards and staff in the business units.

Once completed, the data collected in such questionnaires can be more formally coded into a document typology repository. This repository – and a registration process, described below, for handling and accepting such typology information – will form a central part of your reference XML framework, thus building the overall picture of your information types and vocabulary.

Deciding what to keep

You may need to develop the initial vocabulary and framework in several iterative passes, first recording a maximum of information without too much care for redundancy and repetition, then refining that information to build a wide vocabulary that fits the enterprise picture.

Do not do this unilaterally – keep your IR stewards involved and informed. The more they are involved in this process, the more they will keep a management focus and ensure that your framework really reflects the needs of the enterprise.

The registration process

It is not sufficient to undertake a comprehensive typology audit and gather detailed information. You need also to validate and register this information in a controlled and managed process.

Whatever process you decide to use, agree it, document it and stick to it. Opt for a republic rather than a monarchy – see page 84 – at least as a starting point, and bring in your IR stewards and other analysts. In the registration process, you will need to agree:

- Who can propose an addition to the framework

- What issues or situations can trigger a review, revision or update of the framework

- What consultation procedures are foreseen before adoption of changes

- What are the criteria for accepting new material

- What needs to be checked or validated before it can be added

- How it is agreed, and by whom

- Who and what systems need to be notified of the addition or change

All of these questions and their answers need to be a part of the framework itself. You need to prevent developers from working in ignorance of corporate guidelines and rules for XML development. You should therefore ensure that they know what exists, and demonstrate that any questions they have are going to be handled properly.

Deciding what to discard

Deciding what to keep is only part of the story. It is also necessary – and often painful – to decide what to discard. Although this is the ideal opportunity for thinning out redundant material, you should only discard proposals for element names, attributes, typologies, and so on that are demonstrably without any semantic grounding in the activities of your enterprise. If in doubt, keep them in.

**Content
ownership**

Important questions of responsibility arise with regard to all information and content management systems. In the context of the framework, we should be even clearer: certain business units should feel that they actually 'own' parts of the framework and that, without their permission and guidance as to use, others cannot use their 'assets'. You should thus make a distinction between:

- *Ownership of document typologies.* These can be owned by your IR stewards individually or collectively, depending on the decision-making and maintenance procedures you have established.

- *Ownership of elements, attributes and metadata types.* These should belong to the business unit managing the framework.

- *Ownership of content.* Business units may produce content for someone else or for the enterprise as a whole, but it is this 'someone else' that will ultimately be the owner.

- *Responsibility for document content.* This, however, is clearly the business unit(s) responsible for producing particular content.

What is important is that a sense of responsibility and ownership is associated with each of the above. It is obviously much better for a business unit rather than an individual to be the responsible owner – as individuals within any organization change. In addition, as these represent business assets, the chain of responsibility and ownership must be maintained across reorganizations and be managed accordingly.

With regard to content itself – that is, *instances* rather than *classes* – ownership and responsibility should be established at the lowest level necessary. If a document can be made up of a series of content chunks, it is possible for different business units to be responsible for different content chunks, all of whom might need to give their approval for a particular use.

Take the case of data protection legislation, for example. It may be a requirement of such legislation for any information about an individual to be managed and audited strictly by an identifiable business unit. In such a case, any reuse or further processing of a content chunk containing such information would need to be known to, and possibly cleared for use by, the originating business unit.

Conclusions

The purpose of establishing a central repository of permissible building blocks is to provide developers and content managers with a reliable and predictable infrastructure. In this manner, any business unit, development team or contractor can develop 'knowledge moulds' appropriate for a particular content and context. How those moulds are developed, and how content itself is generated and managed, is the central theme of Chapter 10.

8 Building Momentum

Think big, start small, scale fast and try not to look too amazed when you get it right first time.

Anon

Introduction

With work underway as outlined in previous chapters, you should be building up momentum, bringing different business units into your XML project and involving them in an enterprise-wide strategy on their terms.

In this brief chapter, we seek to build and maintain momentum for the overall strategy and look at a number of issues that should be kept in mind.

Project management

The work being undertaken must be considered and managed just as any other project. This means paying attention to the key questions that drive successful projects forward.

You must be able to compare your progress against some external benchmark and agree your criteria for success. For example:

- How is the XML framework impacting critical business processes?

- Are any business units actively seeking out your XML framework for guidance?

You should be honest and realistic. We have seen from the start that is proposed as a strategy for implementing XML can and should be implemented as good information management. It is important therefore to assess the proportion of the achievements made purely due to XML, and that which is more related to a management-driven approach to data management. Both are important, but knowing the proportion each contributes will help you to prioritize your work accordingly.

Throughout the project, it is important to monitor progress. This can involve:

- Regular reporting, whether through a well-prepared Web site, or more 'classic' means through the corporate hierarchy.

- Review meetings: don't just organize review meetings for the sake of it, but ensure that everyone knows why they are participating, what is expected of them and the value of their respective input.

- GANTT chart or other milestone monitors, keeping an overview of progress made and the main timelines involved.

- Revising and iterating your project plan to cope with changing circumstances.

Developing XML expertise

Even if 'learning XML' is not going to be a core competence for many staff, you will accumulate considerable expertise and knowledge, whether this has come originally from document and information management fields, or from IT staff.

Whatever its source, such knowledge neeeds to be harnessed and made available to drive your project forward. This can be achieved in a number of areas, detailed below.

Knowledge base

There are numerous offering on the software market for corporate 'knowledge bases' or 'reference centers' that allow you to 'capture' and manage centrally all aspects of information and documentation relating to a particular project or undertaking. Some of them also provide messaging and discussion forum facilities.

The danger, unless very carefully structured and managed, is that such facilities degenerate into centralized dumping grounds for documents and ideas. Whether you use off-the-shelf discussion forum software, or other such infrastructure, you will need to be able to:

- Publish internal notes, ideas or exchanges between colleagues

- Update them regularly

- Notify select audiences of important updates and changes

- Discuss issues and organize them according to themes

- Learn from the experiences of others

- Evaluate products, initiatives and ideas

The ideal is to manage such an infrastructure itself in XML. However, you should not let 'learning by doing' burden your project objectives unnecessarily. It would be useful to ensure that standard templates are available for each type of contribution, using the same content and typology analysis described in Chapter 7, that can be transformed into XML at a later stage.

You should be critically aware of the phenomenon of 'solution glut': in the same way that there is probably too much information 'out there' for any particular issue, we are starting to see that for any particular problem, we are bombarded with solutions. The problems themselves should dictate what solutions are needed. Use the availability of new applications and tools as a way of comparing similar functionalities and deducing 'best of the class' characteristics. Through experimentation you may be able to reverse engineer some functions that tools offer you.

User communities

User 'buy in' and active participation in the work being undertaken is an important success factor. You need to keep the confidence and enthusiasm of users. It is useful to remember that the more users and business units there are validating the different stages of your XML project, the more likely its recommendations are to be followed and implemented.

You should check back with users and prompt them for input on all aspects of your assumptions about how information is used and processed. Much valuable 'processing' is still locked away in the minds of users, whether as intuitive leaps between otherwise seemingly unrelated processes – which could benefit from being known and modelled – or an understanding of why a particular document is used in a particular way and thus needs to be processed.

Network momentum

You can build a virtuous circle by drawing key staff from across your enterprise into a human network of XML-based development experience, and by demonstrating that such a network is a valuable reference point for others.

This knock-on effect not only adds to the overall levels of shared and available experience, but also adds weight to the XML framework itself, reinforcing its credibility.

Make sure that are seen to be open and inclusive in your treatment of other projects. Recognize constructive initiatives for what they are and bring them into your project as appropriate without taking them over.

Demonstrations and prototypes

If a picture is worth a thousand words, a demonstration is worth even more. Whether or not you have a functioning prototype at an early stage is not really as important as being able to show *something*. This could be as simple as a tool that extracts and builds XML elements from a structured word-processing document.

More ambitious examples might be a series of stylesheets that present a core set of information, or a document displayed in different formats and different devices. These both involve a certain investment in time and energy, but these are costs worth bearing, given the return in greater understanding of, and support for, the scope of your mission.

The purpose of such demonstrations is as much about means as ends. Traditionally, demonstrators or prototypes aim to validate that an application does what sets out to do. Although the client for a particular application may be rightly concerned with application development methodology and curious about the behind-the-scenes management systems put in place, end users rarely are. For the user, the application must simply work and do the job expected.

In your project, however, the means *are* also important. You are holding up XML as a model to be followed, one that cuts out a lot of the 'black box' mechanics. In your demonstrations, you want to be able to show this, to 'expose' the processing methods. This is not as complex as it sounds.

XSLT is a prime contender for such a demonstration, as is the Scalable Vector Graphics standard. It is limiting to think of SVG as just a simple vector graphics language that happens to be written in XML. Rather, you can use it to demonstrate that, *because* the graphics are described in XML, you can process and manipulate them just like any other XML document, including extracting any 'meaning' associated with a particular line or shape. Coupled with an ontology and using a Topic Map, for example, SVG could provide the basis for a very powerful graphic interface for semantic-level browsing.

Promoting successes and learning

Nothing drives a project like success. However, if it follows years of project failures, its impact might be somewhat muted. *Early* successes are therefore important.

Though cynical, you should factor this consideration into your choice for pilot projects. If you want a successful pilot study to be an engine for further interest and momentum, consider your criteria for choice very carefully:

- *Non-critical*: do not jeopardize your entire information systems infrastructure by trying to replace a key application at an early stage

- *Added-value*: ensure that there is something new in your pilot project that users and business units can appreciate, ideally some feature that wasn't available or possible previously

- *Low cost–benefit ratio*: favour an initiative that offers a high impact for a low investment

- *Pointer to future possibilities*: even if offering little itself, you maybe able to give a flavour of what is to come if the logic demonstrated by your pilot project is applied elsewhere

Only discussions within your enterprise will reveal the best ways to advance and determine which information types and systems to tackle as a priority. It is difficult to identify sure-fire 'win-win' scenarios, but the following are likely to be high on any list:

- *Data-centric* documents and/or information sets that are used between heterogeneous information systems. One of the staple diets of XML developers is the field of Enterprise Application Integration (EAI). Although the methodologies involved do not mandate XML-centred solutions, XML is an obvious contender to be the *lingua franca* at the hub of such systems.

- *Multi-channel publishing* required in a short turnaround environment. This area of application is another ripe for XML applications to deal with the issues raised by the separation of content and presentation.

Both of these are well documented and well supported by tools and expertise. Less so, but of major importance in organizations with highly text-oriented work is:

- *Text analysis* and *intelligent searching*: with well marked-up content, it is now possible to extract content from complex documents in response to highly-targeted criteria and queries.

Maintaining pace

A common remark from developers of large, complex projects is that it is more important to keep to an overall timetable than stick to the detailed timetables of specific sub-projects. To manage this, you need to prevent too many inter-dependencies being created between project tasks.

This is important in a project such as enterprise-wide XML implementation, as XML can be important in creating a 'feel good' factor. You must be able to build momentum without getting snagged by critical path blockages. If other initiatives are under way that are not dependent upon your resources, do not place any of their deliverables on your own critical path.

You need to take care however – too much change at once can be a major source of insecurity and lead staff to balk at change. Ensure that you protect systems that work well from unnecessary XML 'zealotry'. If you have a well-designed and implemented relational database system, for example, why change to XML? Such major applications can be earmarked for a later stage.

On the back burner

In addition to the main, high-profile work that constitutes the core of the XML framework, it will also be necessary to take a number of smaller accompanying measures.

Non-XML solutions

The promises of supposedly sophisticated document management solutions all too often fall short of client expectations, but not before tying up considerable human and financial resources in trying to make them operational. There is a similar risk in presenting an up-front all-XML strategy – it may not work. Achieving enterprise-wide XML use is a major undertaking. It is therefore wise to think about practical management policies that can be applied to existing systems and infrastructure. By doing so, you are both leveraging the most from current investments and laying down principles that can be picked up easily when XML-centred systems are available and operational.

For example:

- *Electronic mail.* If you have established a corporate policy for a minimum metadata set to be applied to all documents, why not use them in electronic mail messages in a 'semi-structured' manner. Systematically include project references and keywords in the subject line, while using hyperlinks within messages to point to documents and resources on-line, rather than using file attachments.

- *File system.* Your directories can be organized according to a corporate taxonomy of document typologies and responsible authorities, while making filename structures transparent and predictable using a file-naming convention.

- *Text processors.* Associate stylesheets and document styles with semantic structures rather than with distinct presentational styles, use the development model of Cascading Style Sheets to work from generic to specific styles to create both generic and business unit-specific document templates.

- *Conversion tools*. Examine the market for conversion tools, for example to extract XML from a word-processed document or to create metadata records for each document from its content, and validate what they can and cannot do.

Investing in these information management solutions will help smooth out the rough road towards a possible later all-XML approach.

XML asset management

Whatever reference elements you create with your XML framework, they should be considered and valued as business assets. They need to be managed, secured and valued as with any other asset.

This should be implicit in the creation of a framework repository, but a specific application and infrastructure will probably be needed to manage these assets, ensure that they are properly protected against modification or misuse and permanently available to everyone who needs them.

Internationalization and localization

Working in a hermetically-sealed unilingual environment or limiting their sphere of activities to a single country is the exception rather than the rule for large organizations today.

XML's original design is imperfect in that it limits the characters that can be used within XML element names, even though any character can be used within element content. Although valid arguments can be made over compatibility, this issue is now being addressed in by XML Blueberry Requirements, raised by the World Wide Web Consortium's 'internationalization initiative' and mediated by its XML Core Working Group.

This has led to the first proposed revision of the XML core standard, XML 1.1. If you are working with multiple language content, you should consider whether to keep the following the same across all languages:

- Element names

- Metadata or attribute names

- Metadata and attribute values

If the names are the same, there are obvious advantages in tracking and identifying similar content types across separate languages, even if all the content thus identified cannot necessarily be read or understood. If you want attribute or metadata values to be language-independent, you should consider assigning abstract or numerical values to particular words or terms in a 'controlled vocabulary', such as a business terminology dictionary or thesaurus. This can only work if there is widespread agreement on the values to be employed – the 'encoding scheme' – but if used, offers further transparency across languages.

An alternative approach involves the development of 'metaschema' that provides for an abstract schema class, which is then translated into a language-specific schema as required. This allows also the mapping of semantically-equivalent structures across different languages, with obvious benefits for translators and others.

If you are working with different content in different languages, you should still attempt to identify semantic equivalence and make a reference back to your XML framework. The simple mention of such parallels in a schema or ontology can be valuable later.

Conclusions

The purpose of this chapter was to step back and look briefly at peripheral issues.

XML must be seen as part of a more general information integration strategy and not a competitor to it – it is important to keep its role in perspective in your overall strategy:

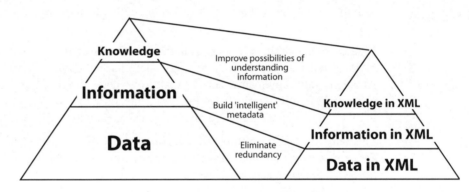

Figure 23. Work is involved in each layer when moving to a target data architecture

Looking at the layers shown in Figure 23 in turn, XML provides a solid base for the target pyramid by ensuring a high degree of data-level integration. It provides a contractual handshake between information systems that acts as a pact to interchange data in a particular manner. Our focus is on finding common structures for the data itself.

The layer above in the pyramid has traditionally been the most labour- and human-intensive. It involves the translation of data into usable information and its movement between applications. Our focus in this layer is on finding common application methods and procedures.

Finally, at the top we are concerned with *doing* something with the information that is captured. This involves all aspects of processes and workflow, and is the focus for what drives an enterprise forward.

It is with this picture in mind that we turn in the next chapter to some of the nuts and bolts questions relating to application development.

9 Application Development

The proverbial phrase 'if we build it, they will come' does not apply to information technology.

Thomas Davenport and Laurence Prusak, *Working Knowledge*

Introduction

It's fine having a wonderful professional XML framework in place that lays down the law regarding XML development, but if nobody actually uses it to produce anything it will be just so much hot air.

Much of the implementation of an XML-centred strategy will depend on users and managers seeing something that works. However, you want to be sure that tools that are developed respect the principles of your framework and ensure maximum inter-operability.

In this chapter we examine the different types of XML tools that exist and the criteria to bear in mind, both when choosing and assessing existing tools and when building your own.

Application architecture

It is worth recapping the role that XML is playing in wider information management strategies.

The last two decades have seen a number of seismic shifts in the way application needs have been translated into toolkits available for users. From centrally-managed computing centres to the desktop, then to the client/server and later 'n-tier' architectures, all have had one characteristic in common. Whether bought-in, customized or bespoke, applications and application suites have been implemented and managed *within* an enterprise.

The 'always on' Internet and the growth of services other that Web pages now means that we are faced with another major shift. Today parts of applications or some tiers of a multi-tier system can be distributed across the Internet. They only form part of a coherent whole when seen as part of the overall *logical* architecture of the system. The implications of this are enormous: it requires not only that data is integrated and inter-operable, but that applications are too. Access to data is no longer sufficient, we need to ensure access to the business rules, processes and logic that drive and manage the applications.

XML on its own is not going to achieve that level of application integration. However, care in the development and use of XML tools, coupled with specific standards described later in this chapter such as XMI and XIF, can and will make the whole process easier. XML must be seen as part of the wider canvass of system integration and change management.

Food for thought

A word about terminology

An 'XML application' should not be confused with an application that uses and/or generates XML.

In formal terms an XML application is a specific vocabulary or use of XML, such as SVG or MathML: it is an *application* of XML.

'Applications' in the more general use of the term refers to specific software tools. To avoid confusion, when we talk about applications that use and manage XML, we refer to them as 'XML tools'.

XML toolkit

You need to be familiar with the different types of tool that make up any respectable toolkit, to help you see through the marketing when a tool is promoted as being 'XML enabled'. Use of such unhelpful descriptions will hopefully diminish as use of XML standards starts to move more into the mainstream.

General considerations

Asking the following questions may help guide you in your choice of XML tools and suppliers:

- *What role is claimed for XML in a particular product?* Remember that the market for 'pure' XML products is relatively immature, and for many vendors XML is merely a means towards another end.

- *Is XML used in a way that can be reused by another tool or environment?* If the XML vocabulary is tightly tied to, and opaquely defined within, a specific environment, it is likely to be little better than a proprietary vendor-dependent standard.

- *Is XML used to encapsulate business logic or content transformation?* If so, are the business or transformation rules themselves accessible and reusable outside the tool's specific environment?

- *Are various schema and frameworks supported?* Some vendors tie the user into one particular approach that might be suitable at first, but may inhibit growth in the longer term.

- *How do the tools manage XML assets and transactions?* You want to keep control over what you produce in a way that you dictate.

- *Are official standards used?* There is no W3C certification system for XML usage, but a number of public authorities are indicating the requirements that must be met for their data and information management needs. This can be a useful indication of current trends.

Conformance testing

All tools must conform with the standards that they are designed to use. This includes:

- *Producing well-formed XML.* If a commercial tool does not do this, don't waste your time with fixes and work-arounds. The interface should ideally prevent the user from performing illegal operations such as manual introduction of badly-nested elements or unmatched start and end tags.

- *Producing valid XML.* If you are working to a schema, the interface should be context-sensitive and only offer to the user those actions that are valid in a particular context. Examples are limiting the choice of elements that can be nested within the current element, or forcing attributes to be set and valued.

- *Avoiding 'over-literal' and over-zealous tools.* For example, suppose a user centres a paragraph by preceding it with a series of tab stops. An over-literal processor might consider every tab as a significant act, rather than 'understanding' the user's intent. Or suppose a user masks part of an erroneous drawing by creating an opaque white rectangle to place over the offending area. An XML graphics processor is not going to 'understand' the significance of this operation either. Similarly, many text-to-HTML converters that pepper their output with unnecessarily-complicated code in an attempt to reproduce the original *exactly* rather than canonically. Such actions are most usually related to presentational questions such as text formatting and positioning rather than content and structure.

- *Respecting the XIXO principle 'XML in, XML out'*. This may not be enough by itself, however. You may require that the XML output by a tool respect *your* vocabulary absolutely. Watch out for tools that add their own proprietary code. Some tools add their own elements or attributes, either as a means of optimizing the particular tool's performance or for tracking work progress. The net result may in practice mean a degree of vendor lock-in. This cannot always be completely avoided, and its use is not on its own a criterion for throwing out an otherwise impressive tool. Such proprietary output should be carefully monitored and managed, however.

- *'Transient fault' tolerance*. While a tool should always ensure that XML documents are well-formed and valid, it should not be so inflexible as to prevent the user from, for example, saving an interim or unfinished document because it is not conformant. This is especially true if it's nine o'clock on Friday evening and the tool is demanding that you complete fifty required attributes that were not entered earlier. Nothing should prevent you from saving interim work, even though the tool should eventually require the missing data before XML is flagged as complete.

Compliance and performance testing

A number of questions arise from interpretation of the W3C standards. Although conforming tools 'must' or 'must not' behave in certain ways, other parts of the specification state that tools 'should' or 'may' do other things. This flexibility was built into the standards to permit rapid developments around the core features and allow other developments and tools to move ahead without compromising the overall standard.

You want to ensure that features that are *important for you* are fully supported, that they are compliant to *your* criteria. Conversely, if you are retaining or building on an older toolset, you may need to think about which features of prospective XML tools can or cannot be used to ensure full inter-operability with legacy tools.

This is particularly true if you have costly SGML tools that are perfectly usable for processing XML documents, but handle other issues differently. For example:

- *XML comments*. Do you need these to be preserved? Many XML processors discard them. If you are putting anything significant in a comment, ask yourself whether you should not define a specific element for this purpose. Just because there is content within a valid element does not mean that must always be displayed or passed downstream. As there isn't a simple solution to the preservation of comments, it's best to avoid the problem arising in the first place.

- *XML processing instructions* (PIs). Do you depend on these? PIs are 'escape' paths from normal XML processing. There are no conventions for their naming or expected behavior *within* a processing instruction. If you are using tools that interpret or generate PIs, be sure that they understand the right ones in the right way. There is no concept of 'namespacing' for processing instructions, so if two tools can both act on a particular PI, you could be heading for problems.

- *Level of user support and user-friendliness*. XML has to come out of the back office and computer centres and this is only possible if the tools resemble something that ordinary mortals use, not just Perl hackers. IT training is becoming the biggest part of many organizations' professional training budgets, so don't add to the burden.

  There is another important business issue here. Familiarity with popular tools implies an easier learning curve and greater productivity. This may be important to you if you experience high turnover or much of your work is outsourced.

- *XML element and attribute names*. These are case-sensitive, but some older SGML tools are not, and may systematically convert element names from lower- to upper-case. If you depend on such older tools, make sure that this issue is factored into your element naming conventions.

- *Respect for your vocabulary.* A tool may be required to respect your vocabulary, and thus the XML elements that you have agreed as part of your framework. If you cannot control how elements and attributes are generated, this could cause problems.

Background research

You should conduct your own background research in this fast-evolving area. A useful portal site is `http://www.xmlsoftware.com`, a site that organizes and presents tools according to their function and use. This does not provide any evaluation of the products listed, but links to other resources.

Information on conformance and test suites can be found at OASIS' comprehensive reference site, managed by Robin Cover:

`http://xml.coverpages.org/xmlConformance.html`

Types of XML tool

We will examine a series of criteria for tools that are available for:

- *Design*. The flow from initial idea, through a modelling of a particular information typology and use – tools that help you design and develop your schema and initial infrastructure.

- *Production*. Tools that help you prepare, create and transform XML, from ensuring that a document is well-formed and usable in a particular application through to publication.

- *Storage*. Tools to manage everything you produce, from simple database solutions to comprehensive XML-based repositories.

Design tools

Even before producing actual XML *content*, you need a series of tools that help in two major areas. Firstly, to design and model your overall infrastructure, including document schema, and secondly to design and 'populate' your vocabulary of terms, definitions and ontology that represents your information territory.

Architecture   A *schema editor* will probably be at the top of your shopping list for XML tools. This is the toolset that allows you to design and build the 'moulds' that will constrain your authors. If your focus is less on text, data and process modelling tools are also important.

Criteria for choice   A range of products is available, and you should consider which selection criteria are important for you:

- *Ease of use*. You will want a development environment that is straightforward, intuitive and ergonomic, particularly if you have little scope for deploying dedicated document analysts.

- *Quality of user documentation*. Even the best tool is blunted if it is not thoroughly and intelligently documented.

- *Integration with UML design tools*. As UML plays an important role in application and overall system designs, it is valuable to be able to 'borrow' or extend some of UML's popular and more familiar concepts when developing document design. If you have experience in the use of UML, there are tools that will help you build on this to develop your overall XML infrastructure.

- *Ease of understanding for non-specialist users.* The use of graphical representations of document, data and processing models and document trees not only helps non-specialists, but can also help to identify problem areas quickly and promote discussion aimed at finding particular solutions.

- *Support for multiple schema standards.* Depending on the complexity and nature of a particular document type, you may want to use different schemas such as XML Schema, Relax-NG, Schematron and so on.

- *Conversion between different schema standards.* You should be able to develop your information models at an abstract level, apply a specific formal schema vocabulary and syntax as appropriate and convert between different standards as needed.

Who designs the schema designer?

One issue not currently taken up by any schema design software relates to our earlier considerations about a common vocabulary.

All schema editors allow the document typology designer to specify which elements and attributes are required and their relationships to one another. None of them, however, allow you to constrain the design of a schema itself to certain boundaries, such as your 'information territory'. In other words, no schema design software allows you to configure it, for example, in such a manner that only element names from a controlled common vocabulary can be chosen and included as valid.

If you use the XML Schema, a solution is at hand, given that any XML Schema document is itself a conformant XML document written entirely in the syntax and grammar of XML. With a bit of thought, you can develop a 'metaschema' that defines precisely what any individual schema may contain. In this sense, the individual schemas that are developed would actually be instances of XML documents created in conformity with the master schema.

Such an approach is not for the fainthearted, however, and would involve the production of a rather massive metaschema document. There would also be maintainability and versioning problems as vocabulary elements were added to your information territory. A more realistic approach would involve an interface to your controlled vocabulary that is available at any point where an element can be added to a new schema design. Ideally, designers would be constrained to choose from a pick list linked to the currently acceptable vocabulary entries when they wished to add a new element or attribute type.

A similar problem arises in the use of modelling tools such as Unified Modeling Language. UML provides for the textual representation of its graphical model diagrams with XML Metadata Interchange. This allows UML class objects to be translated into XML elements, object attributes to child elements or attributes and so on. Particular care needs to paid to the generation of the XML vocabulary that is output. The tag names and attribute names thus generated can be used as a 'quick and dirty' solution to test a newly-generated DTD or schema, but they should be carefully validated and mapped to an agreed vocabulary. It is not acceptable to argue that XSLT can convert it all later – by doing so, you condemn yourself to an unnecessary additional layer of complexity.

Vocabulary and ontology

In earlier chapters we made use of a series of 'core components' to build our vocabulary, using the principles and elements of the exXML Core Components Technical Specification.

It may be sufficient to maintain the primitive information about each of your building blocks in a simple table or spreadsheet, as the Universal Business Language, UBL, does. We will see more of this in Chapter 11.

Your vocabulary management, however, is like a dictionary and may well be used interactively. It is therefore useful to manage and maintain it in XML, using with a tool that offers this functionality, rather than as a 'flat' file.

Production tools

Once you have established the toolset necessary to design your infrastructure, you need to determine the range of tools for actually producing XML content, as well as transforming, formatting and processing it. You also need to be aware of the growing number of ancillary tools that help handle link-management, web services and generation of reference documentation.

XML editors

Generic editors

A simple ASCII text editor can be used – and is often used – to create 'raw' HTML documents. You could in theory produce any set of HTML documents manually. You could, but you are unlikely to, beyond a certain limit of simplicity. We have come to rely rather on the relative comfort of advanced text processing and formatting tools.

Many so-called 'XML editors' offer little more than an XML equivalent of such ASCII text editors. They enable a user to create XML documents, sometimes constrained against a specific DTD or schema, and occasionally check and validate them.

For there to be any future for generic XML editors, the nature of XML is such that an additional layer of user interface will be required. It is not sufficient to restrict users to the associated schema and provide pick lists and other functions to conform to the schema – they also need to be provided with support for more complex operations in XML, such as describing graphics, processes or document management policies.

However, such an approach risks the same criticisms of 'bloat' that are levelled against some current word-processing packages.

Context-specific editors

Each user, each work situation and each process has different needs. These needs should be addressed by context-specific applications, rather than a generic tool that attempts to do everything.

XML's value and flexibility is that it does not roll all aspects of document production, management and dissemination into a single 'black box', but allows an enterprise to separate each individual responsibility and process. If a specific user is only ever to approve, review or reject particular texts, for example, it is not only inappropriate, to provide that user with a complete XML development and editing suite, but also a waste of resources. It is far more appropriate to provide a minimum tool set that ensures that these tasks, and nothing more, are possible. This might seem like an unnecessarily Taylorised[1] approach to the management of documents and information, but it underlines the point that your information may be created, edited, transformed, manipulated, stored and distributed in different ways, by different users and at different stages.

Further, although the 'content', formally-speaking, is always XML, different XML documents can contain anything from a schema or a complex graphic, or a business process to a simple text document. Although a generic editor can create and edit all such types in the same manner, context-specific editors will get the job done more efficiently.

An important point here can be illustrated by the Scalable Vector Graphics (SVG) standard. The graphics in SVG are expressed as a set of mathematical vectors stored as an XML text document. Most users would however prefer to draw graphics using an interactive tool rather than hand code an SVG. In such a situation, the advantage of storing the graphics in XML might be less obvious. The key point is that the XML that makes up the SVG can be manipulated by any other XML processing tool. Not only does this mean that your SVG could be generated in the first place by any XML processor – according for example to a set of XSLT transformation rules – but also that the graphics can be interactive, with the graphics code being processed and controlled – hence what is displayed being changed and controlled – by any application capable of handling XML.

1. Named after F.W. Taylor, an American engineer: the strict management of the work performed by individual workers on a production line as a result of detailed time-and-motion studies, which he named scientific management .

There are however a few categories of generic editor that can help users design document types and produce documents that conform to a particular typology. We look at some of the characteristics of these architectural and instance tools next.

Instance tools   It goes without saying that any tool designed to produce XML documents must produce *well-formed* documents – documents whose elements correctly nest. If the documents to be produced are instances that must conform to a schema, the tool should also ensure that the XML document output is *valid*. However, many users and developers complain that their tools generate too many buggy documents.

It is all too easy to blame the tools: there was a painful two-year wait for the XML Schema standard to be agreed, during which many vendors tried to predict the likely profile of the standard from draft specifications. This did not always work out.

Some problems related to 'comfort' with user interfaces, particularly amongst users familiar with the features of word-processing packages. If the production of document instances requires users to be constrained, they may come unstuck when they find their actions limited, compared with the relative freedom of the word-processor. As a well-formed and valid XML document is by definition a strictly constrained entity, it is difficult to find the right balance between conformity and ease of use.

If your XML documents are heavily data-oriented, remember that there is a wealth of resources and experience available that can help you in the often difficult task of form design: good, ergonomically-designed user interfaces are important in facilitating large-scale date entry.

The same cannot be said, unfortunately, for XML documents that are heavily text-centric. If authors feel that their document production tool is too rigid – if it *feels* like filling in forms – they may not be able to work comfortably. However, as XML *does* prescribe structure, the net effect is to put content into containers, hence the idea of 'pouring' content into a 'knowledge mould', as we see in the next chapter.

Instance tool types   An XML document instance can be anything that conforms to a parent schema. It does not have to be a text document – it depends on the nature and context of the specific XML application or markup language being used. It is worth looking briefly at different instance types to get a flavour of what is already available, irrespective of the tools likely to be developed in narrowly-defined contexts. These include:

- *Text*. This is certainly the principal orientation of the generic XML editors as well as those offering more sophisticated word-processing support. In addition to the core structuring and text-processing functions, an XML text editor should offer support for the creation and insertion of links and the insertion of attribute values from pick lists when they are constrained by a XML Schema datatype. Some editors will also allow you to match keywords that appear in the text against a concordance table to be picked out and tagged automatically (for linking purposes, for example).

- *Graphics*. Scalable Vector Graphics (SVG) is an XML application. A number of SVG-specific editors are available commercially and also being developed in specific industrial and commercial contexts. A good graphics editor must offer a set of predefined graphics and tools that the user can use immediately, plus the ability to import and convert from other graphics packages.

- *Stylesheets*. Extensible Stylesheet Language Formatting Objects (XSL-FO), Cascading Stylesheets and DSSSL are all formatting 'languages' that can convert an XML document into a specific end format and medium.

- *Transformation templates*. XSLT templates, themselves XML documents, contain patterns to be matched in the source document, instructions on how a particular pattern is to be transformed in the output document and programming instructions. An XSLT tool is likely to be the most sophisticated of all the instance production tools. A well-designed tool should allow the user to preview the transformations that are defined, offer find and replace functions and show associations between source and target elements. It should also have a set of more programming-oriented functions such as breakpoints, 'watch' windows and trace functions. Some allow you to specify the structure of a target XML document and help build the XSLT necessary to get there.

- *Business processes*. Whether using graphic models from the Unified Modeling Language (UML), EDI or other systems, processes, workflow, decision charts and so on can be modelled directly in a specific XML vocabulary or markup language.

- *Mathematical and scientific notations*. MathML and ChemML are specific XML markup languages for complex mathematical notations and the three-dimensional representation of molecular structures respectively.

Any of the above can be manually generated using a generic XML editor, in which the specific markup language would use its schema to guide the editor's functions. An analogy is that the XML editor can be thought of as acting as your 'operating system' with the markup vocabulary's schema acting as the application.

As an XML schema document is itself written in XML (unlike the earlier DTDs), it follows that it must be *well-formed*. As the vocabulary and grammar for creating a schema are laid down in the XML Schema standard, it follows also that an XML Schema document itself conforms to a particular very specific *model*, and is thus also *valid*. We can therefore have an XML schema for XML schemas! The advantage of this is that the rules that are laid down for the construction of a schema can be slotted into an XML editor, so that an author is constrained to create a valid and well-formed schema

Criteria for choice   This section lists possible criteria guiding your choice of tools. They will be of varying importance to you, depending on the nature of your XML documents and the experience of your users.

Depending on your XML document types, an XML instance tool should:

- Be a *good word-processor*, particularly if you are producing largely document-centric XML. This seemingly obvious statement is still overlooked by tool designers that come from the data, rather than the document, world. It does not mean offering all the latest frills in page layout and design, nor even necessarily a choice of typefaces or styles (except for user comfort) but must offer the essentials of text editing and composition. Any restrictions that are imposed on authors familiar with the freedom of commercial word-processing packages should be the subject of clear guidelines and good training. The disciplines of authoring for XML are examined in detail in the next chapter, *Content Management*.

- Support *co-authoring*. Most off-the-shelf word-processing and data-entry packages work well with the file locking functions of network file systems, preventing two users simultaneously working on the same file. However, as with well-designed database systems, different users should be able to work simultaneously on different parts of the same document, and only be locked out at the lowest level of content conflict. Further, users should be able to check out part of an XML document for editing – for example an element that contains a section of a document – without problems. The editing tool should not reject either the master document or the element being edited as invalid. This will become an increasingly topical issue as authoring environments move away from traditional file system-based storage and management to more interactive and peer-to-peer environments.

- Support *link creation and management*. XML goes beyond simple one-way hyperlinks that are familiar from HTML. Links in XML can be complex queries, bi-directional and multi-functional. Tools will soon be expected to handle such complexity as part of their core functionality. Some of the issues raised by complex link management strategies are handled in Chapter 13, *Navigation Strategies*.

- Offer an *adaptable user interface*. The solution to this problem is in the nature of XML itself. As an author is encouraged to concentrate on content and structure, the presentation of the editing environment should be arbitrary. If a user happens to want 36-point bold text on the screen while editing, this should have no impact on the real formatting or presentation of the content under consideration. With sophisticated use of stylesheets, or even a user interface language using XML (such as UIML or XUL), the user could be presented with an editing environment that imitates a familiar word-processing package.

In the area of change management, minimizing unnecessary changes is extremely important. The importance of customizable user interfaces does not end with user ergonomics, however. They can also be used to manage and grant specific access or editing rights to particular users or profiles. The way in which the content of a particular XML document is presented to the user could be tightly controlled with an associated stylesheet, granting limited editing access, for example, to a particular element type or attribute set. We will examine these questions in Chapter 11, *Process Management and 'Web Services'*.

In the following chapters we examine how the XML standards encourage the production of 'nimble' bespoke applications tailored to very precise needs, that is, applications that are very efficient in a specific context. If you find that no one off-the-shelf tool matches your criteria, you perhaps need to reflect further about the nature of your toolkit. The essential point is that the authoring interface must be adapted to the specific needs and context of your user communities.

Processing tools

A whole host of tools come into this category, given that XML is designed to be open to processability. There are a number of discernible types.

Conversion tools

There is a range of conversion tools that allow you to handle existing data and documents and 'XML-ise' them. These include conversion of:

- *Word-processing formats to XML*. These can be tools that convert from the portable Rich Text Format (RTF), itself an intermediate exchange format, or tools that handle vendor-specific word-processing text formats. Many word processors mix document structure and presentation. The conversion tools will either discard the presentation information (text formatting, positioning, and so on) or analyze and save it separately for possible later use as XSL-FO stylesheet information. The text content left will be structured to a greater or lesser extent depending on the underlying logic of the original word-processed document. Some word processors do allow some emphasis on logical document structure, for example by separating out formatting rules from structure using internal stylesheets, and this can make the job of conversion to a well-structured XML document that much easier.

- *Database to XML*. These can be tools that convert 'comma-separated value' (CSV) or 'flat' – plain ASCII – file data, or complex data structures in object oriented databases. Such tools differ from document-oriented conversion tools in two important respects. Firstly, as a database table is a set of structured records, the XML output is a *serialization* of the database or spreadsheet: the set of records is presented as a repeated pattern of XML elements, with each field of the database record represented as an element or attribute. Secondly, in particular for object-oriented databases, data that would otherwise appear only once, for example in a lookup table, is imported and repeated in every record that refers to it. These points should be borne in mind as they will have an immense impact on performance and effectiveness of any conversion tool.

• *Electronic Data Interchange (EDI) to XML.* Whether encoded in EDIFACT, X12 or other EDI vocabularies, tools will emphasize batch processing, as the source data is already in a highly structured and predictable syntax. The tools should allow the user to 'map' rules from the source data model to target XML elements and attributes.

• *Metadata and records management information to XML.* Whether interpreting specific library-style records (using for example the US or UK MARC or Z39.50 standards) or extracting or inferring metadata from documents, such tools are likely to be an important and early addition to your toolkit, given the great impact that XML-encoded metadata can have in your overall information management strategy.

Transformation tools

There is a special category of conversion tool concerned with transforming one source XML document to another target XML document using the XSLT standard. These conversions are made according to the rules laid down in an XSLT transformation template and may be done one at a time, 'on the fly' or by batch processing, depending on the context and need.

Such tools construct a tree of the target XML document on the basis of the instructions contained in an XSLT template document. They will often offer predefined transformations, for example from XML to HTML. Some will be activated from a command line interface (CLI), accessible either directly by a user, programmatically or from an API. The tool may run as a separate application or as a Web server module providing real-time server-side services.

Formatting tools

This is the family of one-way conversion tools that take an XML source document and create something in a non-XML end format. These include Portable Document Format (PDF), PCL5 and EPS for defining the printed page, the Wireless Markup Language for displaying an XML document on a WAP-compliant mobile telephone, or various proprietary page design formats such as Quark Xpress, Adobe Framemaker and Macromedia Flash.

Object serialization tools

These tools make up the core of Enterprise Application Integration (EAI) and Business to Business (B2B) solutions and messaging systems. They involve taking data and information objects from one system, together with any programming functions or procedure calls, serializing them and passing them as messages to another system, and finally translating them into the target system's data model and functions.

This so-called 'Message-Oriented Middleware' (MOM) is the backbone of e-commerce. Such tools should normally be able to handle high volumes of data with high levels of availability and integrate seamlessly across different applications and information systems.

Processing methods

For all of these tools, it is important not only to consider which is the most appropriate to the legacy data that needs to be processed, but also to the manner in which they are to be processed:

- Some tools import and handle files one at a time, which can be frustrating if you have tens of thousands of documents, particularly if they are all identically or similarly structured.

- Some tools require user input and 'tweaking' of individual files. This can be very useful when you have documents that are very heterogeneous, and for which you want to maintain a high level of overview and quality control. It may be tiresome, however, if you want to convert large numbers of similar text files.

- Some tools are oriented to batch conversion with little or no user input. This is good news for high-volume routine processing, but if the content is too heterogeneous, such processors are likely to reject many files that do not fit a definable pattern, requiring additional effort on your part to handle exceptions.

Parsers

We introduced the parser in Chapter 3, the tool that prepares an XML document for subsequent processing. The choice of parser is not often nor seriously enough considered in any project.

The *stream* or *event-based* parser processes an incoming XML document a byte at a time and passes it directly to an application, whereas a *tree-based* parser builds up a complete and accessible picture of the whole document. Many parsers are packaged into other XML applications or themselves offer far more than the core functions required by the XML standards. The consequences of this are often negligible, but in any large-scale undertaking there are a number of considerations.

Keep it simple

Try to avoid choosing a parser that offers too much. This might sound a little bizarre, but the logic is simple. If you start to rely on a parser to do things that should really be passed to the XML application proper, you run the risk of being locked into that particular parser. You might realize, for example, that a tree-based parser is more appropriate to the sort of documents you are dealing with that a stream-based parser. If you are using a stream-based parser but also relying on other of its processing functions, it will be more difficult for you to extract your system from the dependency so created.

Conversion is always possible

It is useful to remember that there are tools that can convert a DOM-style document tree into a sequential data stream and vice-versa, if you need to. It is important, however, to remember that every extra step or layer of processing adds to your overheads. If in doubt, do a cost-benefit analysis.

Stream or tree?

You need to consider the trade-off between the respective advantages and costs of the two types of parser.

A *tree-based* parser:

- Is nearly always more resource-intensive, even if you are dealing with relatively small documents

- Needs to be able to load the entirety of an XML document into memory so that the application that is to work on it has access to all of it

- Is useful when you are dealing with known document types and schemas

- Takes on the brunt of the document processing, offering 'clean' interfaces to the main application

- Is necessary when the modifications or actions to be performed upon a document are interactive, unpredictable or do not necessarily follow a particular pattern

A *stream-based* parser:

- Is nearly always faster

- Can handle any size of document with equal ease

- Is useful when the XML document is not of a type known in advance and thus of unpredictable content

- Passes the processing burden on the main application

- Is valuable for filtering or data mining – 'gold panning'– when you know what you are looking for in a particular document but have no idea where it might be found in the data stream'

Whatever the parser, it must be fast. You should test parser performance over a wide set of criteria, as the parser will be the workhorse of much of your infrastructure, preparing XML documents for use within a particular tool. You should test with a range of XML documents, data-rich as well as text-rich, large and small, both 'flat' and heavily nested in their use of elements.

Link management tools

XLink now offers a whole host of options beyond the simple one-way HTML-like hyperlink. Any tool is going to support the creation of simple and extended link traversal and be able to create and manage 'linkbases', external sets of linking information that can be referred to by an XLink.

Tools should also be able to build XPath expressions, highlighting their effect and occurrences in a target document's nodes, and allowing a user to move through matching nodes.

Web service tools

Such tools should enable the creation of Web services using WSDL and SOAP – see Chapter 11. It should be able to offer support to Web service resource discovery functions, such as those specified in the UDDI model, and help users import document typology libraries such as xCBL and UBL.

Security tools

Specific tools are starting to emerge that support the XML Signature and Canonical XML standards, as well as encryption and access management, from the level of an entire suite of XML documents, down to a specific element, and other standards such as X.509.

Documentation tools

There is a permanent need to keep track of all the areas of XML development within an enterprise, whether design, production or evaluation. We have argued earlier about the need to avoid using XML comments that might be discarded by a processor. Documentation tools should be able to pick up elements from designated XML documents that are intended as user or technical documentation, such as the explicit documentation elements foreseen in the XML Schema standard.

Coupled with XSLT and XSL-FO, such tools should be able to generate documents available to the user as HTML, PDF or help files.

Storage tools – databases and XML repositories

Your XML data or text content, schemas, processes, graphics or other content, needs to be stored somewhere. The way in which it is stored and managed will have a key influence on how the XML documents can be used.

Relational database management systems (RDBMS) have proved their efficiency in handling large volumes of data and managing complex data models, and are very efficient at handling complex queries. However, the hierarchical model of XML does not fit well with the relational model of such databases. Alternative object-oriented databases fit the XML model much better, and are much more efficient at supporting navigation through document trees.

Some XML repositories consist of an RDBMS that creates 'virtual' XML documents as required, thus XML is not the native storage format. If a high proportion of your XML content is data-centric rather than document-centric, you are likely to benefit from the inherent strengths of such an approach. Moving the content between its XML representation and its stored relational form, however, involves additional translation stages that involve resources of time and cost.

Other repositories are closer to the object-oriented model and are likely to store the XML content in a proprietary binary format, more efficiently than the native character-based format of XML. The process of generating an XML document from the stored format is also likely to be more efficient, as it is closer to the XML hierarchical model. In very data-centric systems, however, there will be high levels of data replication and redundancy. This is the cost that must be paid to have 'object permanence' – hard coding every value for a particular record rather than inferring many of them from the hierarchically-organized parent objects – which then is the source of the efficiency of such systems. Access to the content using queries is less easy due to the hierarchical organization of the content.

Some tools offer hybrid solutions, storing XML content using the object-oriented model, but re-using key content – held in elements that most resemble data fields – as metadata in a relational database, to improve querying, indexing and searching capabilities.

Your choice of tool will be influenced by its intended purpose. A good overview of criteria and use scenarios is provided in Quin's *Open Source XML Database Toolkit* – see *Further Reading* on page 309 – which covers many of the relevant issues:

- *Resource discovery*: whether your biggest problem is finding what you have produced and being able to refer to it in a query, link or other resource identifier

- *Archiving*: whether your content has historical importance or needs to be maintained indefinitely and in a stable manner, such as online legislation

- *Cooperation and co-authoring*: whether you need to support protocols such as WebDAV or whether XML production is tightly integrated into a business process

- *Version control*: whether you need to update content regularly, keep track of changes and offer commit and rollback solutions

- *Component management*: whether your XML is made up of separately-managed entities, content 'chunks', stylesheets, schemas, all of which can be updated and changed independently

- *Security and access management*: whether access to different content and processes depends on user or business unit profiles or explicit security clearance

- *Application interfaces and communications*: whether your XML is essentially to be accessed by automated processes and program interfaces

A word of caution, however: the current paradigm for content management is the repository, the idea of a central, well-managed and secure place where all content is registered and stored. The growth of peer-to-peer applications undermines this centralized repository approach. As individual users or business units become increasingly responsible for the management of their own resources, including what they produce and how they make it accessible, we are likely to see an increase of more decentralized content management models.

Adapting existing systems

'Big bang' approaches in IT rarely work. You should rather devise an intelligent and comprehensive migration strategy that allows you to move from a current infrastructure to your target infrastructure.

However 'non-XML' parts of your current infrastructure might seem, it is possible to build on and adapt them to make them more amenable to XML-type manipulations. One important topic in this respect, pursued in more detail in the following chapter, regards the use of commercial word-processing packages. An agreement to use, for example, document styles or structures in a consistent manner for particular content types, offers two advantages:

- It exposes and renders explicit the implied semantics of a particular content 'chunk': 'this is a title', 'this is a legal preamble', 'this is an article of a decision' and so on.

- It paves the way for easier translation to XML in the current working environment and facilitates the move to an all-XML solution at a later stage. If individual content structures are consistently and clearly identified, they become identifiable by automated processes, allowing easier processing later.

While users continue to use such non-XML word-processing tools, you can still investigate how to couple them with conversion tools. The key to success is to get users to be more disciplined in how they use their word processors – in particular, which features to use or avoid. Establishing a clear pattern of use makes the job of predicting how to convert content thus prepared into XML much easier.

Building your own tools

Given the vast wealth of XML tools on the market, why would anyone want to reinvent the wheel?

One of the biggest criticisms of the 'enterprise application' was often that it tried to do everything. With very few application development opportunities available, everyone tried to throw in their requirements, as they didn't know when the next opportunity would come. Systems developed like this were not only big, but very inflexible, and although they may have included everything except the kitchen sink, once developed they were difficult to modify.

As XML offers interoperability between different systems, such systems can be much smaller and more focussed, down to the level of a simple set of functions or a single process. This can be achieved in the knowledge that data can be transferred between different components rather than having to be hard coded into and maintained in the proprietary format of one central system.

This modularity becomes all the more important as applications development is shared between teams and spread across different enterprises or business units.

Although not a comprehensive guide to XML tool development, the next section lists some issues that you need to address when deciding whether you should develop your own XML tools.

Objectives   You may well want to proselytize the use of XML by demonstration. Although you can do this through the use of any combination of off-the-shelf solutions, there is nothing more convincing than a home-made demonstrator tool: not only do you have complete control of what is being demonstrated, but you are deliberately choosing content and context with which your users are familiar. Choose a demonstration therefore that actually addresses, and hopefully represents a solution to, a real and tightly-scoped problem, even if it is a small one.

The main reasons for producing your own tools are:

- *Cost*. Many large enterprises equip their staff with a computer configured with a standard software set. Such a computer will come equipped with a set of generic tools, often exceeding the needs of many users. It is easier to manage such configurations, but there is a price to be paid. Why pay for hundreds or thousands of licenses for 'do-everything' tools when more than 80% of their features are never used?

- *Agility.* It is a useful principle to keep XML tools small and agile. If there are two jobs to be done, do it with two tools. Because XML documents are self-describing, they carry with them much information that previously might have been hard-coded into specific applications.

- *Precision.* Generic tools may be satisfactory for many jobs, but occasionally you may benefit from a bespoke development that creates a tool that meets your needs completely with no unnecessary features.

Choice of developments

You may consider creating tools that support any of the areas of functionality catered for by XML and its associated standards:

- A specific development tool that allows the creation of XML schema within a specific vocabulary, using only a permitted subset of schema development functions and in conformity with your vocabulary or Framework.

- A documentalist's tool that allows for the controlled addition of an abstract, keywords and other information to an existing document, or a tool that only adds and checks links placed within a document. Such a tool could, for example, provide a translator with a source text and a target editing area that replicates the source schema for the target language version.

- A management-oriented tool that manages access policies to a set of documents and updates appropriate XSLT scripts accordingly, or an interface tool to an XML-encoded workflow or process management system

Finally, there are tools that are likely to be oriented more to storage and repository management questions.

Methodology

Many Computer Aided Software Engineering (CASE) tools are available to programmers and developers. Many of them use and store valuable data and information about the data managed by the application under development.

Data interchange standards exist that allow you to retrieve such data in XML, including the XML Interchange Format, used predominantly in application development environments using Microsoft's DCOM, and XML Metadata Interchange, used predominantly in CORBA-based systems.

If UML is used as an application design and development methodology, there is also value in representing processes and use-cases in XML. Again, tools exist to help you map the UML models to target XML output, in which different UML-specific constructs are mapped to an XML schema or DTD.

The value of all this being in XML is, once again, interoperability and re-usability: metadata about applications can be used elsewhere than in the specific environment in which it was originally created and foreseen. Data models can be 'understood' and manipulated by other tools. XML is again playing the role of a *lingua franca*.

The role of dummy and pilot projects

As with traditional application development, do not underestimate the value of feedback from your target users. In addition to testing specific functionalities and assessing conformance of a particular approach to user requirements, it can be valuable as a more general 'proof of concept' that allows you to demonstrate the areas which XML developers may be able to penetrate.

Load balancing

In the days of mainframes, data, processing and applications were located on a central system. As desktop systems appeared, the processing load started to shift onto local computers and away from the central system, with file servers appearing to act as repositories for files, data and backup.

Client-server systems started to see a reverse shift, with lightweight 'clients', often based on Web browser technologies, acting as the equivalent of the mainframe's 'terminal', but with the local processing power. Simple HTML pages sent from a Web server are an example of this architecture.

More recently the balance has shifted again, as XML permits large and complex documents to be sent from the server to a client for substantial processing via available application interfaces. At the same time, the server side of such systems system is becoming more complex as the treatment of different processes is spread across different layers and systems. Most recently the problems of load balancing have moved designs beyond the confines of the single application development environment towards architectures in which different modules of an overall application run on different servers, even in different parts of the planet.

Because of such shifts, you need to consider who is able to support each part of the overall load in any development:

- Within the enterprise, one component of the overall architecture that can usually bear considerable load is the desktop computer, as the percentage of time that their processors remain idle is often substantial. Processing load can often be shifted away from bottle-necked application or Web servers onto the local clients.

- Between enterprises, load balancing will require discussion and negotiation. The respective infrastructures of each party will have an influence on both application development and the models that are created.

- Beyond the enterprise more caution must be exercised, particularly if you are developing systems that require client-level processing. You should afford the benefit of the doubt to the client and assume only a minimum of available processing ability, or develop in a manner that is both context-sensitive and aware of the different possible types of client end-systems.

Conclusions

In this chapter we have looked briefly at the changing landscape of application architectures and how the XML family of standards can bring some stability to it.

Starting with the next chapter, we examine a number of specific areas of XML use in detail, and assess the specific architecture and working environment required for each, starting with content management.

10 Content Management

Introduction

Many traditional ideas of content management are often little more than approaches to 'container' management. In other words, the focus is on the packing, labelling and storage of containers of information, but does not go as far as managing anything within the container itself.

In this chapter we are going to start from the beginning and examine how our content is conceived and generated, and how the various ingredients are managed before becoming finished packages.

Planning for knowledge

Our objective is to maximize our opportunities for handling and interpreting information or knowledge and minimizing the effort spent on handling and disentangling data.

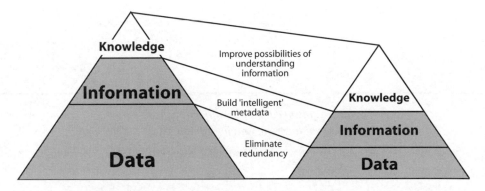

Figure 24. Even in a smaller pyramid, we now have more room for knowledge

We can see from the diagram that with the data layer looked after in XML, there is less need for processing resources at this level. This allows us to concentrate more and more towards the top of the pyramid. Note that the overall size of the pyramid has decreased. This is a reflection of the fact that in the target infrastructure, the management of data and information will be much more 'lean' – with greater data reuse and thus less redundancy – even if we are committing more resources to knowledge.

This diagram does assume that there are distinct layers to process and move between. As a result of over-processing or pre-packaging, these distinctions often cannot be so easily made, making the process of moving from data to knowledge more complex.

Information processing

How data becomes information that is subsequently processed as 'knowledge' can be heavily influenced by how content is managed at source and handled during its useful life.

We are often confronted with 'over-processed' information. The individual ingredients are so mixed into wider structures that it is impossible to distinguish them individually, meaning that is also impossible to process them individually. Imagine being asked to prepare a beef and pepper stir-fry but presented with only a pre-prepared Bolognese sauce. It may theoretically be possible to pull it off, but it makes for a risky approach to getting through catering school.

Yet it is amazing how much IT talent and valuable, well-paid human resources are tied up with doing exactly this in information processing and management projects. A worryingly high percentage of human and computing resources are dedicated every day to the extraction and processing of information from the inside of a quagmire of information chaos. One major IT consultancy considers that upwards of 40% of the IT resources of large enterprises are used simply in extracting and converting data from one system to make it available in another.

It may keep a lot of contractors and professionals in business, but there are better uses of their skills and resources.

Quality and choice

Imagine the conditions required for the preparation of a first-class meal. Food prepared from selected ingredients, chosen from known suppliers and prepared in hygienic conditions are necessary preconditions. With the right ingredients, you can combine at will and leave the irreversible steps – the food blender, the sauces – until they are needed. What do you do as a cook if you learn that all your guests dislike one of the ingredients? If it is already in a pre-processed ready-to-eat meal, you are in trouble. If you learn early enough, you could change the meal. If you are preparing the meal yourself, it would be enough to leave out the offending ingredient, if possible.

So it is also with information systems. If your system can only deliver your content in a pre-determined way, in which the ingredients are no longer identifiable, it makes it well-nigh impossible to create a particular composition in response to a specific need. XSLT as a standard is designed for this sort of 'pick and mix' approach to document creation on the fly. Imagine a confidential document that needs to be made public but that contains names that should legitimately be blanked. If the names are clearly encapsulated as specific elements, applying an XSLT transformation means that this can be achieved without fuss. The alternative is going through the document and blanking the names one at a time, praying that none are overlooked.

Irreversibility

If you want someone else to prepare a meal, you have a wide range of choices, from the fast-food joint to a high-class restaurant. The level of discretion you maintain over range of choice and quality will depend on your budget, as well as availability. With the exception of a few salad bars, the food is presented in a *terminal format*, an irreversible stage of processing over which the client has no further control.

When it comes to processing information, and presenting the ingredients in the combination that a particular client requires, we are all too frequently satisfied with a 'fast-food approach'. As text has traditionally been presented in only a terminal format –

already committed to paper – we seem to find it difficult conceptually to separate information ingredients.

Food for thought

Food processing

Throughout the supply chain from farm to table, however short or involved the route,
foodstuffs are 'processed'. Even if the food itself is not altered or added to in any
way, foods are nurtured, harvested, weighed, selected, labelled, packaged, stored,
forwarded, traded, displayed, promoted and sold before being prepared and
consumed.

The whole of this processing can be undertaken by anyone from a single person to
multiple groups scattered across the planet.

'Information overload' is a well-worn adage of our times, but the indigestion caused by
badly and overly-processed information is less obvious and more complex to unravel.

This is not to preclude the use of 'fast food' approach to pre-packaged information
delivery. It is merely recognition that this should be a conscious and premeditated
choice and not the only one on offer. The growth in information management and documentation services over the last decade attests to a resurgence in the importance of
classifying, sifting, analyzing and abstracting knowledge downstream from its source.

Content management – content or containers?

Often when the phrase 'content management' is used it is a misnomer. To the extent that
a content management system is concerned with handling, updating and revising text
files, metadata, and control information, its primary focus is not content management,
but rather 'container management'.

The analogy with food is valid. The concern here is with what is on the label and packaging, so that distributors and clients alike know whether the ingredient corresponds to

expectations in terms of origin, quality, conformity with appropriate standards and dates of validity.

Food for thought

Labelling standards

In some parts of the world, strict standards regulate the use of pesticides and hormones in food preparation. Others have quality assurance labels or guarantees of organic origin.

The European Union's coding system for additives takes the issue one stage further, offering the consumer a standardized and protected coding system to indicate, for example, permitted food additives – the so-called 'E-numbers'.

Various organic farming certification authorities also offer an assurance to a consumer that the contents conform to certain standards.

Content management systems rarely tackle such important issues further up the production chain, at the stage of initial authoring – and most importantly, the preparations necessary for that authoring to be carried out in the best conditions. We can see that to move from the 'fast food' fully-processed approach to a more refined diet, we need to tackle every stage of the production chain as distinct steps in the overall production process, starting with content origination.

This chapter discusses how the XML family of standards can be brought to bear at the origins of content origination:

• In pre-production, by the use of carefully prepared *knowledge moulds*

• In production, with appropriate tools for authors

The methods outlined may require new skills from an author, or at least a different approach to content composition and the tools made available to achieve it. The chapter therefore also addresses some of the human resource and training implications for an enterprise. It is vital that such implications are seen as part of the overall approach, not just as optional 'plug-ins'.

New concepts of 'content'

As content management, document management and information management are too often considered as interchangeable concepts, we should start by being clear about our use of these terms.

- *Documents as content.* We traditionally think of a document as indistinguishable from its content: "I read your document" rather that "I read what was in your document". By this we mean, we read, digested and processed the contents.

- *Documents as containers.* With the ubiquity of desktop computers, we have started to think of documents and files as indistinguishable: "The data you need is in that document" rather than "The data is that file". We start to separate the concept of the content and the container.

- *Documents as vehicles.* The 'document as electronic file' paradigm allows us to make a further conceptual leap forward. A document is no longer just content, just a container, but is also a vehicle for transporting that content: "Send me that document by e-mail" rather than "Find me the information in that document and send the information by e-mail".

In these three scenarios, we see a number of different ideas about the concept of a document. A collection of bytes that are fed into and interpreted by the correct processor may be a valuable information set or a beautiful digital photograph. Without context, however, it is just a collection of data.

We therefore define a document as *any container that can serve as a vehicle for information*. In XML terms, certainly, a document is a stream of characters, with a beginning and end. The internal structure serves as the vehicle for conveying information about the data in the character stream.

Our problem often is that we restrict our understanding of documents to something that appears on paper or its electronic equivalent. We need to widen the scope to ensure that a document can mean not only a word-processed file, but also e-mail, voice annotations, instant messaging, news and discussion forum messages, as well as graphics, processes and other data.

Managers' information needs

For most managers, only a minor part of the information and knowledge they find useful comes from what we would normally call 'documents'. Much more comes from informal discussions, e-mail, meetings and corridor gossip. Nonetheless, much of this other information is available in electronic form, but it just isn't encapsulated and usable outside of a given context. A routine meeting or sales report, an exchange of mail between colleagues, all contain potentially valuable knowledge.

The 'encapsulation challenge'

This has been the dream of knowledge management gurus for the last decade, but without substantial results beyond complex and proprietary systems. With XML we can aim at a more realistic approach. If data is encapsulated firstly as information, content can already be used and reused in different contexts. By associating 'meaning' with particular associations of information content, it is possible to start building systems that reply to the knowledge management challenge.

The definition of knowledge can become insubstantial when you try to pin it down and describe it in formal terms. We should be clear that XML is intended to shape data, to give it a form, to allow it to be described. Once done, it becomes a vehicle for information. Once that information is 'mobile' and accessible, it can be processed and used by human users as knowledge.

How then do we set about giving form to our data, our content?

Why structure content?

Many organizations traditionally use author guidelines, house style manuals and visual identity guides. They are intended to coerce users into the customs and habits of the organization and ensure that a coherent house style is always presented in documentation. This important exercise is not limited to a purely cosmetic attempt to prove a corporate identity, however.

Visual cues

Because of our heavy dependency on visual communications, through the written or printed word as well as images, we have developed sophisticated visual cues that guide our reading and understanding of particular content. Such cues are intended as signals that we should understand something in a particular way. If a word is *emphasized*, for example, it is to draw particular attention to it.

Structure with a purpose

The structure of our documents using such visual cues, therefore, is a way of helping us to process that structure visually and aid understanding. It relies, obviously, on our ability to recognize and understand the cues. In the written word, the conventions of titles, headings, emphasis and captions are familiar. In other documents, you need to be familiar with a particular 'vocabulary' to understand, for example a workflow diagram.

A computer is not going to 'understand' such cues. What it needs is to be able to recognize them and know what to do when it encounters them. That is the point about markup: giving cues to a processor for the actions to perform on specific identified content. For the computer also, therefore, structure has a purpose.

Upstream organization

The problem of content management requires that information is organized 'upstream' in such a way that the individual ingredients are able to maintain their distinctive identity until their point of use, thus leaving the client to choose them individually or combine them at will. Such organization not only makes for clearer choice for the end user, it also allows reuse of the information in different configurations of 'ingredients'.

If information content is strictly maintained independently of a particular presentation, the same content can be deployed in different ways, each appropriate to a particular medium, target audience and format.

The next sections look at four related topics of such 'upstream content organization'– structure, packaging, labelling, and quality control – before examining their impact for authors.

Structure

How often do we drop a hand-written note on the desk of a colleague? It may be a very informal affair, a few lines expressing an idea, a question or a request, and ephemeral. Electronic mail has radically changed that: we now, consciously or not, structure our communications, thinking of an appropriate title, particularly if competing for attention in someone's crowded in-box, and even hesitating about the list of recipients. *Structure* has entered the equation.

Our first concern in content management must therefore be to recognize that text or information content is not just a free-flowing string of characters, but is made up of:

- Information 'chunks' or distinct building blocks of content

- References to other chunks in the same text or beyond it

- Rules that govern how the building blocks can be assembled, which blocks are entitled to be present and their configuration in a given text

Packaging

The second topic is packaging: each information block needs a distinct package if it is not to 'spill', to enable it to be moved, stored and delivered without loss or damage. Each such block must be able to 'live' independently. If normally used as part of a larger whole, the relationship between the parts and the whole needs also to be known.

Knowledge packages

Considerable work needs to be done in any XML-based system even before an author sets pen to paper or bytes to file.

Most of the 'knowledge packages' we create share important characteristics and properties with each other. The key to any automated or managed processing of content lies with predictability. The first step in our endeavour must be to describe these generic characteristics in such a manner as to prescribe structures that offer such predictability.

Anyone who has invested seriously in designing a really useful template for a word-processing package will know this. If the template is designed to constrain authors to follow a certain model, considerable thought and attention to detail are necessary. XML is even more demanding if used well, and offers precisely the predictability sought after.

Food for thought

Why conform?

No enterprise wants to tie itself to a system that imposes constraints without obvious returns and benefits.

Many organizations are already familiar and comfortable with – or resigned to – the idea of rules and procedures and the need to conform. There may be administrative, financial or legal constraints: nothing makes a financial or legal department more nervous than unpredictable actions.

Predictability also permits automation and rule-based processing, by humans and machines alike.

The basic tools for prescribing such structures in an XML environment are the DTD and schema. They can be thought of as formal statements of intent for an identified type of information content. It is this idea of intent, or the prescription of a document's structure and permitted content, that serves as a framework for creating a model or 'mould' with which to conform.

By creating a knowledge mould, not only are you laying down a prescription of the structure, which by definition will be a conformant XML document, but also ensuring that whatever is produced can be processed predictably at a later stage.

Creating the 'knowledge moulds'
This approach to content and packaging is prevalent in many off-the-shelf text-processing packages today. Users are invited to use pre-conceived 'moulds' – document templates, models, standard form letters and so on – provided with the application, or to develop their own using built-in tools such as macro editors or application programming languages.

These moulds establish a series of structures – similar in intent to the fields of a database form – and the contents of which are managed within the confines of the mould.

Whatever the tools or approach used, the objectives are the same:

- To cut out repetitive tasks in the creation of texts that have similar presentation, structure and/or content
- To control the manner in which information is entered

The resultant knowledge moulds are often designed for use as presentational devices, but our concern is that they are used as receptacles for predefined information content of an expected type. By definition, they are designed and created in advance of the specific texts that use them.

If you use the document structuring features of a commercial word-processing package, be sure to use these features by design and not by default. In other words, make the conscious effort to 'map' the use of those features with semantic structures and the building blocks of your content.

XML offers a formal method by which to create such moulds: the Document Type Definition (DTD) and the schema, and it is these two standards to which the technical community will turn when developing XML-centred document management systems.

The manager's concern, however, should not be with the technical details of these two formal representations of a document's structure, but rather with promoting the principles that they represent:

- Most texts conform to a certain knowledge mould, in that they follow a pattern of structure and content and share certain properties.
- By conforming to a predefined model, a particular text offers predictability to automated processes.
- By automating what is the same, authors can concentrate on what is unique, adding value.
- Prevention is better than cure. Ensuring the production of conformant XML documents at source is to save corrective action later in the information management stream.

The first steps in content management must therefore aim to create order in the knowledge moulds that an enterprise creates and uses. If the content is not created in a coherent manner in the first instance, energy is wasted later repairing the damage.

There are two main aims:

- To ensure that the content 'fits' the mould. If it doesn't, don't break the mould – find another in which the content fits: you can't force a sales report, for example, to fit a mould designed for the technical documentation of a piece of software.

- To ensure – despite being 'set' into a mould – that the content is still identifiable by its constituent ingredients. You should still be able to identify, for example, the blocks of text that contain your sales forecasts or the formal description of a process. Always try to imagine that *any* chunk of content might one day be used elsewhere.

Food for thought

Alphabet soup

Imagineabookwhereallthespacesbetweenwordssentencesandparagraphswereomitted andtherewasnopunctuationtheonlywaytoextractmeaningwouldbetolaborisouslyscana nalyseandidentifyeverydistinctinformationelementwordandmentallyorifyouarelucky anddisposeofthebookinanonterminalformatactuallyaddthespacestogiveclarity...

Hard work, isn't it? At least in this example, the letters are in the right order.

Text should be seen as a finely-prepared salad, with each ingredient preserving its properties and bringing its distinctive contribution, rather than such an alphabet soup. The overall taste may be the same, but you will be hard pressed to identify any single ingredient unequivocally.

We can thus see the need for, and benefit of, the thorough analysis proposed in the XML framework, aimed at identifying and providing a description for all the information building blocks that make up an enterprise's texts and information.

Using the moulds   Your knowledge moulds should provide a working environment for authors that:

- Keeps them on the 'straight-and-narrow': ensures that they concentrate on the content and not on the structure or presentation of the document.

- Supports them in the process of adding and validating reference information: if an author needs to add content that is going to be tagged as an element of a particular type, and that should only hold content in a particular pre-defined way, then the mould should ensure that the author is helped in that. This means not just bluntly refusing something that doesn't fit, but helping the author by offering what does, from pick lists, query-driven searches and so forth.

The strong focus on 'all-in' document production, mixing structure and presentation, is what popularized the 'WYSIWYG' approach – you create the look and feel *and* content of your document as you go along. In fact the acronym ought to be understood the other way around: what you get is what you see, content mixed with structure and presentation, as was its intent. This can lead to complications in XML production systems, however, because of the emphasis on reuse and interoperability. You can only reuse content if you can pick it out from the context-specific presentation and format.

We have already looked at the importance of visual cues in information processing. A production environment should present content on an author's workstation in a way that assists validation against such visual cues. Remember that the way in which content is presented to an author's workstation does not have to be the same as the way in which it is stored. The fact that an author sees a familiar page-oriented layout does not preclude the reuse and positioning of that content for another display medium.

Labelling

Labelling ensures that a package is properly identifiable according to a recognized scheme. Clear labelling and packaging is, however, no indicator of the contents nor of the quality of that content.

> *Food for thought*
>
> ### Shelving and display
>
> In supermarkets a customer can expect to find items shelved according to some logic of product classification, and prices adjacent to the displayed goods, rather than posted at the checkout.
>
> Similarly, the supermarket itself can expect deliveries to be bundled according to product. Store promotions are most likely to be presented near the entrance. One would not expect to find unlabeled packages on the shelves and would distrust any with hand-written or improvised labels. A customer would rightly complain about finding washing powder in a package announcing breakfast cereal.

Knowledge 'chunks'

The concept of identifying and separately labelling content 'chunks' within a document is very important in XML:

- Firstly, because of its nature, you can never be sure when one chunk within a document might become a document in its own right or be used in another context. By packaging and labelling each chunk you are optimizing the chances for its potential reuse.

- Secondly, such distinct identification is necessary for the intelligent use of XPointer, XLink and XPath.

- Thirdly, you are 'exposing' the semantics or intent of each chunk, making its use more accessible to those unfamiliar with a particular content or content type.

Quality control Quality control in this context is about determining and managing how content finds its way into a particular package. This includes managing who is authorized to put it there, what quality controls are applied, whether a sell-by date is required and what indications are needed to determine when processing of the content is complete.

New skills for authors

The discussion on structuring 'knowledge moulds' demonstrates that text can no longer be considered as simply a flow of characters. There are a number of characteristics that need to be borne in mind for our knowledge moulds and the tools that support them.

Outlining Some word processors already offer outlining functions, some even going as far as describing such functions as 'thought processors'. This is a radical departure from the 'linear' text processing model, allowing users to structures their thoughts and ideas into manageable chunks that can be manipulated easily and moved around as distinct chunks.

More often than not, however, such outline functions are used merely to help organize the initial structure of a document. Once a document is developed, most authors abandon the outline. A publisher might later be able to recuperate and use the outline, to help create, for example, a table of contents and to identify chunks of content by section headings. It is rare, unfortunately, however, to reuse such outlines systematically as the content chunk 'containers' they so evidently are, which is XML's loss, as well as your enterprise's.

Link management and 'linkability' An author may need to refer to another text or reference. In the traditions of academia, an author would be required to indicate, as a footnote or endnote, the full reference of the text being cited. With the linking functionalities offered by XML, an author needs to consider three issues.

- Firstly, if merely a reference is required, how should a hyperlink be added so that a later user can find the resource being referred to?

- Secondly, the author may want to embed the resource referred to, in which case a placeholder needs to be created at the appropriate point so that, upon subsequent processing, the resource is located and embedded into the flow of the document at the point indicated. This obviously raises questions of intellectual property rights and copyright.

- Finally, the author, or the enterprise for whom he or she works, may want to indicate whether, and how, links might be made to the content being prepared. This might be, for example, to address the copyright questions of the previous point, or to indicate the relative suitability of the specific chunk for as a target for linking.

Controlled vocabularies

If specific names or terms are used, it is better to choose from a controlled vocabulary or validate the choice of terms against it. There are a number of reasons for this.

Firstly, integrity: you can be sure that a proper name or term is correctly spelled or refers to a unique occurrence in a particular group or list. Take our earlier fictional parliamentary debate. We could simply write, in a press release being prepared following the debate:

'Mr Bloggs, on a point of order at the opening of the plenary session, sought to block consideration of the Environment Committee's report…'

But what if there are more than one 'Mr Bloggs', or the author is not absolutely sure whether it might have been Mr Bløgs or Mr Blogg who was speaking?

Secondly, rendering an implicit reference explicit. Using the same example, how do we know to which 'report' the speaker is referring? We would like to be able to associate a reference with the text that indicates the precise details. If neither the formal title nor reference of the report to which the press release referred are actually mentioned in the press release, this sort of tagging would be invaluable.

Thirdly, to ensure that there is no confusion between a name, proper noun or word that has a specific meaning in its context and the same word's more general use and meaning. This is not normally a problem for a human user, but a processor is not going to make the distinction unless given a hint to do so. This hint is markup. The advantages downstream are obviously enormous. Once a processor knows that, for example, the names of Members of Parliament or the official titles of reports are clearly identifiable, it is possible to assign processing instructions to handle occurrences of this markup as and when they are encountered and according to very specific rules. One such situation might be to facilitate the translation of documents, particularly with machine-aided translation systems. They would need to know, for example, that they should skip real names and check whether there are official or already-translated texts available for other marked titles, business terms or specific vocabulary.

Imagine an author's guide:

'In any press release embed, within the first occurrence of a Member's name, a reference to the linkset appropriate to the Member. This will then offer links to the Member's Web site, a summary of the Member's political profile and create a placeholder for a jpeg photograph.'

All the above cases call for the use of lookup tables or other such tools to allow the user to validate their text and having it automatically marked up as having a specific meaning.

A number of methods are already available in some commercial XML editors, including linking to remote database information or importing or defining a 'local' look-up list for use with a specific schema or DTD. Obviously, if you define and develop your own authoring tools, the specific functionalities required can be clearly and explicitly defined.

Other methods involve the downstream processing of the content. For example, a custom parser could be configured to check, for each text submitted to a central repository, for the presence of certain key words that should be identified for special treatment.

The disadvantage of this approach concerns error handling: if the processor identifies an error or ambiguity, and does not know how to proceed, it will need to throw the document out for manual handling or refer it back for correction.

It is probably better to handle controlled vocabularies at source, but that means ensuring that authors are equipped, both in terms of tools and training, to notice the appropriate 'triggers' and act accordingly.

Keywords

Authors should be encouraged to anticipate how end users are likely to look for particular content. Keyword searches and queries are still the most common approach (although we look at a better, conceptual approach in Chapter 13), so it is valuable to identify and tag keywords in the text:

- If a keyword is defined, that content chunk ought to be flagged for link references

- If a keyword is used but not explained, its use might be flagged to be marked up with a reference to the definition

- If a particular content chunk is concerned with the subject matter of a known keyword, that chunk should be marked for indexing against that keyword

These are traditionally a documentalist's skills. In organizations that have professional documentalists and/or librarians, their functions are being required earlier in the document production process, rather than close to the shelving and archiving functions that are often associated with the job profile. In those organizations that do not, authors should be encouraged to provide some of this information.

Alternatively, if document types are sufficiently precise, certain keywords can be associated with the knowledge mould and be inherited by the document instances created.

Identifying semantic containers

Element names are useful for pinning down a particular type of content, for example in a query using XPath. But attention also needs to be paid to labelling the different instances of a particular type, whether within a particular document (multiple occurrences of the same element type) or in different documents.

In our example of the record of proceedings of a parliamentary debate that we created in Chapter 6, each set of interventions was marked with a unique identifier docID:

```
<proceedings date="2002-11-15"
docUID="P5_CRE(2002)11-15">
...
<intervention id="002">
<speech memberID="0678">
Mr. Speaker, I rise here on a point of order.
<interruption type="04"/>
Are you aware that...
</speech>
</intervention>
...
</proceedings>
```

This identifier could also be used to construct our XML document filenames and fragment identifiers:

- If there was a 'docID resolver' behind a particular Web server or service, the record of proceedings for a particular day could be cited simply using our identifier, thus:

  `http://docs.parl.xyz?id=P5_CRE(2002)11-15`

- If a 'hard-coded' URI were needed, this could be:

  `http://parl.xyz/docs/P5_CRE(2002)11-15.xml`

- If we needed to cite right down to the granularity of the specific intervention, it would be enough to cite either 'the fragment-as-a-document', if each <intervention> were saved as a separate file:

  `http://parl.xyz/docs/P5_CRE(2002)11-15(002).xml`

- Or cite the fragment *within* the document:

  `http://parl.xyz/docs/P5_CRE(2002)11-15.xml#002`

The advantages of this approach are:

- There is a single consistent naming policy for documents as well as document fragments;

- The convention is independent of application, technology or physical location;

- The structure of the reference is predictable. As such, context-specific algorithms can be constructed to meet specific needs.

We will see the value of these approaches in Chapter 13, *Navigation Strategies*.

Emphasis on structure and content, not presentation

Too many authoring guidelines still place an emphasis on presentation:

> *'the date should be left justified, 12pt Times Roman; The document reference should follow immediately below, left justified, 10pt Arial Narrow'*.

The separation between visual cues and document structure has not been made. As we saw earlier, a good XML tool, adapted for the purpose, would allow these content elements to be formatted and presented to the *screen* according to those rules without affecting the underlying stored data.

Authors should nevertheless be encouraged to concentrate on structure, even if they want to use the visual cues of formatting to help them navigate a document.

Authors should nevertheless be encouraged to concentrate on structure, even if they want to use the visual cues of formatting to help them navigate a document. For example, we all tend to use 'relative' comments and phrases when we are writing, for example 'in the previous section', 'yesterday', 'further down'. In a situation where an author's content may be reused in a completely different context, it is more appropriate to use absolute descriptions: 'in section 3', 'on 14 June 2002' or 'paragraph 5'.

You may have difficulty in convincing your users to expend the extra effort in checking text, tagging, linking and registering reference information. You might have more chance if they can see an immediate benefit and that other boring and repetitive tasks have been taken off their shoulders, such as formatting, filing, file-naming, and so on, allowing them to concentrate on the job in hand: creating content.

Registration

Whatever the document, it is important to agree registration details and procedures. The registration serves both as a guarantor of correct packaging and labelling, but also an indication that a document has been created according to certain standards. If all documents have to be created using a particular tool and conforming to an agreed schema, make sure that only that tool has access to your 'container' management system, and that the documents are validated against the schema.

The user should be spared from this tedium as far as possible – there is nothing more certain to put users off a content management system than requiring them to fill in a couple of dozen fields of data before saving a document.

Metadata

In addition to committing, or saving, the document, the registration process should also involve the generation of reference metadata.

Much metadata can be inferred from context and environment. Others can be a simple copy of attribute values or element content within the document itself. If this is the case, the management tool must ensure referential integrity in ensuring that metadata values are updated both within the document itself and in any external metadata reference base.

Access rules

The knowledge mould may indicate a default access policy. This may need to be confirmed by a user, or the access policies could be coded into the authoring tool; The access rights to a document might be extremely restricted – to the authors and their immediate collaborators, for example – when a document is marked as incomplete or under revision. You will need to decide how much of this control and access information you want to code into the document itself, and how much should be managed by the authoring tools.

Management of content management

Clarifying and enforcing clear limits of responsibility for content management is essential. Too many so-called content management tools roll together a whole series of otherwise distinct tasks, skills and responsibilities, blurring the limits between them. It is inevitable therefore to look for a corresponding business unit – a content management department – that covers all these tasks and responsibilities. Such a function rarely exists, precisely because content management is such a multi-faceted area of work.

We saw in Chapter 4 the need for clear responsibilities and, if necessary, an arbiter with sufficient power and authority to enforce those domains. It is worth establishing a Service Level Agreement (SLA) between your IT business unit and content generating business units that lays down clearly respective responsibilities, as shown in Table 4, which shows an excerpt from a first outline of a possible SLA, indicating some of the key areas that need to be delineated clearly.

Table 4. Excerpt from a first outline of a possible SLA

	Responsibility for Contents	**Responsibility for Containers**
Area of responsibility	'Intellectual content' of documents	Computing and tools infrastructure
Document loading	Identification of authors and actors cited. Verification and completion of document specific metadata	Unique ID for document. Performance and availability of content management system tools and lookup tables
Access and security	Definition of categories of access and diffusion and association of default values with DTDs and schema for inheritance to document instances	Infrastructure for the validation and authentication of internal users (authors, editors, etc.) and profiles of external access groups
Publishing	Publishing rules (deadlines, target group identification, 'push' and promotion needs)	Infrastructure for handling target groups, notification systems and rules
Search functions	Definition of search criteria required (full text, by metadata, concept, ontological), levels of granularity, and navigation strategies	Evaluation of search tools and implementation and maintenance of search infrastructure

You should draw up a detailed list of tasks and responsibilities, including procedures to follow in difficult or urgent situations and trigger mechanisms that set a procedure in motion. Such a schedule again keeps the issues clear.

Table 5 shows an example of extracts of a possible agreement on divisions of responsibility in the domain of Web publishing.

Table 5. Example of extracts of a possible agreement on divisions of responsibility

Task/Procedure	Initiative and Responsibility
Creation of a new document/ information typology	Business Unit responsible for authoring instances of new typology
• Definition of document structure	Information Resources stewards
• Referencing and filing rules	idem
• Metadata	idem
• Analysis of authoring tools requirements	Information Resources steward → IT User Support
• Volumetrics study	Information Resources steward → Computer Centre
• Conformity of proposed structure with XML framework	Information Architecture service
• Definition of workflow and process rules	Information Resources steward → IT User Support
Creation of a document instance	Business Unit responsible for authoring
• Initial drafting	decided by above per typology
• Revision	idem
• Approval	idem
• Editorial Procedures	
• Work plan and editorial priorities	Editorial Board
• Definition of access policies by typology	Editorial Board → Management Board
• Web Site coherence	Webmaster editorial group
• Definition of 'shortcut' procedures and criteria for their use	Webmaster editorial group → Editorial Board

Table 5. (continued)

Task/Procedure	Initiative and Responsibility
• Creation of a new 'section' on Web site	Editorial Board
• Decisions regarding DNS and URI conventions	Information Architecture Service → Webmaster editorial group
Operational	
• Definition of performance evaluation criteria	Editorial Board
• Stability and Performance of publishing platforms	Computer Centre
• Security (intrusion detection, audit trails, logging	Security Service → Computing Centre
• Content validation tools	Information Resources stewards → Webmaster editorial group → IT User Support

If agreement can't be reached on any of these areas of responsibility, check first that the terminology and meaning behind them are clearly understood ("Oh, that's what you intend by 'performance evaluation'. In that case…"), meaning shared and agreed, before deciding whether to pass it up to a higher authority for arbitration.

Conclusions

There is no point producing and saving content if you can't find it and use it again. We have become too dependent on the desktop computer and lazily compliant with its file management criteria. We have forgotten that what we produce as 'knowledge workers' belongs to our enterprise. We have to ensure that our knowledge production conforms to the moulds that meet the needs of our enterprise and that sufficient hooks are included for XML-based systems to pick up the relevant information that will help place content in context.

This chapter has described how you should carefully prepare all your content in XML, and use conventions to pick out and markup key elements. You have now to decide what you are going to do with it, and thus look at the whole area of process management.

11 Process Management and 'Web Services'

The desire to do something does not automatically confer the ability to do it.

Isaac Asimov

Introduction

In the previous chapter, we concentrated on the 'encapsulation' in XML of essentially text and text-based content. We have also seen how the XSLT language is used to transform one XML document to another according to a set of rules in a third XML document, the XSLT template.

We therefore have a scenario in which one document containing content and markup is converted to another, based on processing instructions contained in a third. The encapsulation of both content and process use the same syntax and grammar.

An interesting question therefore arises: can we use XML to extend and generalize this idea: to 'encapsulate' all sorts of processes, whatever their nature or origin?

In this chapter, we look at how XML standards are used in process management in the broad sense of the term. We will be looking not only at how business logic and process management can be handled in XML, but also how requests for 'services' – delivered across the Internet – can be made in XML. Putting these together with our actual content – also in XML, of course – should enable us to build a new approach. Integration, not only across platforms and terminals as we have seen in earlier chapters, but across business logic.

Processing

You might have all the ingredients you want and need. You might have decided how you want them presented to the end-user. But you still have to get from one to the other. You need to *process* your ingredients. To do this, you use a recipe. There may not be hundreds of recipes for a particular meal, but generally, how you proceed will depend on a number of factors:

- Cost of ideal ingredients and their alternatives

- Time available

- Volume to be produced

- Tools and infrastructure available

- Skills and personnel at hand

- Complexity of the recipe

In other words, it is not sufficient to have your ingredients and a general idea of how to put them together, but you need a detailed and specific recipe.

Figure 25. Throwing all ingredients together does not make a dish, not even a salad…

In sum, we have a process. We can easily transpose this analogy to information management – we can't throw content together randomly, it has to be managed in processes that ensure coherence of outcome.

Figure 26. …while the same is true of information management.

Processing is the core workload of computing applications. As we saw in earlier chapters, the traditional monolithic approach to information system development and management has been to 'roll up' into a single application all three of these aspects: content, process and delivery. The advent of the 'n-tier' architecture has seen the separation of these different layers, with physical and logical architectures developed to handle each layer specifically.

With such architectures, it is imperative that the data transferred between each layer is understood by each component. XML should be a favoured solution for this role.

In the previous chapter we examined some of the detailed ways that content can be encapsulated in XML, but why would we be interested in encapsulating recipes or *processes*? What if we want someone else to carry out a process on our behalf? Someone – or some 'service' – that is perhaps more competent or more efficient in execution due to proficiency or economies of scale.

For this to happen, we need to be able to explain the process in clear and unambiguous language. This is no different to other areas of outsourcing, in which a principal company lays down in detail the services that are expected from a supplier or subsidiary in a contractual form. With the development of the World Wide Web, content is now accessible irrespective of location, original format or support medium, using the TCP/IP, HTTP and HTML protocols. What then if 'services' – however defined – were equally accessible via the Web?

As application development becomes multi-layered, it is starting to reach beyond the confines of an individual enterprise. Different layers and/or components of the overall architecture can be separately located, developed, maintained and deployed by different entities or organizations. In such circumstances, it is not sufficient for content to be encoded in a standardized manner to be able to be shared across different domains and systems. We must similarly encode our processes, our business logic.

'Web services' is a generic term that underpins the drive to develop standardized methods of exposing business processes in such a way that they can work with any content that can use those processes. Like remote procedure calls (RPCs, a Unix inter-process communication protocol), common processing methods could be stored in a central library, remote from but accessible to a particular application that calls them into service when needed.

This chapter considers different concepts of *processing*, from straightforward data transformations permitted by XSLT, through to the complex use of Web services that are becoming possible using XML-based standards and protocols. Common throughout is the concept of starting with a set of data and processing it to arrive at a second or further sets of data.

Process management

Processes are everywhere in our enterprise environments – embedded in application logic and implicit in our everyday work. Many older information systems wrapped content together with processes and delivery mechanisms in a single 'black box'. Not only was it difficult to access the content independently of the system, it was also well-nigh impossible to access – let alone understand – the processes that drove the system. One IT journalist in the mid-1990s estimated that more than $60 billion of mainframe software running in the USA had no source code. Couple that with often poor documentation, and you have a massive problem understanding an application's processes.

Today we see similar if not identical processes cropping up in different applications and different enterprises. Together with this, we see an increasing need to inter-operate between such applications and across otherwise separate enterprises. Further, we face an increasing demand to be able to quantify the work we do and the processes that we employ. The way in which processes are managed is, therefore, also changing. We demand greater agility from our information systems, greater transparency and less dependency on a single software or solutions vendor.

What is a process?

One of the father's of business process design and engineering, Thomas Davenport, offers the following definitions in *Process Innovation: Re-engineering Work through Information Technology*:

Business activities should be viewed as more than a collection of individual or even functional tasks; they should be broken down into processes that can be designed for maximum effectiveness, in both manufacturing and service environment…

A process is a specific ordering of work activities across time and space, with a beginning, an end, and clearly identified inputs and outputs: a structure for action.

Business logic and business process integration

How is XML to be used, therefore, not just to encapsulate content but also to encapsulate what might be done with it? We can imagine XML input and output, in line with the above quotation, but can we imagine an XML-enabled process?

Content can often only be used if a given process 'knows' what to do with it, or a process bound to the content instructs an application what needs to be done. So we need to reflect on:

- How to encapsulate business rules to generate or trigger processes according to particular variables – for example, a metadata or attribute value– or conditions being met

- What rules should be associated with content at source

- What is actually delivered to the end user

After looking briefly at different processing needs and processing types, we will look at categories of process management, including:

- *Transformation management*: how to transform the content of one XML document to another according to certain processing rules

- *Process integration*: how the actual processing rules themselves are managed, and themselves transformed

- *Business messaging*: how to pass information from system to system without losing anything in translations between one format and another.

We then look at a number of example scenarios that demonstrate the value that XML can play in them all.

Why have other approaches failed?

Before doing this, it is worth examining why other approaches to encapsulating and managing business processes have failed, or have not delivered on their promises. We need to consider both the realms of business processes, and that of business messaging, as a means of accessing and triggering those processes. The main 'culprits' were, respectively, Business Process Re-engineering (BPR) and Electronic Data Interchange (EDI).

BPR

BPR involved the radical overhaul of an enterprise's workflow and positioned IT as the key enabler for a clean, new system. The biggest reason for BPR's loss of support was probably that its often gigantic, enterprise-wide projects were seen and designed as comprehensive but one-off implementation systems. They were notoriously immune to evolution within an enterprise, and thus offered little possibility of incremental or business unit-by-unit change. They were expensive, not just in terms of the actual tools themselves, but in terms of the learning curve and human investment required, which was subsequently tied up with a particular tool.

Secondly, BPR applications were developed within proprietary, although effective, tools: the process definitions were encapsulated within the software and so hard-wired to the specific development environment.

Thirdly, they were invariably developed *within* an enterprise. There was little apparent need and no demand for such process engineering beyond and between enterprises.

EDI   EDI was developed as a specific standard for the exchange of trading information, for example, electronic orders and invoicing, using standard message blocks or 'transaction sets'. EDI didn't fail, but it did not provide the 'silver bullet' of electronic commerce that many had expected.

While BPR sought to handle process management within an enterprise, EDI sought to remove barriers to interoperability and allow processes to work between enterprises. To do this, it required agreement on the format and structure of 'business messages' – documents that conveyed instructions to be executed from one partner to another.

EDI was expensive and difficult to access for smaller enterprises. It was also proprietary, inasmuch as the transport of its documents was conducted over virtual private networks (VPNs) rather than the public Internet.

EDI was bulky. Those data formats that were standardized tended to be global, generic models that were 'highest common denominators'. They tried to contain something for everyone and so inevitably much that was not needed in specific situations. Each set of partners in a particular exchange would trim what was not needed to suit their needs, a process of customization that required considerable skilled investment.

EDI was also too unwieldy for many. The infrastructure model that it supported meant that parties to an EDI agreement could not expose only part of their internal information architecture – EDI required access to the whole model. The only way around this was to replicate that part that you wanted to be 'public', with the consequent loss of referential integrity.

Separation of data and processing layers

Every XML document is made up of elements that consist of content wrapped in markup, for example:

```
<recipe ID="0365">
<title>
Aubergine and Feta Bake
</title>
<ingredients>
<ingredient ID="067543">
<name xml:lang="EN-gb">
aubergine
</name>
<name xml:lang="EN-us">
eggplant
</name>
<quantity measurement="weight" unit="kg">
0.5
</quantity>
</ingredient>
...
</ingredients>
</recipe>
```

In this fragment, the contents are the list of ingredients for a recipe, together with various properties, including descriptions, qualities and quantities of those ingredients.

But of course a recipe involves more than a list of the ingredients. It is also a step-by-step description of the process by which a finished dish is achieved. This information could be simply committed to the XML recipe document as appropriately marked-up text after the list of ingredients:

```
<recipe>
<ingredients>
...
</ingredients>
<procedure>
<step id="1">
<title>
Preparing the aubergines
</title>
<description>
Slice the aubergines lengthways (max. half a cm thick) and place on
an oiled baking tray...
</description>
```

An XML document's content does not have to be 'content' in the normal sense of the word. Here, although the recipe steps are described in text, as in any cookery book, it is possible to make these steps available programmatically.

By now, it should be clear that XML content does not have to be destined solely for the human end user. It can also encapsulate data and information for system and application use. Our recipe XML document could equally easily contain elements that are essentially processing instructions, information destined for machine, rather than human, consumption as in any classic computer program:

```
<recipe>
<ingredients>
...
</ingredients>
<procedure>
<step id="1">
<call>
PrepareAubergines
</call>
</step>
<step id="2">
<call>
PrepareSauce
</call>
</step>
...
</procedure>
</recipe>
```

Processing instructions and metadata intended to influence or direct this processing can therefore accompany the actual data content and become an integral part of the document. Which content elements of a particular document are actually presented to the user will be determined by how each element is handled by the respective XML tools involved. In the above example, reading through the lines resembles the steps of a program that is processing the ingredients.

This seems to sit uncomfortably with received wisdom about proprietary lock-in. If you include what are to all intents and purposes context-specific processing instructions, there is the danger that transparency and portability are sacrificed. In the example above, we can hazard a guess as to the nature of the processes involved but would have no clue from the context what is going to happen and how. We have argued in earlier chapters that XML is not really a programming language, so it would not therefore perform this function very effectively.

An ideal approach would be to ensure that the *description* of the processes themselves is transparent and portable, in much the same way as the content. Doing all the processing internally in XML is not necessarily very efficient. Many information systems rely on using remote procedure calls that send a standardized message to an external process, which then acts on the message and the parameters that the message indicates. What if we are able to invoke a process like this using a message standardized in XML?

Content, processes and messages

The content of the recipe in the previous section is the list of ingredients. Assume that we need to send these ingredients to particular processes throughout the course of the dish's preparation to arrive at the desired result. In the previous code extract, we identified two such processes, PrepareAubergines and PrepareSauce. If we are to separate content and process, then we must encapsulate these.

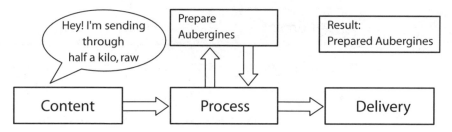

Figure 27. Externalizing part of the recipe, the PrepareAubergines process

In this model, therefore, the process has been externalized from the content and is invoked by means of a message. The message itself contains details of the content to be processed.

However, as we saw above, one of the main problems of process management was traditionally that too many processes were hard coded into a particular environment and therefore were too specific to a particular situation. We could express the same processing need in a slightly different way, as in Figure 28.

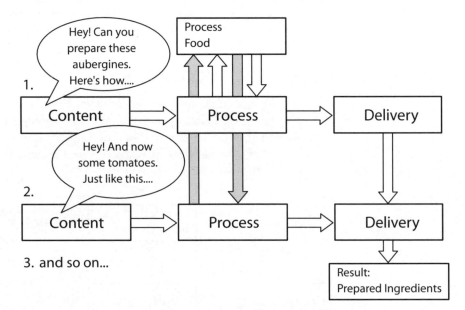

Figure 28. Adding a generic Process Food process

Here second attempt is a little more sophisticated: we have a generic `ProcessFood` process, to which we send detailed instructions and our ingredients.

In this model, we are making a more general call to a multi-purpose food processor, passing more detailed instructions in our message, including an indication of the particular process needed. We might want to go one step further, as in Figure 29.

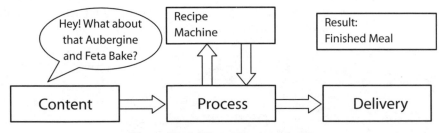

Figure 29. Adding a Recipe Machine

We now have a generic Recipe Machine that will take care of everything, as long as we provide all the ingredients, explain all the steps of the recipe and check that all the necessary equipment is available. In this last model, the whole recipe process is called as part of a broader activity. This situation is tantamount to handing over a basket of groceries and a cookery book, pointing to the right page and stating "do that and have it ready by 8 this evening".

As we will see later in the chapter, XML standardization efforts are under way to encapsulate all aspects of process management and delivery. Before we look at those, we should look further into various processing needs.

Processing needs

A range of different processing needs influences the way in which XML is designed and used for a particular information management problem. Processing can be either of the 'black box' type, implementing a predefined path from one step to another, or can be interactive with a user or other external systems that follow specific processes according to rules, triggers or other factors.

Before we discuss the implementation of a particular processing model, there are a number of issues that we need to address.

Making a recipe work

In the processes that we wish to encapsulate and share, we will also be concerned about these issues, which are referred to as:

- Service discovery
- Service invocation
- Message composition
- Interoperability
- Verification
- Authentication and authorization
- Confidentiality and security

We will look at these issues in turn.

Your first concern is finding a process that fits your needs. To return to the cooking analogy, you may leaf through a cookery book and decide on a recipe for a particular occasion. You will check your supplies and shop to find missing ingredients. Alternatively, you may have a bare larder, the shops are closed, and you want to dream up a recipe that can be made with a limited set of ingredients (service discovery).

Once you have an idea for a recipe, you want to call it up and set to work (invocation). You of course want to be sure that the recipe can actually be carried out in your particular kitchen and does not require equipment you don't have (interoperability). Further, you want to be sure that the recipe is composed in a logical manner – for example with your Grandmother's hand-written notes in the right order – and is comprehensible (message composition).

However much confidence you might have in the authenticity of the recipe or of the authority of the cook proposing it, you will not leave any of the steps to chance. If a particular step requires you to 'bake in the oven for 40 minutes', you will nevertheless verify it from time to time. If thick smoke is coming from the over, you will suspect there is something amiss – you want to be able to handle such errors (verification).

If you are defending a treasured family recipe from some speculative food processing company keen to add it to their product line, you want to be sure that you protect confidentiality, not just by limiting access to the recipe, but also to the kitchen when the recipe is being executed (confidentiality and security).

Service discovery

In our approach, we are proposing that the processes we use within a particular business context be externalized from a single application or system. If this is to be effective, we need:

• To manage them in a coherent manner

• To be able to find them when we need them

Many enterprises have taken the approach of centralized 'process libraries' where all processes are managed together, often in the same location, and are accessed according to a method – often an application programming interface (API) – and a syntax that is common to all the processes. Specific applications that need to make a call to a specific process then effectively know where to go and what to say.

This is relatively easy within the context of a single-site enterprise, but more complex when the processes are managed in a subsidiary enterprise, on a server on the other side of the planet.

The World Wide Web is a useful comparative model. Documents are scattered across Web servers across the world and are managed locally. Global search engines and organized online directories can help us to discover what is available and where. We then point our browser in the right direction and fetch the document for which we are looking.

You should be able to do the same with your processes. The point about 'Web' services is precisely that they are usable across the Web. They use the same ubiquitous naming and addressing approach that is used to identify and access content resources. You can therefore think of Web services simply as process Web resources, as distinct from, for example, content Web resources.

The Web currently uses HTML to encapsulate the content of a resource, URIs to address the resource once available, and HTTP to manage the transactions to request and send the resource from Web site to client browser. Web services are no different, and use specific standards to encapsulate the service being offered, to make the service accessible via the Internet, and a special 'envelope' to deliver the messages between client and server using HTTP.

As with content resources, some sort of 'metadata' needs to be used to describe a process resource, such as what the process is intended for, how it is used and what the expected and intended outcomes are.

Service invocation

Having discovered that there is a process 'out there' that meets our needs, we need to be able to invoke it. The beauty of the Web services paradigm is that it builds simply and elegantly on the invocation method used to access any Web page. In a hyperlink, there is:

- A standard method, the 'nuts and bolts' of the HTTP request sent by a Web browser connected to the Internet using the HTTP and TCP/IP protocols

- A standard syntax, built into the simple `<a href>` hyperlink tag and containing the invocation and the target page to be fetched

We want to be able to invoke a Web service in the same manner.

Message composition

We need to invoke a process with a message that gives the service all the information it needs to execute properly and in the way that the host service is expecting. This could be simply a couple of parameters, or it could be a complex set of information, documents and calls to other processes, for example, to bill a credit card for the use of the service.

Interoperability

When we invoke an external process, we want to be sure that it can be used in our environment and that it responds as we expect. It is not enough that the service invocation message is properly composed and that the service at the other end is properly configured and able to process your request. We need to be sure that systems at our end of the service are able to handle what is generated. Where the Web service invoked is only part of a longer workflow, we need to be sure that its invocation does not block the rest of the procedure, but integrates seamlessly within the whole.

Verification

It is often not enough to know where information has been sent. Some indication is needed that it has actually been received and even that has been processed or forwarded as intended.

This is particularly critical in situations where the outcome of one process is necessary for the successful execution of another.

Authentication and authorization

When information is passed from one user or system to another, it is often necessary to be sure that senders really are who they say they are – *authentication* – and that they are entitled to do what they are doing – *authorization*.

In information processing, it is not always possible to verify personally every aspect of a transaction or a process. Forms of certification are available. Trust is involved. These are possible because standards and regulations are in place that act as reliable reference points for users, consumers, businesses and government.

In information processing, we need:

- To be able to verify the identity of the person or system that is involved in a particular stage of a transaction

- To know that such persons or systems are authorized to do what they are doing

- Some means to ensure – as with a contract – that they cannot go back on an undertaking they have made, or not be able to claim that such an undertaking was not actually made by them (so-called 'non-repudiation').

Recent work on XML-based standards is demonstrating that all these needs can be expressed in secure and reliable XML documents by using the XML Signature and Canonical XML standards and the XML Encryption processes.

Confidentiality and security

As with critical internal parts of our information architecture, we want to be sure – whether we are in the position of client, service or both – that our transactions are safe from prying eyes, cannot be intercepted or modified en route to execution.

Communication between sender and recipient

An essential element of first-year communications studies is the understanding that in order to communicate a sender and receiver need to have a common means of encoding and decoding what is communicated. It is not sufficient just to create a message. It must be encoded in a way that can be transported through a particular medium, and it must be able to be decoded and thus understood at the other end.

Such encoding is usually context- or medium-specific. What XML offers is a generic and standardized means of encoding information that can be exploited independently of context or medium. By encoding not only data, but also the information about how to understand that data, XML offers an efficient means of communicating between parties.

If the parties communicate regularly, and they wish or need to formalize the 'data exchange contract', they can do this by agreeing XML schemas that reflect their data and information models. If they do not, but nevertheless want to make the data understandable to an unknown or future system or user, XML at least offers a generic model to which understanding can be more easily associated than with proprietary data formats.

In both cases, the important concern is that information is understood in the way intended by all parties that use it.

From processes to Web services

Having identified the issues that must be met in generalizing and externalizing processes, we can now look at what emerging Web services standards offer. It should be stressed that these standards still represent work in progress, even if well advanced in some areas. The objective here is not to examine the details of each standard or initiative, but rather to give an idea of how they fit together and what their respective functions are.

Web services infrastructure

Let's visualize – using our recipe analogy – what we are looking for when we talk about a 'Web service'. This is illustrated in Figure 30.

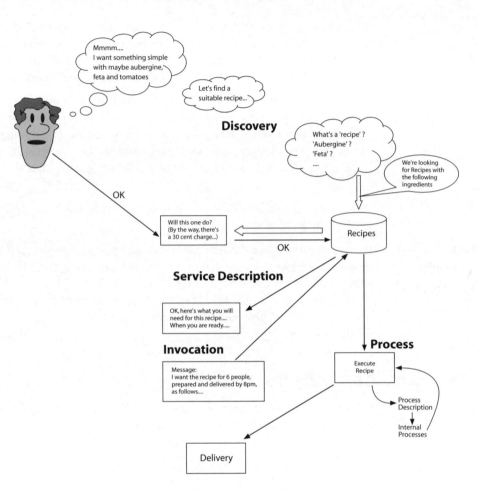

Figure 30. The complete recipe process

Clearly, from initial idea and investigation through to final delivery requires a series of clear steps.

Discovery: UDDI and DAML-S

Two main approaches to XML process discovery are under development. One uses the analogy of the telephone 'yellow pages' – some central, discoverable directory that can be interrogated according to certain criteria of service being requested, by analogy: 'find me all entries under catering, recipes, cookery and entertaining.' This is 'Universal Description, Discovery and Integration' or UDDI.

UDDI started out as a commercial effort and has now grown to be managed as a member section in the OASIS consortium. It is intended not only to organize information about services provided, but also a mechanism for consulting online UDDI registries. Its intended use is for service providers to 'advertise' their services in the registry using a schema and to enable Web service users to interact with such registers to identify suitable services.

The second approach adopts a more 'fuzzy' approach and builds on the semantics of the underlying process models, by analogy: 'if this process takes food ingredients as input and provides finished dishes as output, we can deduce that it is in the business of making recipes, even if it doesn't say so'. This is DAML-S.

DAML-S, short for DAML-Services, has grown from the collaborative efforts of two 'Semantic Web' initiatives, the mainly US-sponsored 'DARPA Agent Markup Language' (DAML) and the mainly EU-sponsored 'Ontology Inference Layer' (OIL).

The Semantic Web – which we look at in more detail in Chapter 13 – is concerned with inferring relationships between resources on the Web. Its objective is to render machine-processable the sorts of assertions that we – as humans – make every day about such relationships: for example 'Yes, this article is written by the same guy, even if his name has changed in the meantime'.

DAML-S is more explicitly concerned with semantics, and it is thus able to 'discover' services from any combination of data known about them, rather than just the limited information set that UDDI offers.

DAML-S intentionally covers much more ground than UDDI. It is thus not limited to Web service discovery, but also supports detailed descriptions of processes, their invocation, execution and verification, and the composition of messages.

Discovery doesn't tell the whole story, however. You may also need to ask questions such as 'tell me what specific services are offered, how these services operate and how good they are'. We need to add here two other issues:

- *Integration*, by which we can be sure that the specific service invoked will integrate within our specific workflow. For example, some services may be described in the same way but actually provide different services, and *vice versa*. Some semantics are needed.

- *Quality of Service* (QoS), by which we can gain an objective assessment of the service under consideration. When you are managing all your elements within a closed system or application, it is relatively easy to qualify and quantify the service being provided. When you are using services from across the Internet, this is less obvious, yet you need such assessments when building your overall application.

As well as integration and QoS details, we further need information about how the abstract model of a discovered process is bound to a specific Web service implementation language.

Service description: WSDL

Once we have a high-level view of services that are available and suitable for our use, our local information system will want a detailed description of what the service does and what input it requires to be used correctly.

The 'Web Service Description Language' (WSDL) provides this information. WSDL is not yet an agreed standard, but a proposal submitted to the W3C, who are currently working on refining Web service description requirements and Version 1.2 of the language.

Upon request to a Web service repository, a WSDL document is sent to the client that contains, for example, information about:

- Specific endpoints that a service exposes, the addressable point to which a request for the service must be sent

- Data formats expected and supported, whether for the invocation message or for the actual content be processed

- Transport protocols used

This information helps the to client decide on whether to use the specific service the best ways of doing so.

Invocation: SOAP and XProtocol

Once you know what a Web service does and are familiar with its specific operating instructions, you are ready to compose a specific invocation of it. As with remote procedure calls in traditional application environments, the Web service will be expecting a message of particular format and content that invokes the service and returns the results to the client.

This message is structured in a standard manner using the Simple Object Access Protocol (SOAP).

Transport: HTTP, MIME, FTP

When both the client and the Web service have collected the required information about each other, they need to agree on what *transport bindings* will be necessary. These are the mechanisms will be used to transport the service content and messages between client and service. Although HTTP can be used, others are possible, depending on the process requirements and needs of the client.

Process modelling: BPML, BPEL4WS and XPDL

We might also find that the service itself, described as a set of internal processes, is modelled in XML. There are a number of possibilities for such encoding:

- The Business Process Management Initiative (BPMI) is another industry consortium that is developing Business Process Modeling Language (BPML). This seeks to go much further and express aspects of process management in XML, using standardized business messages as the key transport mechanism for process data.

- The Business Process Execution Language for Web Services (BPEL4WS) is a commercially-developed modelling language that brings together the earlier XLang and Web Service Flow Languages.

- The Workflow Management Coalition's XML Process Definition Language (XPDL) is strongly oriented to workflow needs and the importance of passing 'transition information' between different steps of a workflow process. Process definitions as such are themselves outside the scope of this markup language, as the actual content that is encapsulated is mainly for coordination and transition data (that is, temporary control data with no inherent value to the process) rather than the process details themselves. It is likely to be valuable, however, in situations aiming at integrating existing process steps.

Message Modelling: xCBL, UBL and ebXML

There has been growing recognition that a lot of business processes can be classified into a small number of generic models or principal business activities. For example, there are probably many thousands of models and structures of 'purchase order' in use every day around the world.

The Universal Business Language (UBL) is an initiative organized under the auspices of OASIS that builds on the successful ebXML standard. Through that work, and its liaison with different standards organizations, including the ISO, UN/CEFACT and the ITU, UBL has a very real chance of becoming a *de jure* standard for international e-commerce.

UBL takes as its initial input the Core Components model developed for exXML and xCBL – XML Common Business Library, itself a major collaboration led by CommerceOne in the USA. Core components were mentioned in Chapter 5 and Chapter 6. The Core Components Technical Specification is a set of standard semantic building blocks for developing specific information models, and is used to build a UBL component library and a number of XML Schema of business documents.

Orchestration: Web services and workflow

A particular development in an information system might involve may tens or hundreds of processing steps, many of which might be externalized. These steps might involve invoking processes from different sources, involving the orchestration of a wide range of online resources.

The entire process will not only be executed once. A new instance might be triggered every second or every day. Many instances running in parallel might need to be supported.

In addition, a number of more specific initiatives offer 'shrink wrapped' solutions, sometimes only tentatively based on XML, that concentrate on specific e-business needs of certain industry sectors or operational infrastructures.

Styles of processing

Processing methods fall broadly into two main models: synchronous and asynchronous.Table 6 highlights the key differences between these models.

Table 6. Comparison between synchronous and asynchronous processing

Synchronous	Asynchronous
Interactive, 'real-time', online	Sequential, 'production line', offline
Works well with HTTP (used in 'client/server' paradigm)	Works well with SMTP (used in e-mail 'store and forward' paradigm)
Uses XML Protocol and Simple Object Access Protocol (SOAP)	Uses XML Messaging
Does not favour bidirectional or object lifecycle tasks	Does not favour many-to-many transactions
Favours lightweight and low-volume tasks	Favours heavy-duty and batch processing

In synchronous processing, there is usually some interaction between different actors in a given process such that such that the overall process can only advance in response to specific actions being taken. This could be anything from simple confirmation by a user of information contained in an online form to a complex algorithm that one system executes in response to triggers provided by another.

In asynchronous processing, each processing step is normally a discreet step that passes control to the next once completed but does not have other processes, users or systems awaiting an output.

XML offers solutions for both types of processing. It is true that the older EDI standard supports both these requirements, but it presents one major drawback: to work, it depends on the availability and use of dedicated Value Added Networks (VANs) that handle all the traffic and transactions.

To complicate matters, it has been the experience of many EDI users that a single VAN does not cover all processing needs, such as that established between a group of trusted enterprises for specific interworking. If one of your suppliers is not part of the same network, you will need to establish a separate VAN for transactions with their organization.

XML-based processing however builds on the ubiquity of the Web infrastructure and the TCP/IP protocols of the Internet, eliminating the need for any dedicated network, often a major cost for such operations.

Dangers

When considering what processes are likely to be brought to bear on any particular content type, some thought should be paid to where and how to store your XML content. There have been a number of scares about the vulnerability of systems to attack because protocols like SOAP seem to sneak application logic behind a standard Web access protocol, HTTP.

It is true that anything *could* be wrapped into a SOAP message, but that does not mean that it will actually be able to do anything. A SOAP message will be expected to act in a certain manner, as described in the message envelope. If it does not, a firewall should be configured to stop it. As with other areas of Web security, it is not by the banning of a particular process that security will be improved, but by the judicious application of security policies and ensuring that SOAP is used correctly and transparently.

It is important to think also about processing overhead: how much processing will actually be involved with a particular approach or method. XSLT is not the most efficient of transformation systems, and will involve considerable transformation operations and processing overhead.

Performance   If you are to invest in Web services and business process management, then you will not be able to afford disasters. If critical processes are split physically between different servers and sites, and possibly different companies, the risks are high if the systems are not performing optimally and in perfect harmony. A slight change in the coding of one process step or a minor error in an XML schema could bring a whole e-business infrastructure to its knees.

In fairness, this is also a failing of any big 'all-in-one' application developed with insufficient documentation or testing. The advantage of the XML approach is transparency.

One of the design principles of HTTP was originally to cut down on the number of data transfers required to establish a connection and download data between client and server. Limiting the number of data exchanges needed to perform a process, and using the full power of XML to encapsulate both the content, intended and required action in the process request and the subsequent resulting return trip should therefore be important considerations when designing and developing Web services.

It is important therefore to establish objective metrics by which to assess the overall quality of service that a particular Web service offers.

Security questions

It is possible for element content, the presence of a particular attribute or an attribute value to trigger a back-office process. In such cases it is vital that a processor is able to identify and validate the source of a particular request and execute it within the context of the requestor.

Coupling the use of such services with strong authentication protocols, encryption and integrity checking can make this secure. XML is transported using the TCP/IP and HTTP protocols that form the backbone of the Web, and these allow XML processes to be secured using the same mechanisms that are used for the Web generally, S/MIME and Secure Sockets Layer (SSL).

It is important to remember that software and application code can pass within a plain text data stream. Until it is processed by a tool that understands it, its purpose is entirely unknown. This provides an opportunity for malicious code to find its way past a corporate firewall. However, this danger needs to be put in context.

'Pure' HTML code sent to a browser cannot harm any process or operation on the client side, as it is a language designed essentially for presentation within in a browser. Problems start, however, when the HTML has other code embedded, for example in the form of scripts that either launch processes on the client machine, or attempt to invoke remote processes that try to access client resources. Security management software within firewalls and proxy servers cannot always identify the nature of HTML traffic.

Although many of the security concerns posed by such scripting languages are known and addressed, there has been considerable concern about SOAP, as it uses the same protocols to access and call procedures residing on remote servers. It is important to remember, however, that XML has been designed specifically *not* to require prior knowledge of an XML document's intended use, so we seem to be faced with a paradox.

Security answers

It should be an axiom for managers that the security of any particular content, whether an information artefact, a process or an attribute, should be managed on the object itself. Content movements and interactions are too numerous for security to be managed at an application level. Security therefore needs to be part of the XML entity itself and not a part of the applications that manage them. Examining security questions only when looking at SOAP objects, for example, should therefore provide a warning that security has been left too late in your information architecture design.

In the case of SOAP, one known problem is however thrown up at the processing level over 'non-validating parsers'. Parsers are not required to process default attribute values defined within a DTD, and some therefore do not. This could cause problems if critical processing information embedded in an element's attribute is assigned a default value that is not explicitly handled and passed on by a processor.

The lesson to learn is to avoid using default values in DTDs, instead explicitly defining them using #required or, better, phasing out the use of DTDs altogether and replacing them with robust schemas.

Work on a number of related standards is important here:

- *XML Signature* is a joint W3C and IETF initiative that has produced a number of standards. It has already produced a recommendation on *Signature Processing and Syntax; Canonical XML* to allow comparison of documents that might have slight syntactic differences but be otherwise logically equivalent, and an *XPath Filter* to help process and sign digitally only parts of an XML document.

- *XML Encryption* has so far produced an *Encryption Syntax and Processing* recommendation that is intended to ensure that transaction processing is not compromised through the use of weak encryption or poor authentication and authorization mechanisms.

- Beyond the W3C, OASIS is also involved in standardization work in this area, notably on exchanging authentication, entitlement and authorization information using the Security Assertion Markup Language (SAML) and the Extensible Access Control Markup Language (XACML).

Role in inter-application exchanges and EAI

XML is rapidly providing the underlying data standards for encapsulating content that is moved between different information systems, providing a basis for content exchange and transparent understanding of processing instructions.

It is important to avoid encapsulating complete transaction definitions within specific XML schemas. We have seen that one of the golden rules of XML underlines the importance of separating content and presentation. This is equally true for separation of content and processing.

In our recipe example earlier in the chapter, we saw the importance of dissociating the processing from the actual data. If the processing needs are too closely associated with the content data model, it will make the particular DTD or schema too proprietary, in the sense of being too tightly bound to a particular process. The emphasis should rather be on developing schemas for particular content models, and separate schemas to act as process models, each based on a respective common vocabulary.

'Political' problems

Many have argued that the sheer processability and transparency of XML are themselves a threat. There are concerns that XML-based processing will allow and encourage data automation in fields never before contemplated, with a consequent risk to jobs, even if these are largely unfounded.

As before, it is important that all users and business units are kept fully involved, so that they can see the benefits of XML's processability for everyone. In the short term there may be resistance, but in the longer term users currently locked in the drudgery of manual data processing and transformation might be better used in developing more sophisticated, but previously inaccessible, data management. Keep in mind the quotation that opens Chapter 2, '*The bane of my existence is doing things that I know the computer could do for me*.' One of XML's objectives is to facilitate that automation.

Web services development

Although still in its infancy, Web services could transform the way the Web is used, moving it from the current medium for delivering content and information to a global platform for service and process delivery.

- The standards emerging around SOAP, XProtocol and WSDL, will provide the foundation for these developments

- The security and encryption standards emerging from the W3C will encourage confidence for all to commit to and develop on that infrastructure

- Initiatives like UBL will offer smaller enterprises the means implement Web services without heavy initial investment

The considerations around the choice of text processing software and the need to avoid vendor lock-in are equally valid for Web services. Products are coming to market on the bandwagon of XML-centred service delivery, but often in very proprietary implementations. The key to stable and open standards for the Web services infrastructure will be the same as for XML information management itself: prior agreement through negotiated and commonly-developed schemas that describe extensively and explicitly the services and processes that your organization needs – nothing more, nothing less.

Conclusions

XIXO (XML In, and XML Out) is a mantra that is worth repeating, no more so than in the areas of information processing that we have looked at in this chapter. If XML content is produced in strict compliance with standards at source and validated against a schema, only valid XML can appear from your content-producing business units. This has the immediate and obvious benefit of easing the processing burden downstream automatically. So much effort – from the manual interventions of the 'desperate Perl hacker' to sophisticated transformation processes – can be saved if enough thought is applied at the point of creation.

One of the design principles of XML is that one shouldn't need to know where and how particular content might be used, transformed or processed. The processing burden, however, ought to be restricted to that which is strictly necessary and be able to be tied into the enterprise's business strategy.

In summary, in order to make XML-based process management and Web services a reality, we need:

- Clear definitions of our processes

- A messaging system between user and Web service

- An agreement on the transport being used

- Effective security in place

- A means of 'knowing' about and accessing available process definitions

The final point brings us to the last substantial area to be considered in the book: that of semantics. In the next chapter, we will see how XML-based standards help us navigate intelligently through the increasing volume of information, content and services that are coming on-line.

12 Delivery Management

Semantic Web, my behind. I just want to order a pizza, not have mozzarella explained to me

Len Bullard

Introduction

We have looked at managing content and at managing the processes that handle and manipulate content. In this chapter, we will look at a further and important area of content processing – how content is actually delivered to end users.

The key here is how the same content might need to be delivered and in different ways appropriate to particular circumstances, user taste and preference, technical and infra-structure capacity or other context-specific criteria.

> ### Food for thought
>
> #### There's soup and there's soup
>
> My three sons will all eat vegetable soup. Two of them will not, however, if the soup contains identifiable 'lumps' of vegetable. A quick pass through the liquidizer and everybody is happy. Same ingredients, same soup, different presentations.

What is the point of delivery?

It's not enough to have information if nobody is ever going to use it. The World Wide Web broke down the barriers between information systems by offering a standard inter-face, the Web browser, through which users could be presented with content from such systems. The browser paradigm has remained intact despite the 'browser wars' of the mid-1990s when competitiveness over functionality risked undermining browser-independent access.

Despite the liberation that Web browsing presented, it nevertheless requires a Web browser running on a computer. The advent of other end-user devices such as mobile telephones equipped with WAP readers, Personal Digital Assistants (PDAs) has presented Web developers with a dilemma. With so much invested in browser-oriented production systems, there has been a fear that similar infrastructure might be required for every different end-user device coming onto the market. The problem is that the number of device types that could be available within a decade my be in the hundreds.

The next revolution for Web technologies, after breaking down the barriers posed by different information systems, will therefore be to break down the barriers between possible end-user devices. This is possible because of the massive convergence of four information delivery and communication systems, as shown in Figure 31.

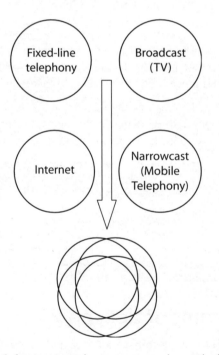

Figure 31. Four key infrastructures have converged massively over recent years

Mobile computing, and in particular mobile telephony, has been at the forefront of this new revolution. If we look at some of the factors that characterize its use, it is easier to understand where the challenges lie:

- *Low processing power.* Despite massive advances, the on-board processing of even the best mobile telephone is still dwarfed by the most modest personal computer. Any browser or user interface has to operate within these limits.

- *Limited user interfaces.* Very small screens, whether text only or graphical, and limited text input through the standard 12-key keypad. Alternatives such as voice recognition are still immature.

- *Hard-coded applications.* The on-board chipsets are less adaptable and need to work properly first time without the luxury of the updates, patches, and plug-ins that characterize computer-based browsers.

- *Narrow bandwidth.* Information throughput is improving and likely to make a major leap forward with the introduction and use of third-generation mobile telecommunications standards. Despite these advances, bandwidth is still and will remain well behind that available to terrestrial-connected systems.

- *Limited client-side manoeuvre.* Because of the limits of processing power and memory, devices are limited in the extent of client-side operations and manipulations that can be undertaken, including validation and well-formedness checks against schemas and DTDs or the use of style sheets to effect transformations.

These factors mean that the content delivered to such terminals needs to be processed before delivery and that the delivered content, as well as requests, queries and other output from the device back to any content server need to be small.

These are some of the considerations that arise from the deployment and use of a single user device type. Taking on several dozen or more device types to satisfy a heterogeneous client base could be much more complex.

The advantage of XML is that it offers economies of scale in such situations: the same family of standards can be used to re-purpose content for any end-user device type. It is no coincidence that the markup language developed for use with WAP-enabled mobile telephones, Wireless Markup Language, or WML, is based on XML. It consists of a specific vocabulary of XML developed and optimized for use with low-bandwidth, slow and unreliable network connections. Using an XML vocabulary enables WML systems to build on the legacy content of HTML-based systems and to re-purpose content relatively easily. Even more elegant approaches are in store, as we will see shortly.

In assessing how to make use of XML for delivering context-specific content, therefore, one early and major consideration must be the processing burden that can be supported at the client. As the amount of processing that is possible and/or desirable at the client decreases, so, therefore, the amount of processing increases at the server end, the point of content creation and processing.

Before looking at this in more detail, we ought to clarify our understanding of end-user or 'terminal' formats.

Understanding terminal data formats

Bureaucrats, lawyers and accountants are dependent on paper records. Laws, contracts, undertakings, agreements, accounts all require it. The universally-accepted form of proof is still a signature on a piece of paper. Paper is the ultimate terminal format and defines the main features of this concept:

- *Intended for human consumption*. It is not designed for computers but for the humble human user. It is tangible, transportable and ubiquitous.

- *Irreversible*. Once committed to paper, content cannot easily be tampered with or changed without those changes being detectable. It is the 'end of the line'.

- *Definitive and authentic*. Until the computer and laser printer allowed easy creation of multiple drafts of a document, it used to be the case that if a matter was on paper, not only would it form the final word, but its existence, coupled with the necessary seals, headed stationery and/or signatures, would be an indication of authenticity.

With the advent of digital signatures and authentication, and the increasing reliance on electronic file and record management, rather than its paper counterparts, this is starting to change. The biggest paradigm shift will come when we move from considering a paper document to be definitive and its electronic equivalents merely copies to an acceptance of the electronic version as definitive and authentic and paper as merely being a copy. This will be particularly true in the public sector, with its responsibilities towards the citizen, business, other organizations, agencies and administrations, as a guardian of laws and treaties and as a reference point for standards and public policy.

This is important, as we should be able to add a further item to our list of characteristics of terminal formats: that they be *disposable*. It should only be the source and original content that it considered as authentic, everything else being but an ephemeral and disposable copy.

The idea of a format being terminal is that it is not intended to be processed or manipulated further – hence the power of a signed paper document. If a document is to undergo further processing, it should not be committed to an irreversible format.

XML allows us to maintain this distinction. The initial delay in producing the XSL standard was in part due to bundling the two transformation issues together. As a result, two separate standards that have emerged:

- XSLT. Transformation from one source XML document to another document, usually, but not necessarily, XML, allows scope in the target document for further manipulation and/or transformation if needed.

- XSL-FO, on the other hand, is primarily concerned with transforming a source XML document into a definitively and irreversibly-formatted terminal format

Content repurposing

One of the great selling points of XML has been that you can easily reuse or 're-purpose' your content in different contexts and for different users. We will now briefly look at the different approaches to content reuse, and the implications and considerations they raise.

Different approaches

The different approaches available to content repurposing reflect the different possible criteria and uses:

- *Batch processing*. This is appropriate when the volume of material to be processed and formatted is more important than the speed with which it is done. This type of repurposing is well suited to 'off-peak' processing when processing throughput may not be high because of lack of performance or power. It is not suited in circumstances when content is updated frequently or a time lag in delivery would make a significant difference.

- *On-the-fly repurposing*. This is appropriate in the case of real or near real-time repurposing of content delivered to a user, usually in response to an explicit request. This is probably the ideal scenario for any systems designer or engineer, but has to be tempered with the realities of the processing overheads it implies in any volume-delivery system.

- *Format-based repurposing*. This is appropriate when producing output in conformity with a known format. The more predictable is the scope and constraints of the target format, the easier it is to develop standardized transformations that achieve the desired end.

- *Client-based repurposing*. This is appropriate when producing output in conformity with the personal preferences of and/or access rights granted to a specific user.

What underpins all of these approaches is a qualitative shift away from the 'stovepipe' production systems of the past. The principal concern should be to maintain original contents in its native format for as long as possible. Repurposing, to be really effective, should be done at the latest possible stage, as close to the end user as is possible both in terms of timing and needs. Original content chunks should always maintain their identity and referencing. Only repurposed content should be considered as ephemeral and disposable.

Legal and political considerations

As content becomes more ephemeral, changing from one invocation of a specific Web page to the next, a number of questions arise:

- Is today's 'on-the-fly' production the same as yesterday's? Some form of time/date stamping of output may be required if content delivered from a specified location such as a Web site URI is likely to change from one access to the next.

- If an end-user downloads and reuses personalized content, how is it possible to distinguish that content from another download of the same content by another user? Imagine for example that you are dealing with highly classified and confidential documents. You may want to ensure that if an authorized user is entitled to print out or copy a particular document, that the document becomes personally identifiable as part of the output process. By associating distinguishing marks with an immutable terminal format, you are ensuring that every copy of such a classified document is accountable.

The priorities identified and processes chosen will consequently have a major impact on infrastructure. More importantly, the range of potential impact is likely to be much higher in this area than in any other.

We saw in Chapter 3 the importance of agreeing a common vocabulary. Despite that, there are those who continue to argue that – for example – using a semantically identical element name in one way in one system and another way in a second, is of no importance, because XSLT simply allows you to translate from one to the other as needed. This is an abuse of the idea of content re-purposing, however, and is both an unnecessary and avoidable overhead. The ability to correct poor design and mistakes should not be taken as a license for creating them in the first place. Rather, XML element names should be harmonized between systems as part of the development of the common business vocabulary.

Personalization

Data has little value out of context. A dull list of names for one person may be a valuable data information source to another. Everything depends on context. The value is realized when the data is put into a specific context for a specific user.

This is the importance of personalization, which goes well beyond simple considerations of the selection and filtering of content to find specific information, although such processes are at the heart of the mechanisms of personalization.

Selecting and filtering available content

It is important to identify the bases upon which selection or filtering might be applied to an available content set. These include:

- *Type of content* – news, research, executive summaries, raw data and so on
- *Type of presentation* – text document, graphics, tabulated data
- *Themes or subject domains*
- *User preferences* – type size and format, level of detail, delivery mechanisms
- *Security and restrictions* – the access rights of the user

Matching rights and requests

Access management is concerned with presenting a subset of the total content available that a particular user or user profile is entitled to access. This subset is not necessary or exclusively a number of documents within a document set, but can also be personalized access to parts within a particular document.

Although 'classic' network file systems and document management systems are reasonably efficient in managing document-level access, they are not able to control access within a document, hence the term 'container management' that we have used for this type of control. With the judicious use of XSLT, it is possible to manage intra-document access, provide high levels of personalization and restrict information access down to the 'chunk' level, as necessary.

It is important to plan how access rights management is executed in practice. This will depend on enterprise policy, which of course should be known and explicitly defined, not just assumed in the development and application of policies at the implementation level.

Traditionally, a user submits a request to a search engine that checks the query pattern against its data and returns a list of 'hits' – database matches – that correspond. Assuming that this contains every document instance that matches the query, but that the user is only entitled to access a certain category of those documents, we have three potential scenarios for data presentation to the end user.

In the first, the search engine first compiles a full list of every hit that matches the search criteria, for example as an XML document with the access rights for each hit indicated. That document is then be passed through an XSLT processor with a stylesheet that correlates a user's access rights with the access policies associated with the content defined by the hits. The output document is then sent to the user in appropriate form. In this scenario, users therefore only ever see hits that corresponded with their access rights profile.

In the second scenario, a similar initial compilation is undertaken, but the full result list is presented to the user with indications of access level. Inaccessible documents might be included in such a list, but any reference to their location or hyperlinks could be excluded from the information presented. This might seem like a paradox. However, many organizations and public administrations are both:

- Obliged by freedom of information legislation to indicate *what* they have

- Entitled to classify and restrict access to certain content

In these circumstances, the second approach satisfies such needs.

In the third scenario, user access rights are included in the initial query, reducing the result set much earlier in the information preparation chain. This reduces processing overheads, but it also allows less scope for search optimization and caching of results. This is because every query is personalized according to individual or group profiles and thus varies.

Whichever approach is chosen, XML provides the necessary encoding possibilities.

Privacy – P3P   P3P, a recent addition to the fold of Web Consortium standards, adopted in Spring 2002, provides a way of matching what a Web server intends to do with certain information and what a user is prepared to accept. A common area is the processing of 'cookies', the small data files often placed on the hard drive of a client's computer by a Web server, and used either to maintain information about the user – for example, personal data and preferences – or to trace previous visits by the user to that site. One Web site might issue and read them, and allow third-party sites such as an advertiser to do the same. If the user is however only prepared to divulge data to the originating Web site, the browser or other client device must be able to limit the access.

P3P offers such data in a standardized machine-readable XML form both on the server and client side. The P3P recommendation lays down the minimum set of data that any compliant Web site or browser must carry, together with a standardized mechanism for adding other data as needed.

In use a P3P-enabled browser or other client terminal limits the behavior of the browser to the policies laid down by the user. It also reports to and, if necessary, prompts, the user, if a visited site requests greater use of private information than that granted by the user.

Questions of timing

There has been an animated debate in the Web standards community over the definition of a 'document', and how it differs from a 'resource', given that documents on the Web are pointed to, referenced and retrieved using uniform *resource* identifiers, URIs.

One valid distinction that can be made comes down to a question of timing: a resource is, in theory, always present. A document, on the other hand, could be considered as being a snapshot at a given moment. Philosophers will tell you that you can't step into the same river twice.

Whatever your particular philosophy, you should think about naming conventions as a way of addressing this problem. One approach is illustrated in Figure 32, which makes a distinction among three concepts of versioning.

We can see here that there is one version that is by definition always the most recent, whilst two other version types represent snapshots at given stages:

* A 'snapshot' version, a numbered or time-stamped instance, gives a picture of the state of a document at a particular moment. Reference to this version is always stable, but there is not necessarily any indication of subsequent updates or versions of the document in question.

* The 'latest' or 'most recent' version is given a fixed reference, even if the file is updated with the same reference to reflect updates in its contents. This is useful when you want to point unambiguously to the most recent version of a resource that may still be under preparation, irrespective of its version number.

* The 'release version' is the public face of the resource, devoid of any versioning information and representing the most recent version released by a business unit.

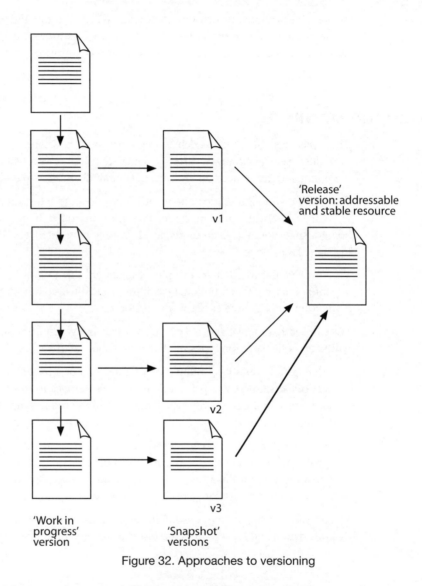

'Release'
version: addressable
and stable resource

v1

v2

v3

'Work in
progress'
version

'Snapshot'
versions

Figure 32. Approaches to versioning

Which approach you use will depend inevitably on your needs.

**Download or
notify?**

Should a document written yesterday be named or referenced differently from the slightly modified version created today? This question raises the whole area of version control and content management, but the important issue for us here is how to manage delivery or retrieval of content over time.

Imagine a subscription management system offering e-mail delivery of documents that are also available on a particular site. If a particular document evolves over time due to revisions and corrections, it will be difficult to know how often to offer updates to users.

On the other hand, consider a notification system, whereby a subscriber merely receives a notification that a particular document is available, but leaves the user to fetch it only when required. In this scenario, assuming the evolving document is maintained with the same resource name, the document would always by definition be up to date and accurate at the time that it was accessed by a subscriber. The downside is that the subscriber may not be able to access the document at the moment required, making the subscription system look attractive again.

A hybrid approach might be to download content as and when it is produced, but allow intelligent re-assembly of constituent parts as updated sections, corrections, and additions become available.

This is why a comprehensive naming convention is critical, as it allows you to manipulate the smallest practical content chunks while being able to associate constituent parts to the whole.

Presentation

Early chapters discussed the importance of presentation as a means of structuring a user's attention, in particular using visual cues to impart certain meaning or emphasis. Presentation provides cues as to the importance, nuance or other issues the content provider attaches to particular parts of the content. These cues will predominantly be visual in screen- and paper-based terminal formats, but can also be aural, such as the volume, timbre and tone of voice used in a voice-synthesized browser.

It is important that the presentation chosen is appropriate to:

- *Content type* – for example, matrices of data best presented as two-dimensional tables, text is best presented paged, whereas program listings not and so on

- *Publisher* – corporate identity is reinforced when visual identity guidelines are strictly adhered to

- Terminal format – full research papers are not a suitable content for browser running on a mobile telephone, while a five line summary might be

- *The user's capabilities* – complex graphics or small typefaces may be of little use if the user is visually impaired or color-blind

Visual identity and entity mapping

If you have carried out the activities described in Chapter 7, *Mapping the Old to the New*, you should have identified the main structures that make up your documents. You should also have been able to map different structures to their principal presentational constructs for different media, principally Web browsers. Our concern is to structure a user's attention through visual, aural and other cues, much in the same way that we use formatting of the printed word.

The 'what you see is what you get' (WYSIWYG) paradigm has severely distorted our sense of functional roles and separation of content and presentation. This was discussed in detail earlier in the book, but it is worth remembering an important lesson.

The format in which information is ultimately delivered should be considered at the start of the whole document production chain. It can even have a positive influence on how you mark up your content in the first place. But presentation – of the content as it appears to the user – must be kept strictly separate from content and its representation – how the content is logically structured – otherwise there is the risk of locking your content into a particular output channel or format.

Conclusions

In this chapter, we have looked at how content, structured and organized at source in XML following a logic devised by the content's originators, can be delivered to end users in many different ways according to needs and conditions of use.

But how are users going to be able to identify what it is that users actually want 'delivered'? This is the central concern of the next chapter.

13 Navigation Strategies

Knowledge is of two kinds. We know a subject ourselves, or we know where we can find information upon it

Samuel Johnson

Introduction

This book has largely focussed on documents and information 'objects', and how they can be created, managed, processed and transformed by human and machine.

Even if the best of intentions are coupled with the best technology, there is an increasingly difficult further issue – how to find what you are looking for. In this chapter, we look at some of the organizational and management issues that arise when we attempt to tackle the elusive issue of 'knowledge management', and examine two final standards that can help in that work.

Information organization and access

Think of a newly-constructed supermarket that we have visited to collect ingredients:

- In a well-organized and signed supermarket, the main areas will be clearly delineated. We should be able to find our ingredients according to the layout of the store: first by category and then, when we are in the correct aisle, by browsing the shelves until we find what we need.

- Alternatively, if there is an information desk, we could go through the list of ingredients with an assistant and identify the exact shelf location for each before venturing deeper into the store. If we are lucky, we might be given an indication whether the store stocks each product and the stock level. This could save fruitless browsing.

- We might be lucky: stores occasionally make promotions and temporarily regroup everything needed in one promotional area. Visit that, and we can pick up everything we need in one go. If we are a regular customer with a loyalty card, we might even have received notification via post or e-mail about promotions and so be able to save even more time.

These three analogies correspond with the principal ways in which we can currently track down and retrieve information within a particular information collection such as a Web site:

- Many large Web sites have sophisticated content navigation pages that offer users lists of contents or menus. These are organized according to classification schemes from which users can choose more narrowly-defined categories of information.

- Alternatively, search engines allow a set of search criteria and/or keywords to be used for a search, creating a list of items that appear to correspond with our request and that can subsequently be accessed directly using hyperlinks.

- An e-mail notification from the Web site might arrive when a new document is published that matches our set of criteria, stored in a user profile on the Web site.

Limitations   There are a number of limitations with these approaches, as well as a series of conceptual and organizational problems that can frustrate us in our search for particular content.

Set Theory   It is an often complex task to decide on the classification of a set of documents or information. The advantage of a Web site or other electronic information system, compared to a 'paper' library, is that although a document may be stored in one location, it can appear 'virtually' wherever required. It can therefore be classified simultaneously under different headings and categories.

This might however make life more difficult for the end user, not being able to visualize the classification scheme clearly, and for the Web site manager, in terms of maintenance of the multiple menu entries. On some sites, there is a strict separation between navigational pages and content pages. Navigational menus can be updated and maintained more easily on such sites than where content is locked into a particular navigational structure.

Noise and silence   The greatest frustration with search tools is that they often are not 'find' tools. Several hundred 'hits' may be returned from a query that do not contain a reference to a particular document that *does* exist and which conforms to the search criteria.

The accuracy of a search depends on a combination of factors, including:

- The quality and range of the metadata
- The uniqueness of the search criteria
- The quality and nature of the pattern-matching algorithms the search tool uses
- The patience and vigilance of the end user

Deciphering search results can still resemble looking for a needle in a haystack, even if the haystack has been reduced in volume. Further, navigating the results usually involves going back and forth between the results list and potential matches, like navigating an enormous labyrinth of blind alleys.

Whose site is it anyway?

The menus and search facilities made available will depend on:

- How much effort has gone into defining and using categories to which different content objects are assigned
- The power of the algorithms used by the search engine to make 'intelligent' deductions from the keywords a user deploys
- The rigor applied by authors, data managers and documentalists in associating metadata and other reference information with the content for which they are responsible

Even with the best search tools, the organization of these categories is still based on the information owner's view of the world. As a user, you might have to get inside such a world view to understand the intent behind by a site's organization model, and become familiar with the terminology and vocabulary used.

There are various ways that such shortcomings can be overcome, and we examine them below. We will also look at a new approach, 'conceptual navigation'. As we will see, this involves navigating between concepts and associations between them – a far more intuitive exercise for the user. This approach builds on the standards currently emerging to support the Semantic Web.

Knowledge management

Data analysis thrives on volume and computers excel in number-crunching activities. The paradox of knowledge management, however, is that 'less is better' – the emphasis is on qualitative rather than quantitative assessments and analysis of information. We saw at the outset of the book that we are not necessarily consuming more information than in previous years, despite the massive increases in volume available. We are, of necessity, becoming more selective.

In the knowledge pyramid shown in Figure 17 on page 144, the objective is to decrease the overall volume while increasing the proportion composed of information and knowledge. Any strategy that helps to select and filter more effectively should be welcomed.

In developing an XML-centric information architecture, we are already putting the focus on an enterprise's information assets rather than on the processes and tool sets that manage them. We ensured that these assets were properly packaged, labelled and stored and we have developed a standard set of reference data – metadata – to inform us about the assets. Further, the internal markup allows us to identify and access the semantic building blocks of any information object.

All of these approaches lend leverage to information access and, ultimately, knowledge advantage in our enterprise. The levers that we look at in this chapter are:

- A series of *resource navigation* strategies, the emphasis being on improving user access to your information resources

- A *concept navigation* strategy, driven by the most recent Semantic Web standards

User navigation strategies

There are four main strategies at the disposal of users for seeking information:

- *Zooming-in*. Starting form a relatively broad base, even from the 'Welcome' page of a Web site, users can search successively more detailed categories until they find the level of granularity for which they are looking.

- *Zooming-out* and 'panning'. In contrast to the above, the user is presented with too much detail and wants to pull back to get a wider picture.

- *Querying*. Whether in the context of a specific decision support system, or because the user knows that there is a specific document 'out there' that they need, an exact match that often required, as precise sometimes as a unique instance.

- *Notification*. In this strategy the user is 'pushed' information about content via e-mail or a similar medium on the basis of criteria that the user or content provider has defined.

It is also possible to follow 'out-of-hierarchy' links: a key word, an association or other trigger leads the user to move outside the path a taxonomy provides, to jump to another topic that may be related to the specific resource, but not necessarily to the subject taxonomy within which that resource is classified. Such transverse links are often the most difficult to develop and maintain.

Despite the power of HTTP and HTML, it is often only the first of these strategies that is exploited in any depth or effectiveness, due to the work of implementing the others.

Classification and sets

Establishing and maintaining a classification scheme is time-consuming. It is an important investment in the architectural design of a large Web site, providing the principal mechanism by which menu navigation schemes are developed. The work involved is still only a fraction of the human effort involved in maintaining such a Web site.

As an information navigation device, a classification scheme supports the 'zooming in' strategy. It however requires that:

- The user is familiar with concepts of classification or taxonomies

- That taxonomies exist that the user can navigate

- That duplication and ambiguity be kept to a minimum

Classification schemes and taxonomies do not always have to be created for a particular environment. Many are already available and freely accessible, often focussing on a specific domain or theme, for example the 'workhorses' of library management such as the Library of Congress Subject Headings (LCSH), Dewey and the Universal Decimal Classification. Others are becoming available in electronic form, such as the DMOZ Open Directory Project, whose complete taxonomy is available in Resource Descriptor Framework (RDF) form, as described in Chapter 3.

What is important is that you have a classification scheme that works for you. Conceiving, planning and constructing your taxonomy is an important exercise. It will give a high level overview of your organization's scope of interests, and often some surprises. It should be taken seriously, not to be left as an afterthought to a database manager, HTML coder or Web page designer.

A thesaurus is a complementary resource to a taxonomy, useful not just for offering a standardized set of keywords to facilitate searches, but also offering synonyms and relationships between terms that help user and machine alike develop search and linking strategies.

Links and metadata

Having a set of key words or a taxonomy is not enough: using 'Brown' as a search word on a Web search engine, for example, will give you upwards of 25 million hits, without any distinction between references to the color and to the family name. Context is required, for example an indication that occurrences of the word in the context of its use as a name, not as a color, are wanted.

Properly structured and used, however, metadata associated with your documents provides a valuable set of hooks to information retrieval, irrespective of content type or format.

Building linkbases

The advent of the powerful XLink standard opens new possibilities for information linking. As links are no longer restricted to the one-way traversals familiar in HTML, it becomes possible to develop 'link sets' – specific and separately managed XML documents that maintain links as a discreet resource set.

These can be developed as thematic classifications, providing you give control to documentalists and librarians and allow such link sets to grow alongside your content.

Link placement

Embedding hyperlinks in content rarely seems to involve content providers – authors – as much as it should. As we saw in *New skills for authors* in Chapter 10, it should be part of a new approach to authoring to reactivate the old art of citation and cross-referencing, encouraging authors to include appropriate links at the time of writing.

Unfortunately, in reality such information is often not available so early in the production cycle and only becomes so when texts are committed to the Web. If you have a thoroughly integrated information architecture in place, in which every information resource carries a unique identifier, it is possible. In theory, the identifier by which you refer to another resource in an editing environment should not differ from the identifier used on the Web site, as we will see in more detail in the next section.

There are three distinct methods for managing the inclusion of links:

- *Manual*, in which the links are hard coded, either by the author or further down the production chain during the 'Web-isation' of the content

- *Query-driven*, in which an author or editor finds a reference to a resource to be linked by means of a query mechanism, embedding the hyperlink code and reference once the target resource has been identified

- *Algorithmic*, in which a text, once completed, is run through a link-management module that looks for occurrences of certain key words, XML elements or attributes and, after validation, builds the links into the finalized text

To be used well, these require an understanding of the importance of managing any XML attributes and naming conventions, because of their potential valuable use as 'hooks' for XPath. As links can be two-way or multi-dimensional in future, it is also important to understand that both ends of a particular link are important. It should be a matter of policy to identify content (or content types) that are not suitable to be the destination of links.

If you have a search engine associated with your corporate Web site, useful information can be found by analyzing data on failed searches. By analyzing user search terms, you can build a picture of what might be useful in your labels and metadata. This is also a valuable exercise in building 'subject indicators' using the Topic Maps standard, XTM, as we will see later in the chapter.

Content identification and discovery

Before we can set about discovering content, however, we need first to be able to be able to identify it: you don't head off down the supermarket aisles without an idea of the groceries you are looking for. Further, users want results and should be able to find content without having to refer to or even know the identity of the originating authority or business unit.

What, then, constitutes a content identifier?

The strength of the World Wide Web lies in its ubiquitous use of Uniform Resource Identifiers, which allow a user to direct a browser to an unambiguous address and retrieve the content that it finds there.

Web sites or proprietary systems that hide or otherwise disguise discrete content identification from a browser using session-specific URIs or other mechanisms are increasingly unpopular with users and business units keen on promoting content discovery. You cannot direct others to specific content if its address keeps changing or is never fully divulged.

Even when the content seems to have a unique address, unresolved issues often remain, and their resolution is the subject of fierce debates within on-line development communities.

The first problem comes in the debate over the distinctions between content, usually expressed in terms of a resource, and a document. For example, is a unique identifier required for:

• Distinct content, or

• A distinct representation of that content, for example in a particular file format or language?

In semantic terms, a unique identifier for the content or resource is required, to distinguish it from semantically different content. In technical terms, however, the unique identifier needs to address a specific physical resource: the URI of the Internet has to point to a specific file on a specific machine if it is to retrieve specific content.

In most circumstances, however, it is a false dichotomy – we need both, because:

- Users choose or identify specific content
- Systems must then use that content identifier to resolve to a particular file

To work effectively, this resolution process needs to be context sensitive, including:

- *File type*, whether HTML, XML or a proprietary text or other format.
- *Human language* – some browsers and servers use a 'content negotiation' protocol in HTTP to allow delivery of a document in the user's preferred language, on the basis of the header information the browser sends to the server
- *Version management* – automatically offering the most recent version of a document unless a specific version is requested

Whatever processes are involved on the server side to decide which file is sent to a client, it is clear that the content identifier and other variables need to be sufficiently clear to allow algorithmic resolution of the initial request.

A coherent and complete naming convention allows such an infrastructure to be built and become operational with relative simplicity. It is also valuable in its own right as a means of:

- Maintaining *semantic singularity* – for example, replacing the file type extension `.htm` by `.pdf` in a file name or URI should yield a predictable result: the same content in a different format. The same should apply also for language versions of a text or versions.
- Avoiding broken links. It is remarkable how many Web sites seem to 'disappear' after a major overhaul. Your application infrastructure should not manage file naming. For example, if your whole site were managed by one system that generated dynamic Web pages with names such as:

`http://www.example.com/example.asp`

you would have problems with sites linking to your pages if the same page appeared as:

`http://www.example.com/example.htm`

after an application migration.

If links are created using the URI of a particular physical file, you are potentially heading for trouble. You either need to ensure maintenance and permanence of the filenames or look for another solution. This could involve declaring public document identifiers and encouraging users to use them, together with, for example, Web services that use the document identifier to collect the relevant file:

```
http://www.example.com/doc?example
```

- Simpler organization – content, whatever its version, format, language, is organized together

Fragments and internal pointers

Once specific content is identified, the additional question of identifying distinct parts within the document often remains. The XML standards offer two main approaches to this:

- Identifying a distinct fragment with a known and labelled identifier, for example 'Part 1' or 'N°123';

- Identifying a fragment according to particular criterion, for example 'first section with a title "xyz"' or 'any element with the name "paragraph"'

There are two mechanisms by which internal fragments of a document can be presented to a user:

- The fragment is identified at the server level, then delivered to the user, for example:

```
http://example.com/document.htm?part1
```

- The fragment is identified at the browser level, within the entire document already delivered to the browser, for example:

```
http://example.com/document.htm#part1
```

There are advantages and disadvantages to both approaches:

- With server-level processing, only the required fragment would be transferred to one client. This speeds up delivery, but if a user is navigating between different parts of a same document, there will be a lot of traffic between server and client.

- With browser-level processing, the fragment identification is carried out after the entire document is downloaded. The transfer will take longer, but once done, navigation within the document can be conducted off-line, as all fragment identification is done locally.

Different factors will determine which of the two approaches are used:

- The size and complexity of the main content. If linking within a document is likely to be a major issue, server-side fragment identification is probably to be favoured.

- The need for feedback from users and applications. For example, many major Web sites use 'click stream analysis', identifying patterns of user actions. If most navigation is performed within a large document *after* the entire document has been transferred from the server, the Web site is not going to have access to such feedback. In any URI browser request of the form:

  `http://example.com/document.htm#start`

  the browser does not send the `#start` to the server. It is therefore difficult to assess what part of a document is being sought or linked to with any level of granularity.

It is clear that the XPointer and XPath standards open the door to sophisticated search, identification and retrieval mechanisms within an XML document's structure. However, support for these standards is not yet mature. XPointer can, for example, refer to ID attributes associated with specific content elements, but without an accompanying DTD or schema and a browser able to validate their use, the client interpreting the specific pointer will not be able to tell which attributes are of the specific type ID.

Language versions

In much the same manner that there are endless debates over the question 'what is a document?', there are debates over language versions.

A key point is the question of whether a direct translation of a document is in fact another document or merely a particular version of the first document. If they are the same, the same identifier can be used for both, and you would simply qualify which language version was required in a particular context. Some browsers permit the user to specify language preferences; if a link points to an identifier rather than a specific file, some servers configured for language negotiation can check a set of rules to decide which file to deliver. If a standard naming convention is used, the whole process becomes easier.

This issue is not always an easy one to resolve, particularly in situations when there is a deliberate lac of correspondence between two language texts. The intent is important, saving arguments over semantics and linguistics:

- If the intent of the authority responsible for a document set is that document A and document B are semantically equivalent, they should be identified as one

- If the intent is otherwise, or unclear, consider different language versions as distinct entities

- In all cases, try to avoid any language-dependent semantic content in filenames and identifiers, in the same way that they should be avoided in all XML constructs

Knowledge management and XML

A growing number of commentators are remarking that knowledge management is not about technology. Once we move away from the relatively safe ground of data into the quicksands of meaning, interpretation and understanding, we can easily lose our footing.

Where does XML come in? Although the really hard work in building a knowledge management infrastructure lies with managers and documentation specialists, XML and its family provide an excellent set of standards on which to build. Even if XML does not offer semantic understanding of itself, it does provide a standardized means of achieving it. Although XML tools are important, XML does not of itself give you the knowledge extraction and advantage that you are looking for.

A central issue in XML-centred information management is to make one set of data understandable in a context other than that in which it was originally conceived. XML vocabularies and schema aim to encapsulate certain terms and meaning in a way that allows them to be exchanged and used by other systems.

In the first part of this chapter, we have looked at different ways in which we can improve our chances of honing down a vast collection of data – better metadata management, better identification of our resources and better access to the information objects. From this large data set, we hope to create a more manageable and relevant information set, from which we can extract the essentials of what we need.

The limits of metadata

Metadata is certainly the key to good information management – up to a point. We face a paradox that we are potential victims of our own success. If the ever-growing volume of data and documents is being properly marked up and labelled, it follows that a rapidly growing volume of valuable information is also being created, in the form of structured metadata.

Given our limited capacity to digest information, we need to be sure that our ability to filter and select ever more thoroughly can keep up with events. With the current paradigm, we may run into trouble.

Portals became the popular in large enterprises or closely-knit information communities as a means of providing an umbrella over a series of independent and separate resource sets and Web sites and a single point of entry to the various resources beyond this entry point. By providing a level of navigation above that of the individual sites, the desire is to make user's navigation easier. However, as the volume of the corresponding sites grows, so does the volume and complexity of the portal. As it becomes clear that external information sources exist that share similar ideas and information territories, there is talk of a 'portal of portals'.

This problem occurs simply because portals do nothing to simplify the volume of information available, but merely offer a more refined way of navigating it. Their involvement also usually stops at the level of the information object or container. It is rare to see a portal that links material on the same theme at the sub-document or element level. Portals also require very high levels of maintenance, and all information resources that are referenced by the portals require stable pointers and addresses.

There is however a more substantial problem with this basic architectural model, and that concerns by whom and how the terms – or keywords – are chosen to describe particular content.

Problems of keyword choice

Humans become attached to a personal choice of jargon and keywords. Imagine that you hear a radio programme discussing the proceedings of a particular piece of legislation or government policy and want to find out more from official sources:

- The official terminology may be refer to a 'committee of representatives', but the press will still refer to the Washington or Brussels bureaucrats

- The official terminology may refer to 'Bovine Spongiform Encephalopathy', but we are more familiar with 'BSE' or 'mad cow disease'

We may need to be familiar with much related terminology if we hope to discover information by browsing the Web site. If a new item, we might be in luck, but otherwise we are likely to have to rely on a site search using key words. Worse for us, the subject of discussion as we formulated it may not even appear in the document we are seeking.

An appropriate search might be obvious, particularly in context. More often, however, it can be implicit within a particular information set. Think of a book, in which some terms appear in the index and offer references to sections in which the actual word is not used, but the related subject is nevertheless discussed. In other situations the subject may unintentionally refer to something else: in the context of agriculture, for example, 'rape' is more likely to refer to 'oil seed rape' than anything more sinister.

We seem to be in difficulties. XML can only offer an open and inter-operable representation of the content of our documents and metadata, but it cannot convey semantics. As users, we still have problems in attempting to understand contextual meaning.

How we can relate terms together cannot be encapsulated in our information typology models. Schemas can indicate that a structural relationship exists between two elements – 'is child of', 'requires element x' – but offers no semantics. The problem is to bridge the gap between subjects we understand and resources that someone else offers, labelled according to a context-specific taxonomy.

Two hemispheres of knowledge

We can visualize knowledge representation as shown in Figure 33.

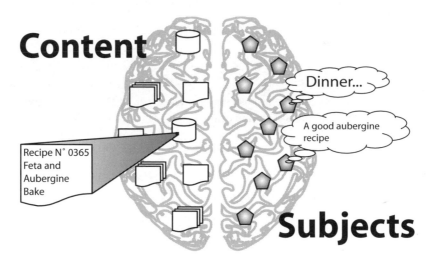

Figure 33. The separation of data and concepts

Two hemispheres, one full of content represented by addressable resources, the other full of vague terms and concepts, related to each other by our understanding of their meaning[1].

On one side of this imaginary brain we find all our content: documents, processes and so on – the entirety of our digital objects, addressable by reference to resource identifiers. These resources are well labelled and packaged. The user has access to the terminology base and classification schemes that will help locate a particular resource, particularly if the guidelines in this book have been followed.

---

1. I am grateful to Anne Wrightson for introducing this idea and sparking my neurones. What I have made of these hemispheres, however, is entirely my responsibility.

This hemisphere represents the domain of discoverable and addressable resources.

On the other side of the brain, we find all our subjects, sometimes vague, possibly ambiguous. Without becoming philosophical, we find here anything we can talk about without necessarily being able to define.

Some of these subjects – 'a good aubergine recipe', 'yesterday's debate on mad cow disease' – may be clear enough for us to be able relate to particular resources. Others – 'dinner', 'a no-confidence vote' – will be harder to pin down to a particular document or reference.

This hemisphere represents the domain of the Semantic Web.

Bridging the gap

The reality for most of us is that we think and organize much of our work around such objectively vague concepts.

When we are looking for specific resources that covers a particular concept, on a Web site, for example, we must make a conscious effort to adapt our search to a particular vocabulary, rather than staying in our personal domain of fuzzy terminology. We do this by making a link between a vague idea and a specific resource and traversing it, based upon our experience and interpretation of what we think is needed in a particular context.

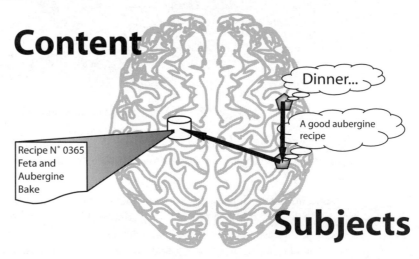

Figure 34. Relating data and concepts

Knowledge representation

It is not this book's intention to offer a crash course in knowledge management theory in its final pages, but rather to see how our work in building an XML-centred information architecture will pay dividends in knowledge representation. To do this, we will look at a few key concepts along the way.

From resources to meaning

Until now we have been concerned with building an information architecture in which resources are created, clearly packaged and labelled, stored and addressed in such a way that they can be permanently accessed. We are building a 'mini-Web' of interconnecting resources and allowing others to connect to it by establishing and enforcing clear and open naming conventions, preferably coupled with an addressable (Web) service.

But what do we do with a concept like 'mad cow disease' if it doesn't point to anything? If there is no resource with any mention of it in its content or metadata, should we just 'warn' the search engine that if the term crops up in a search it should direct the user to 'BSE'? It is necessary to move beyond the world of resources into a 'web of meaning'.

Resources and subjects

We have established a rich collection of addressable resources on one side of our imaginary brain: we now need to work on the other half. We need to establish and maintain a navigable set of concepts or subjects that tell us about themselves and their relationships to each other.

We first examined this challenge in Chapter 7 in the section *Presentation analysis and ontology*, establishing that we needed more than the XML schema could offer us. We also need an understanding of how different semantic building blocks relate to each other. With this, users should be able to follow concepts until they find the information they need. Only then can we pass them to the 'other side' of our imaginary brain, by making a link to an addressable resource.

An advantage *en passant* of this approach is that is more 'lightweight' for the user and the service provider alike – rather than wading through thousands of documents, complex searches and time-consuming browsing, users skim the content via a map of subjects and relationships. Only when exactly the right intersection of interests has been found do they descend to the level of actual documents. The queries necessary to identify the resources that correspond to their concepts can then be built dynamically.

Having a vocabulary for our information territory is not sufficient, however. If we are to share it, then as with schemas we have to agree over intended meaning.

Topic Maps

Both the RDF and Topic Maps standards use similar concepts. However, we only elaborate on Topic Maps here for one main reason – RDF remains concerned with resources.

It was developed as a standard to represent relationships between addressable resources using those resources' metadata.

Topic Maps, on the other hand, allow the creation of navigable maps of subjects and associations without necessarily relating or connecting to a specific resource. If you want to make the leap between the two imaginary hemispheres, content and subject, and link to the XML-structured content on the other side, each subject and association will have to be linked, either manually or programmatically.

A Topic Map is made up of a set of *subjects* linked by *associations*:

- A subject can be 'anything that can be talked about', in the sense of a subject or topic of interest. So both 'mad cow disease' and 'BSE' would be distinct and valid subjects.

- Subjects are linked by different types of *associations* that make knowledgeable *assertions*. An association can be freely defined, for example 'means the same as', 'is owned by', 'votes on', 'is friend of' and so on.

- Associations can have direction, in the sense that they can only be used one way round in a particular relationship between two subjects, such as 'A is part of B', or can be symmetrical – such as 'A is another word for B'.

- Subjects can have *roles* in different associations. For example, in an association 'votes for', a subject 'citizen' plays the role of 'elector' while 'Joe Bloggs' plays the role of 'candidate'.

- Both subjects and associations, together with identified resources, are *topics* that are given names and an identity. It is via the identity that meaning is subsequently attached, usually in the form of another association to a resource that describes, defines or *is* the subject being referred to.

Human developers of a Topic Map make the assertions. This is a key issue in the use of the standard. If Topic Maps are to allow and facilitate the aggregation of knowledge across domains, many assertions have to be made, for example:

I believe that this piece of legislation regulating the management of herds infected with mad cow disease is an implementation of the EU directive on the subject. I am an authority on the subject. I thus assert my belief by creating an association 'implements'.

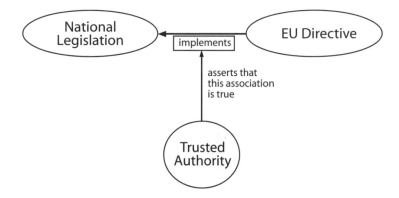

Figure 35. Human assertions give authority to associations

Anyone can make assertions. Some will be true, some will be intended to be true but in fact be false or only partly true, while others might be deliberately false with the intention of misleading. Building relationships of trust across information territories is thus extremely important. Public repositories of 'published subjects' will allow such assertions to be made and validated in the public arena.

The process of identifying subjects, their associations, types and roles involves building an ontology.

Building an ontology

An ontology is a set of concepts and their relationships that together describe objects in a particular information territory.

Our information territory

The first step should be to give a name or expression to all the objects in a particular territory. In the territory of legislative work, for example, this could include subjects for the different types of actors, documents, procedures, activities, bodies and relationships. It does not have to be exhaustive. Indeed, by its nature, a Topic Map will evolve as new terms and ideas enter into the information territory. An analysis of the search terms that users employ can also be provide for an ontology.

By this stage of your XML deployment, you should already have a mass of material available for subjects: metadata types, metadata value sets, indices of document repositories, business terms and semantic definitions used in building your schema. The vocabulary you build under the XML framework is immediately of value here as part of your ontology.

Identifying and defining relationships

As subjects are defined, so too must types of association between them. Some may be very general and be employed in many areas, such as the 'means the same as' mentioned, while others may be specific to a pair of subjects.

Identifying instances

Once 'classes' of topic are identified, such as 'policy area', 'Member of Parliament', 'Executive', 'legislative procedure' above, instances can be enumerated. If value listings for use with metadata elements exist, you can populate your ontology with these entries. If you are using a mandatory reference data set, you should create 'published subjects' of these. These public indicators act as stable anchors of meaning, to indicate, for example, that 'Joe Bloggs' referred to anywhere in your domain is the Joe Bloggs indicated in your published subject.

Developing knowledge management projects

Developing a knowledge management project using an ontology will have many characteristics typical of any large-scale information technology project. However, the great advantage with Topic Maps and XTM compared with 'proprietary' knowledge management solutions is that it can be tightly managed with distinct steps that avoid locking your enterprise into a single vendor solution. Some of your standard XML tools can be used in the development work. More specific tools can be used, but their output should be well-formed XML that can be validated against the XTM standard's DTD.

Your project should include:

- A feasibility study, possibly coupled with a small pilot project, to demonstrate the use of the Topic Maps standard, and in particular, the intelligent reuse of the XML information architecture already developed. This stage should aim to build your business case for investing in this approach to knowledge management, and demonstrate how knowledge can be acquired and modelled from existing resources.

- A requirements analysis to acquire the knowledge within your particular territory, or part of it, and to construct a 'first cut' informal ontology. At this stage, you should be aiming to tap your metadata sets, schemas and business vocabularies in order to build a first list of potential topic subjects.

- A more formal ontology should then be constructed. At this stage you should bring your experts and 'knowledge managers' into the project, the people who can make and defend the 'assertions' that will form the main bindings of your associations.

- A period of iteration and refinement of your ontology, to check it with users and allow it to evolve with use.

- The definition of a process and internal procedures for maintaining the ontology.

Management of knowledge management

We saw earlier the drawbacks of portals – as the information resources base grows, so does the workload of maintaining and extending the portal. The whole point of an XML-centred architecture is reuse, therefore it should come as a relief to realize that your 'knowledge' is going to grow with your resources.

As documents and other resources are created, metadata will be generated and maintained. This metadata in turn will help link – make assertions between – the resource and subjects in the Topic Map. This will start to work in the other direction too – as the Topic Map grows and associations are made between subjects, metadata creation can become more context specific, users being prompted for a greater or lesser number of entries according to the information associations defined and asserted by the Topic Map.

Some experts have suggested following the patterns of work of key users in an enterprise. This can help to gain insights into the terminology and vocabulary that can be usefully referenced, simply by examining the way that such users file documents and label information, messages and files.

Conclusions

Whatever personal terminology or pet phrases you use, you should be able to build a knowledge map and facilitate knowledge navigation using the Topic Maps standard.

This 'map' will only be a representation of your information territory – it will be down to users to establish 'grounding points' to pin down the abstract representations of the map to specific addressable resources.

So the next time someone asks you "Where's the beef?", you can reply in context:

- Not on a 1984 hamburger commercial

- Not with Gary Hart, 1984 US Presidential hopeful, according to his rival Walter Mondale

- In aisle 16, just past the poultry.

Bonne digestion!

14 Conclusions

Avoiding the responsibility of studying a plan thoroughly at the beginning guarantees having to explain its failure at the end.

Anon

Project management

Much of this book has been about management. In particular, it has been about treating the whole approach to developing an XML framework and coherent information architecture as a *project*, not just as a set of loosely-defined rules and best practices tucked away in the minds of XML specialists.

A few key messages need to be kept in mind.

Resisting end-to-end project development

We all have a natural tendency to want to get it all done, to see the whole picture. The 'stovepipe' model of application development should not have been killed off only to re-emerge in the guise of narrowly-defined XML schema implemented by few and understood by fewer.

Keep focus on the subject not the verb – on the content objects, not the application processing. In this way, application and tool development will fit in with the needs of the information objects, rather than the objects being created by the applications.

Using dummy prototypes for management

Establishment of an XML framework is not primarily a technology project, but rather a strategic business opportunity to leverage the full power of your information assets. You cannot afford to lose the opportunity because of insufficient management 'buy-in', yet the work to be done prior to actual XML application implementation is difficult to visualize and will not necessarily show tangible results very quickly. Prototypes have always been useful to gain insight and feedback. They are also an important tool here, in the 'armory of conviction' that a serious information architect needs to convince a sceptical senior management.

Pilot projects   It is impossible to change the whole enterprise way of thinking and working with information overnight. A well-targeted and much publicized pilot project should be chosen for its impact, ease of implementation and – an added bonus – core value for the overall architecture.

Information architecture

As more and more businesses focus on the value of their information assets, the more this emerging area of information architecture will become critical. No buildings architect is going to imagine, design and help create without standards and without commitment to those standards by all those involved in a particular construction. It is no different with information.

Securing data in a transparent architecture   The architecture proposed to your developers must be useful, understood and available. They must be assured that, by following your framework, they can build something that is going to last and fit other parts of the enterprise's data management. They need to be sure that the framework to which they will refer and upon which their systems will build is secure and reliable.

Keeping management focus   A building developer is not going to let electricians and plumbers design the building or allow them to take decisions outside of their areas of responsibility. A chain of command passes down through the developer, the architects, the foremen down to the people who do the actual construction work. So it should be with information architecture.

Maintaining technology independence   However tempting it might be to reach for an 'off the shelf' all-in-one solution, resist it if you can. 'Off the shelf' is rarely 'out of the box' – there are always customizations, preferences and configurations to be done. In addition, once the tool is out of the box, it is also likely to be out of the hands of management.

The standards battle

XML applications today number in the thousands, with widespread redundancy as competing groups struggle to agree a common vocabulary for their particular territory. The clean, standards-based world of XML suddenly seems like a Tower of Babel. XML has become a victim of its own success. Because anyone can develop a specific XML implementation, anyone does. The XML standard does not prescribe a mandatory method or process for arriving at a new application.

The W3C rightly points out that their function is to act as a stable reference point for standards, and not to dictate on their implementation or use, in the same way as does the ISO. However, the success of the OASIS standard process for developing XML applications has made it possibly *too* easy for a handful of active players to form a new standard. No-one checks and compares, encourages or forces cooperation to avoid overlap, or to revise scope to exclude an 'information territory' that has already been claimed. At the same time, some standards, such as XQuery, Xforms and XPointer from W3C or UBL and Relax-NG from OASIS, are eagerly awaited. Some might claim that both organizations were dispersing themselves too much.

Some have pleaded for a regulatory authority for XML, akin to the 'maintenance agencies' that come with many ISO standards. Others suggest that we simply need an agreed methodology for developing standards, akin to the Universal Business Language's proposed design rules.

There is however another approach, one that takes account of all our human shortcomings. An interesting and valuable project would be to direct the power of the Topic Maps standard towards establishing a clear 'mother of all maps': a map of the information territories defined and declared as specific XML markup languages and published schema. The developers and maintainers of the different standards identified would be able to make assertions about the semantic equivalence of items appearing in different languages, helping to take some of the sting out of choosing between them, or those parts that are useful. Such a map would allow a more sanguine assessment of the need for another XML markup language.

This last idea might be just an idle thought over a final coffee, but it highlights one central concern of this book: if the power of XML has not yet been fully unleashed, it has been because XML has been over-hyped as a *technology*, and even offered as a solution to problems that it cannot possibly address. Its true power in the long term, however, will be as a universal business tool and corporate asset.

XML must move center-stage and be integrated into the earliest considerations of information system design. This is where information architecture will come into its own: an open, standards-based and stable architecture for the most complex systems imaginable. This is information architecture with XML.

Reference

This part of the book presents a guide to all the key standards and specifications that make up the XML Family. It is split into two parts: those standards that are the responsibility of the World Wide Web Consortium (W3C), including the core XML standard itself, and those standards created and managed by other bodies or initiatives.

W3C recommendations

Organization of references

All the references in this section are to work undertaken under the auspices of the W3C. Each entry indicates the title, an indication of status of Recommendation, Proposed Recommendation or Candidate Recommendation as of January 2003, the editors/ authors, the publication date and the main URI to the reference. Text in quotation marks is from the respective reference, taken from the abstract introducing the work.

Recommendations

This is the status that represents the W3C equivalent of a standard:

'A Recommendation is work that represents consensus within W3C and has the Director's stamp of approval. W3C considers that the ideas or technology specified by a Recommendation are appropriate for widespread deployment and promote W3C's mission.'

Proposed recommendations

This is an indication that the work is probably approaching completion and that it has some demonstrable implementations to show that it actually works:

'A Proposed Recommendation is work that (1) represents consensus within the group that produced it and (2) has been proposed by the Director to the Advisory Committee for review.'

Candidate recommendations

This is an indication that the work now reflects the objectives it set out to achieve and is a call for implementation experience:

'A Candidate Recommendation is work that has received significant review from its immediate technical community. It is an explicit call to those outside of the related Working Groups or the W3C itself for implementation and technical feedback.'

The main W3C specifications that are covered in this book are listed below, arranged alphabetically by their usual acronym.

Canonical XML Version 1.0

Recommendation:

15 March 2001
John Boyer

http://www.w3.org/TR/xml-c14n

'Any XML document is part of a set of XML documents that are logically equivalent within an application context, but which vary in physical representation based on syntactic changes permitted by XML 1.0 [XML] and Namespaces in XML [Names]. This specification describes a method for generating a physical representation, the canonical form, of an XML document that accounts for the permissible changes. Except for limitations regarding a few unusual cases, if two documents have the same canonical form, then the two documents are logically equivalent within the given application context.'

Cascading Style Sheets, Level 1 (CSS1) Specification

Recommendation:

First published 17 December 1996
Revised 11 January 1999
Håkon Wium Lie, Bert Bos

http://www.w3.org/TR/REC-CSS1

'This document specifies level 1 of the Cascading Style Sheet mechanism (CSS1). CSS1 is a simple style sheet mechanism that allows authors and readers to attach style (e.g. fonts, colors and spacing) to HTML documents. The CSS1 language is human readable and writable, and expresses style in common desktop publishing terminology.

One of the fundamental features of CSS is that style sheets cascade; authors can attach a preferred style sheet, while the reader may have a personal style sheet to adjust for human or technological handicaps. The rules for resolving conflicts between different style sheets are defined in this specification.'

**Cascading
Style Sheets,
Level 2 (CSS2)
Specification**

Recommendation:

12 May 1998
Bert Bos, Håkon Wium Lie, Chris Lilley, Ian Jacobs

`http://www.w3.org/TR/REC-CSS2`

*'This specification defines Cascading Style Sheets, level 2 (CSS2). CSS2 is a style
sheet language that allows authors and users to attach style (e.g., fonts, spacing,
and aural cues) to structured documents (e.g., HTML documents and XML
applications). By separating the presentation style of documents from the content of
documents, CSS2 simplifies Web authoring and site maintenance.*

*CSS2 builds on CSS1 (see [CSS1]) and, with very few exceptions, all valid CSS1
style sheets are valid CSS2 style sheets. CSS2 supports media-specific style sheets
so that authors may tailor the presentation of their documents to visual browsers,
aural devices, printers, braille devices, handheld devices, etc. This specification
also supports content positioning, downloadable fonts, table layout, features for
internationalization, automatic counters and numbering, and some properties
related to user interface.'*

**Document
Object Model**

This is now an area of activity for the W3C, rather than simply a single recommendation. The main activity is described at:

`http://www.w3.org/DOM/`

*'The Document Object Model is a platform- and language-neutral interface that
will allow programs and scripts to dynamically access and update the content,
structure and style of documents. The document can be further processed and the
results of that processing can be incorporated back into the presented page.'*

There are currently seven different DOM recommendations, covering different aspects
of DOM use:

- Level 1

  `http://www.w3.org/TR/REC-DOM-Level-1`

- Level 2 Views Specification

  `http://www.w3.org/TR/DOM-Level-2-Views`

- Level 2 Traversal and Range Specification

  `http://www.w3.org/TR/DOM-Level-2-Traversal-Range/`

- Level 2 Style Specification

  `http://www.w3.org/TR/DOM-Level-2-Style/`

- Level 2 Events Specification

  `http://www.w3.org/TR/DOM-Level-2-Events/`

- Level 2 Core Specification

  `http://www.w3.org/TR/DOM-Level-2-Core/`

- Level 2 HTML Specification

  `http://www.w3.org/TR/DOM-Level-2-HTML/`

Mathematical Markup Language (MathML) Version 2.0

Recommendation:

21 February 2001
David Carlisle, Patrick Ion, Robert Miner, Nico Poppelier

`http://www.w3.org/TR/MathML2/`

'MathML is an XML application for describing mathematical notation and capturing both its structure and content. The goal of MathML is to enable mathematics to be served, received, and processed on the World Wide Web, just as HTML has enabled this functionality for text.

'This specification of the markup language MathML is intended primarily for a readership consisting of those who will be developing or implementing renderers or editors using it, or software that will communicate using MathML as a protocol for input or output. It is not a User's Guide but rather a reference document.'

Namespaces in XML

Recommendation:

14 January 1999
Tim Bray, Dave Hollander, Andrew Layman

`http://www.w3.org/TR/REC-xml-names`

Also newer Version 1.1, currently in Candidate Recommendation phase, until mid February 2003:

18 December 2002
Dave Hollander, Andrew Layman, Richard Tobin, Tim Bray

`http://www.w3.org/TR/xml-names11/`

OWL: the Web Ontology Language

This is in very early stages, without even any draft specification. The intention is to build on the earlier DAML and OIL standards (see next section). For more information, follow progress at:

`http://www.w3.org/TR/owl-ref/`

'The World Wide Web as it is currently constituted resembles a poorly mapped

geography. Our insights into the documents and capabilities available are based on keyword searches, abetted by clever use of document connectivity and usage patterns. The sheer mass of this data is unmanageable without powerful tool support. In order to map this terrain more precisely, computational agents require machine-readable descriptions of the content and capabilities of Web accessible resources...

'The Web Ontology Language (OWL) is intended to provide a language that can be used to describe the classes and relations between them that are inherent in Web documents and applications.'

Resource Description Framework (RDF) Model and Syntax Specification

Recommendation:

22 February 1999
Ora Lassila, Ralph R. Swick

`http://www.w3.org/TR/REC-rdf-syntax`

'The World Wide Web was originally built for human consumption, and although everything on it is machine-readable, this data is not machine-understandable. It is very hard to automate anything on the Web, and because of the volume of information the Web contains, it is not possible to manage it manually. The solution proposed here is to use metadata to describe the data contained on the Web...

'Resource Description Framework (RDF) is a foundation for processing metadata; it provides interoperability between applications that exchange machine-understandable information on the Web. RDF emphasizes facilities to enable automated processing of Web resources.'

SMIL™

SMIL is a trademark of the World Wide Web Consortium, registered and held by its host institutions MIT, ERCIM and Keio.

SMIL is now a series of related standards, managed under the 'Synchronized Multimedia' activity of the W3C:

'The Synchronized Multimedia Integration Language (SMIL, pronounced "smile") enables simple authoring of interactive audiovisual presentations. SMIL is typically used for 'rich media'/multimedia presentations which integrate streaming audio and video with images, text or any other media type. SMIL is an easy-to-learn HTML-like language, and many SMIL presentations are written using a simple text-editor.'

SMIL currently consists of three recommendations:

- SMIL 1.0 Specification

  `http://www.w3.org/TR/REC-smil/`

- SMIL 2.0 Specification

  `http://www.w3.org/TR/smil20/`

- SMIL Animation

  `http://www.w3.org/TR/smil-animation/`

SOAP Version 1.2

Currently in Candidate Recommendation phase until 24 January 2003, for both sections:

19 December 2002
Martin Gudgin, Marc Hadley, Noah Mendelsohn, Jean-Jacques Moreau,
Henrik Frystyk Nielsen

- Part 1: Messaging Framework

  `http://www.w3.org/TR/soap12-part1/`

- Part 2: Adjuncts

  `http://www.w3.org/TR/soap12-part2/`

- There is also a helpful 'Part 0: Primer' at:

  `http://www.w3.org/TR/soap12-part0/`

  'SOAP Version 1.2 is a lightweight protocol intended for exchanging structured information in a decentralized, distributed environment ... [that] defines, using XML technologies, an extensible messaging framework containing a message construct that can be exchanged over a variety of underlying protocols...'

Scalable Vector Graphics (SVG) 1.1 Specification

Recommendation:

14 January 2003
Jon Ferraiolo, FUJISAWA Jun, Dean Jackson

`http://www.w3.org/TR/SVG11/`

'This specification defines the features and syntax for Scalable Vector Graphics (SVG) Version 1.1, a modularized language for describing two-dimensional vector and mixed vector/raster graphics in XML'

In addition, there is an accompanying recommendation defining profiles for the use of SVG in cellular phones and PDAs:

- Mobile SVG Profiles: SVG Tiny and SVG Basic:

  `http://www.w3.org/TR/SVGMobile/`

XML Inclusions (XInclude) Version 1.0

Candidate Recommendation phase ended in November 2002:

17 September 2002
Jonathan Marsh, David Orchard

`http://www.w3.org/TR/xinclude/`

'*Specifies a processing model and syntax for general purpose inclusion. Inclusion is accomplished by merging a number of XML information sets into a single composite Infoset. Specification of the XML documents (infosets) to be merged and control over the merging process is expressed in XML-friendly syntax (elements, attributes, URI references)*'

XML Linking Language (XLink) Version 1.0

Recommendation:

27 June 2001
Steven DeRose, Eve Maler, David Orchard

`http://www.w3.org/TR/xlink/`

'*Allows elements to be inserted into XML documents in order to create and describe links between resources. It uses XML syntax to create structures that can describe links similar to the simple unidirectional hyperlinks of today's HTML, as well as more sophisticated links*'

Extensible Markup Language (XML) 1.1

Currently in Candidate Recommendation phase, ending mid-February 2003:

15 October 2002
John Cowan

`http://www.w3.org/TR/xml11/`

The original XML standard presented limitations for the naming of XML elements, an issue that was addressed under the 'Blueberry Requirements' This proposed update consists of a number of updates to the original standard.

XML Base

Recommendation:

27 June 2001
Jonathan Marsh

`http://www.w3.org/TR/xmlbase/`

Similar in function and use to the HTML BASE tag, this recommendation specifies a single attribute `xml:base`. This can be used with XLink, XML Infoset or indeed any XML recommendation, to specify a 'starting' URI in a document against which relative links can be resolved.

XML Fragments   Candidate Recommendation:

> 12 February 2001
> Paul Grosso, Daniel Veillard
>
> `http://www.w3.org/TR/xml-fragment`
>
> *'The XML standard supports logical documents composed of possibly several entities. It may be desirable to view or edit one or more of the entities or parts of entities while having no interest, need, or ability to view or edit the entire document. The problem, then, is how to provide to a recipient of such a fragment the appropriate information about the context that fragment had in the larger document that is not available to the recipient'*

This work is currently blocked and has not advanced to Proposed recommendation. See also XPointer on page 303.

XML
Information Set
(InfoSet)

Recommendation:

> 24 October 2001
> John Cowan, Richard Tobin
>
> `http://www.w3.org/TR/xml-infoset/`

This recommendation describes a formal model for the building blocks (or 'information items') of any given XML document that can be used by any application that requires such information.

XML Schema
Part 1:
Structures

Recommendation:

> 2 May 2001
> Henry S. Thompson, David Beech, Murray Maloney, Noah Mendelsohn
>
> `http://www.w3.org/TR/xmlschema-1/`
>
> *'[The] XML Schema definition language... offers facilities for describing the structure and constraining the contents of XML 1.0 documents, including those which exploit the XML Namespace facility. The schema language, which is itself represented in XML 1.0 and uses namespaces, substantially reconstructs and considerably extends the capabilities found in XML 1.0 document type definitions (DTDs).'*

This specification works together with XML Schema Part 2: Datatypes, described below.

XML Schema Part 2: Datatypes

Recommendation:

2 May 2001
Paul V. Biron, Ashok Malhotra

`http://www.w3.org/TR/xmlschema-2/`

Part 2 of the specification of the XML Schema language:

'Defines facilities for defining datatypes to be used in XML Schemas as well as other XML specifications. The datatype language, which is itself represented in XML 1.0, provides a superset of the capabilities found in XML 1.0 document type definitions (DTDs) for specifying datatypes on elements and attributes'

XML Path Language (XPath) Version 1.0

Recommendation:

16 November 1999
James Clark, Steven DeRose

`http://www.w3.org/TR/xpath`

'XPath is a language for addressing parts of an XML document, designed to be used by both XSLT and XPointer'

XPointer

The 'original' XPointer proposal came to a halt at the Candidate Recommendation stage due to a lack of implementation feedback. It was then re-launched as four separate proposals, a 'Framework' defining the language and its general use and a number of 'schemes' for its use in particular contexts:

- XPointer Framework

  Proposed Recommendation, review period ended in December 2003:

  13 November 2002
  Paul Grosso, Eve Maler, Jonathan Marsh, Norman Walsh

  `http://www.w3.org/TR/xptr-framework/`

  'An extensible system for XML addressing that underlies additional XPointer scheme specifications.'

  The Framework is intended to be used as a basis for fragment identification.

- XPointer element() Scheme

  Proposed Recommendation, review period ended in December 2003:

  13 November 2002
  Paul Grosso, Eve Maler, Jonathan Marsh, Norman Walsh

  `http://www.w3.org/TR/xptr-element/`

  'Intended to be used with the XPointer Framework [XPtrFrame] to allow basic addressing of XML elements.'

- XPointer xmlns() Scheme

  Proposed Recommendation, review period ended in December 2003:

  13 November 2002
  Steven J. DeRose, Ron Daniel Jr., Eve Maler, Jonathan Marsh

  `http://www.w3.org/TR/xptr-xmlns/`

  '[Intended] to allow correct interpretation of namespace prefixes in pointers.'

- XPointer xpointer() Scheme

  This is only a working draft at present:

  19 December 2002
  Steven DeRose, Eve Maler, Ron Daniel Jr.

  `http://www.w3.org/TR/xptr-xpointer/`

  '[Intended] to provide a high level of functionality for addressing portions of XML documents. It is based on XPath, and adds the ability to address strings, points, and ranges in accordance with definitions provided in DOM Level 2: Traversal and Range Specification.'

XProtocol   Work on this as a specific proposal is in its infancy. There is at present a working draft of a XML Protocol (XMLP) Requirements document at:

`http://www.w3.org/TR/xmlp-reqs`

More substantially, there is work underway looking at the wider issue of protocols and Web services:

`http://www.w3.org/2000/xp/Group/`

XQuery

A number of working drafts are under consideration, from a basic definition of the proposed query language to more specific issues regarding data models, formal semantics and query use cases. See:

http://www.w3.org/XML/Query

Extensible Stylesheet Language (XSL)

XSL was originally defined as *'a language for expressing stylesheets'* in XML. This original project was split into two: *'a language for transforming XML documents'* and *'an XML vocabulary for specifying formatting semantics'*. This gave rise to two specifications:

* XSL Transformations (XSLT) Version 1.0

  Recommendation:

  16 November 1999
  James Clark

  http://www.w3.org/TR/xslt

  'This specification defines the syntax and semantics of XSLT, which is a language for transforming XML documents into other XML documents.'

* Extensible Stylesheet Language (XSL) Version 1.0 or XSL-FO

  Recommendation:

  15 October 2001
  Sharon Adler, Anders Berglund, Jeff Caruso, Stephen Deach, Tony Graham,
  Paul Grosso, Eduardo Gutentag, Alexander Milowski, Scott Parnell,
  Jeremy Richman, Steve Zilles

  http://www.w3.org/TR/xsl/

  To avoid confusion with the earlier, joint work, and to distinguish it from the XSLT standard, this is often referred to as XSL-FO (for 'Formatting Objects').

  'An XSL stylesheet specifies the presentation of a class of XML documents by describing how an instance of the class is transformed into an XML document that uses the formatting vocabulary'

WSDL

Originally submitted to the W3C as a draft proposal, the Web Service Description Language is now being formalized by the consortium's Web Services Description Working Group. It is intended to be *'an XML format for describing network services as a set of endpoints operating on messages containing either document-oriented or proce-*

dure-oriented information'. A related 'Bindings' proposal will describe how WSDL can be used with SOAP 1.2.

```
http://www.w3.org/2002/ws/desc/
```

Other standards

Other standards mentioned in the book are listed below. The citations come from the basic information presenting each standard, as provided on the reference Web sites indicated.

CCTS   The Core Components Technical Specification of exXML presents:

> '...*a methodology for developing a common set of semantic building blocks that represent the general types of business data in use today and provides for the creation of new business vocabularies and restructuring of existing business vocabularies.'*

Version v1.90 has been sent for implementation verification using a standard UN/CEFACT process.

The latest addressable version is v1.85 at:

```
http://www.unece.org/cefact/ebxml/ccts185.pdf
```

with a 'cache' of version v1.90 on the OASIS/Cover Pages site at:

```
http://xml.coverpages.org/CCTS-V1pt90.zip
```

DAML   The DARPA Agent Markup Language is being developed as an extension to XML and the Resource Description Framework (RDF). According to the daml.org Web site:

> '*XML has a limited capability to describe the relationships (schemas or ontologies) with respect to objects. The use of ontologies provides a very powerful way to describe objects and their relationships to other objects.'*

```
http://www.daml.org
```

DAML-S   DAML-S is *'a DAML+OIL ontology for describing the properties and capabilities of Web services'*. For a presentation, see:

```
http://www.daml.org/services/ISWC2002-DAMLS.pdf
```

DCMES, DCMI or DC

The Dublin Core Metadata Initiative has produced and continually updates a 'core' set of metadata elements and refinements. They represent the 'best of breed' as regards a choice for a minimum set of metadata to be associated with any resource.

`http://www.dublincore.org/usage/terms/dc/current-elements/`

DTD

The Document Type Description, precursor of the XML Schema is strictly speaking not a standard in its own right. It is referred to in the main XML specification and conforms with the concept defined in the Standard Generalized Markup Language (SGML), of which both HTML and XML are specific applications.

`http://www.w3.org/TR/2000/REC-xml-20001006#dt-doctype`

ebXML

Jointly sponsored by UN/CEFACT and OASIS, ebXML is a membership-based consortium that is responsible for a series of standards, notably the Registry Information Model and Registry Services specification, the Core Components Model mentioned above (CCTS) and the Technical Architecture specification. It has become a Member Section of OASIS.

`http://www.ebxml.org/`

MARC

'The MARC formats are standards for the representation and communication of bibliographic and related information in machine-readable form and are maintained by the US Library of Congress.'

`http://www.loc.gov/marc/`

OIL

The Ontology Inference Layer is:

'...a proposal for a Web-based representation and inference layer for ontologies.'

`http://www.ontoknowledge.org/oil/`

Relax-NG

'The key features of RELAX-NG are that it is simple, easy to learn, uses XML syntax, does not change the information set of an XML document, supports XML namespaces, treats attributes uniformly with elements so far as possible, has unrestricted support for unordered content, has unrestricted support for mixed content, has a solid theoretical basis, and can partner with a separate datatyping language.'

`http://www.oasis-open.org/committees/relax-ng/`

SAX

'SAX is the Simple API for XML, originally a Java-only API. SAX was the first widely adopted API for XML in Java, and is a 'de facto' standard. The current version is SAX 2.0.1, and there are versions for several programming language environments other than Java.'

http://www.saxproject.org/

Topic Maps   The ISO Topic Maps standard, ISO/IEC 13250, second edition, May 2002:

'...provides a standardized notation for interchangeably representing information about the structure of information resources used to define topics, and the relationships between topics. A set of one or more interrelated documents that employs the notation defined by this International Standard is called a topic map.'

http://www.y12.doe.gov/sgml/sc34/document/0322_files/iso13250-2nd-ed-v2.pdf

UBL   The Universal Business Language is a set of proposals, promoted by the OASIS Technical Committee of that name, which aim to:

'...develop a standard library of XML business documents (purchase orders, invoices, etc.) [and] ...design a mechanism for the generation of context-specific business schemas through the application of transformation rules to the common UBL source library. UBL is intended to become an international standard for electronic commerce freely available to everyone without licensing or other fees.'

http://www.oasis-open.org/committees/ubl/

UDDI   The Universal Description, Discovery and Integration protocol:

'...creates a standard interoperable platform that enables companies and applications to quickly, easily, and dynamically find and use Web services over the Internet. UDDI also allows operational registries to be maintained for different purposes in different contexts.'

It is managed by uddi.org, which is now a 'Member Section' of OASIS.

http://www.uddi.org/

XML Topic   This is a specification from the TopicMaps.org consortium, chartered to deliver *'an*
Maps (XTM) 1.0   *abstract model and XML grammar for interchanging Web-based topic maps'.* The specification:

'...provides a model and grammar for representing the structure of information resources used to define topics, and the associations (relationships) between topics. Names, resources, and relationships are said to be characteristics of abstract subjects, which are called topics'

http://www.topicmaps.org/xtm/

Further Reading

Books

Wayne Applehans, Alden Globe and Greg Laugero: *Managing Knowledge*, Addison-Wesley, 1998

Tim Berners-Lee: *Weaving the Web*, Orion Business Book, 1999

Neil Bradley: *The XML Companion* (Second Edition), Addison-Wesley, 2000

John Seely Brown and Paul Duguid: *The Social Life of Information*, Harvard Business School Press, 2000

David Carlson: *Modeling XML Applications with UML*, Addison-Wesley, 2001

Manuel Castells: *The Rise of the Network Society*, Blackwell, 1996

Melissa A. Cook: *Building Enterprise Information Architectures*, Prentice Hall PTR, 1996

Thomas H. Davenport: *Process Innovation: Reengineering Work through Information Technology*, Harvard Business School Press, 1992

Thomas H. Davenport and Laurence Prusak: *Working Knowledge*, Harvard Business School Press, 1998

John Davies, Dieter Fensel and Frank van Harmelen (eds.): *Towards the Semantic Web*, John Wiley & Sons, 2003

Kevin Dick: *XML: A Manager's Guide*. Addison-Wesley, 1999

Dieter Fensel: *Ontologies: A Silver Bullet for Knowledge Management and Electronic Commerce*, Springer-Verlag, 2001

Brian J. Ford: *The Future of Food*, Thames & Hudson, 2000

Johan Hjelm and Peter Stark: *XSLT: The Ultimate Guide to Transforming Web Data*, John Wiley & Sons, 2001

Inge Kaul, Isabelle Grunberg and Marc A. Stern (eds.): *Global Public Goods*, Oxford University Press for the United Nations Development Programme, 1999

David Marco: *Building and Managing the Meta Data Repository*, John Wiley & Sons, 2000

Jack Park (ed.) and Sam Hunting (Technical ed.): *XML Topic Maps*, Addison-Wesley,(2002

Ian S. Graham and Liam Quin: *Open Source XML Database Toolkit*, John Wiley & Sons, 2000

Louis Rosenfeld and Peter Morville: *Information Architecture for the World Wide Web*, O'Reilly, 1998

Kendall Scott: *UML Explained*, Addison-Wesley, 2001

Simon St. Laurent: *XML Elements of Style*, McGraw-Hill, 1999

Odile Troulet-Lambert: *UML et XML pour le commerce électronique*, Hermes Science, 2000

On-line resources

Everyone has their preferred sites and sources for information on XML and related topics. I list two categories here: reference sites, where most of the formal specifications and related material can be found; and information/news sites. These are my comments and my opinions, influenced by my core interests in architecture and management rather than 'pure' technology.

Reference   *The World Wide Web Consortium, W3C*. The welcome page of the site is well balanced between the latest information and news and a listing of the principal entry points to the work of the Consortium. All formal works – recommendations through to working drafts and notes – are inverse-chronologically listed (most recent first) under www.w3.org/TR/.

http://www.w3.org

The Organisation for the Advancement for Structured Information Standards, OASIS. The welcome page is similarly structured with recent news and information and a listing of the different technical committees that oversee the development of specific standards.

http://www.oasis-open.org

The International Digital Enterprise Alliance, IDEAlliance, is a not-for-profit membership organization. Its mission is to advance user-driven, cross-industry solutions for all publishing and content-related processes by developing standards, fostering business alliances, and identifying best practices. It is also the driving force and principal organizer of many of the leading XML conferences, including XML USA and XML Europe. The proceedings of some previous conferences are available online.

http://www.idealliance.org

The Localisation Industry Standards Association, LISA, is a not-for-profit membership organization. LISA provides best practice, business guidelines and multilingual information management standards. It organizes conferences, training and a range of services for its members.

http://www.lisa.org

The Object Management Group, OMG, is an open membership, not-for-profit consortium that produces and maintains computer industry specifications for interoperable enterprise applications. It is best known for three of these: Model Driven Architecture (MDA), the Unified Modeling Language (UML) and the Common Object Request Broker Architecture (CORBA).

http://www.omg.org

Knowledge on the Web, KnoW, is a collaborative initiative bringing together industrial, commercial, governmental and not-for-profit organizations, consultants, implementers, academics and software vendors

http://www.knowweb.org

Information and news

The Cover Pages. Hosted now by OASIS, Robin Cover's very personal site is a must as the most comprehensive news-feed on XML and all related activities. By his own admission, not always the easiest site to search, it nonetheless is on top of everything important and interesting that is going on. The self-enforced editorial policy of avoiding polemics and concentrating on facts and information is very much appreciated.

http://xml.coverpages.org

XML.com. A site that is now part of the very professional O'Reilly publishers' network of resources. News, comment and analysis, well organized and with excellent writers and commentators.

```
http://www.xml.com
```

XML.org. Established and hosted by OASIS, this portal is a useful reference guide, but also links with much of the research and developments being undertaken in the IT industry and by vendors.

```
http://www.xml.org
```

Diffuse. The Diffuse Project is funded under the European Union's Information Society Technologies (IST) Programme and provides valuable news and research on all aspects of information and data management standards, not just XML. It provides very clear and concise guides and pointers to the wealth of standards and references that exist. The guide to the standards and consortia, `http://www.diffuse.org/fora.html`, is an invaluable guide through the maze, with useful indications of the status and nature of the bodies behind the acronyms.

```
http://www.diffuse.org
```

XML Hack. This is a news site tailored to the needs of XML developers. Simple, elegant and to the point.

```
http://www.xmlhack.com
```

Glossary

API

Application Programming Interface. Rather than accessing the raw code within a particular system, *applications* tend now to access a standard interface that reacts to one or other of a set of known commands and properties, and delivers a predictable result or set of responses from an otherwise invisible 'black box'. An *API* publishes this interface for use by other systems.

Application

In formal *SGML* and XML terms, any specific formalization of the use of SGML/XML to be used in a particular context. *HTML* is an application of SGML; *ebXML* is an application of XML.

Association

A relationship between two objects or, in the *Topic Maps* standards, two Topics.

Canonical

A standard representation of an object such as an electronic *document* that allows comparison with another to determine whether their contents are, in fact, identical, even if their original forms may not be.

CIO

Chief Information Officer. The most senior manager responsible for the information systems in an enterprise principally associated with that enterprise's main business. A senior management rather than a technology responsibility.

Class

An abstract description of any set of objects that together share a set of distinguishing properties and/or behaviors. A *document* class could be represented by a template, *schema* or *DTD*.

Digital rot

The process of erosion of a set of electronic resources through lack of maintenance, neglect or oversight, often based on the axiom that only paper versions of information and *documents* are authentic representations.

Disintermediation

The process of 'cutting out the middle man', or making something directly available without passing through one or many potentially distorting filters or stages.

Document

A distinct, complete and meaningful set of information. In XML, the principal logical structure of information, delimited by the document's root opening and closing tags.

DOM

Document Object Model, a W3C standard – see the *Reference* section on page 295.

DTD

Document Type Definition. A formalization of the expected and intended internal structure of a document destined to belong to a particular document type. A part of the *SGML* standard, also used in the XML standard.

EAI

Enterprise Application Integration. The integration of diverse and otherwise non-interoperable systems that allows coherent and integrated business processes to develop.

ebXML

Electronic Business XML, successor of *EDI*, and a standard of the UN/CEFACT and OASIS – see the *Reference* section on page 295.

EDI

Electronic Data Interchange, a UN standard laying down rules for the exchange of *documents* between different organizations. Largely focussed on trade facilitation.

Encapsulation

The process of including a particular concept or content within a recognized set of delimiting codes, for the purpose of exchange between and across different systems.

Entity

In general terms, a logical ('atomic') unit of construction. In specific XML terms, it is a placeholder for a string of characters in a data stream that are substituted at the time of processing for their intended content. Predefined entities are used in XML to represent the five characters (<, >, ?, " and ') that otherwise are understood as part of *markup* rather than content.

HTML

Hypertext *Markup* Language, the language of the Web. Formally, an *application* of *SGML*, HTML is a markup language that lays down a set of conventions that describe how a *document* sent from a Web server is rendered or displayed in a Web browser.

HTTP

Hypertext Transfer Protocol. The formalized data structure used across the Internet for communications between a Web server and a client.

Instance

A specific, individual occurrence of a *class* of objects. A *document* may be an instance of a document typology.

Markup

A syntax used to encapsulate content in a particular context.

Namespace

An indicator or other mechanism for declaring that a certain set of concepts should be understood in a distinct way in a particular context. Also a specific XML standard – see the *Reference* section on page 295.

Ontology

An agreement to understand a set of concepts and the relationships between them in a particular manner in a given context.

Parser

In XML, a small and efficient program that firstly checks that a particular XML *document* conforms to the prescribed structure and rules (if defined) and breaks the document into data structures that can be manipulated and used by an XML tool.

Proprietary lock-in

The process of becoming dependent on the technologies, products or 'standards', not in the public domain or protected by copyright, used by a particular supplier.

Regular expression

A pattern-matching language used to determine whether a particular string of characters (for example in an XPath expression) match, and thus fulfill, a set of criteria, used normally to qualify the nature of subsequent processing.

Reification

In *Topic Maps* and RDF, the process of making a particular topic or *entity* the centre of attention for the user.

Resource discovery

The process of finding a particular information resource or other digital object on the basis of metadata or other reference information, rather than a directly accessible address.

Root

The outermost enclosing element in an XML *document*, within which the entirety of a given XML document is encapsulated.

SAX

'Simple *API* for XML', a stream or event-based processor of XML *documents*.

Schema

A formalized description of the expected and intended internal structure and representation of any *document* that is to be created as an *instance* of a particular *class*.

SGML

Standard Generalized *Markup* Language, an ISO standard for the formal representation of electronic *document* structure.

SOAP

Simple Object Access Protocol. A W3C standard – see the *Reference* section on page 295.

Tag

The prescribed method for encapsulating content in *SGML* and XML. In *HTML*, and XML, tags are identified using special characters <, > and /.

TAG

The Technical Architecture Group, a high-level working group set up by the W3C to investigate, debate and formulate recommendations on the future architecture and infrastructure for the World Wide Web.

Terminal format

A specific format or presentation of information content that is not intended to be processed further (thus 'terminal' in the sense of 'the end of the line').

Thesaurus

In information management, a set of terms – clearly and unambiguously defined – that are described in a limited dictionary and intended for use as a 'controlled vocabulary', forcing users and agents to an agreed terminology rather other, potentially ambiguous terms.

Topic Map

An ISO standard for the representation of an *ontology* – see the *Reference* section on page 295.

UDDI

Universal Description, Discovery and Integration protocol – see the *Reference* section on page 295.

UML

Unified Modeling Language. A standard of the Object Management Group and a central plank of its 'Model Driven Architecture', offering a standardized notation to describe and model business systems and processes.

URI

Uniform Resource Identifier. A generic name for all types of identifier that allow a service or user to identify a particular point in the information territory that is the Internet.

URL

Uniform Resource Locator. An informal designation, no longer used in formal or technical specifications, of the more popular types of URI, commonly confused with a 'Web address' using the *HTTP* protocol.

URN

Uniform Resource Name:

1. A URI maintained by an authority, institution or organisation that professes a commitment to the persistence of a particular resource identification scheme.

2. A standard of the Internet Engineering Task Force, in the form of a specific scheme for the structuring and representation of resource identifiers that is not dependent on any particular location or technology.

Web paradigm

The model of information management, organisation and delivery that is represented by the World Wide Web and the technology and standards that maintain it.

Web publishing

Electronic *document* and information delivery via the Internet, whether using 'pull' ('come and get it') or 'push' ('here it is') technologies.

Web service

A 'black box' service that can be invoked across the Internet.

Index